Inner Experience

SUNY series, Intersections: Philosophy and Critical Theory
_____
Rodolphe Gasché, editor

Inner Experience

L'Expérience Intérieure

GEORGES BATAILLE

Translated and with an introduction by

STUART KENDALL

© Éditions Gallimard, 1954

Published by State University of New York Press, Albany

© 2014 State University of New York

For information, contact State University of New York Press, Albany, NY
www.sunypress.edu

Production by Diane Ganeles
Marketing by Anne M. Valentine

Library of Congress Cataloging-in-Publication Data

Bataille, Georges, 1897–1962.
    [L'Expérience intérieure. English]
    Inner experience / Georges Bataille ; translated and with an introduction by Stuart Kendall.
        pages cm. — (SUNY series, Intersections: philosophy and critical theory)
    Includes bibliographical references and index.
    ISBN 978-1-4384-5237-1 (hardcover : alk. paper)
    ISBN 978-1-4384-5236-4 (pbk. : alk. paper)
    1. Mysticism.   2. Spiritual life.   I. Title.

B828.B313 2014
128—dc23   2013030143

10 9 8 7 6 5 4 3 2 1

Contents

Translator's Introduction: A Debauchery of Thought   vii

Inner Experience

Foreword   3

Part One: Draft of an Introduction to Inner Experience   7
     1. Critique of Dogmatic Servitude (and of Mysticism)   9
     2. Experience, Sole Authority, Sole Value   13
     3. Principles of a Method and of a Community   17

Part Two: Torture   37

Part Three: Antecedents to the Torture (or the Comedy)   67
     I Want to Carry My Person to the Pinnacle   70
     Death Is in a Sense a Deception   73
     The Blue of Noon   80
     The Labyrinth (or the Composition of Beings)   85
     "Communication"   96

Part Four: Post-Scriptum to the Torture (or the
New Mystical Theology)   101
     1. God   104
     2. Descartes   107

3. Hegel   110

4. Ecstasy   113

5. Fortune   129

6. Nietzsche   131

Part Five: *Manibus Date Lilia Plenis*   159
    Gloria in excelsis mihi   161
    God   165

Method of Meditation

Foreword   169

Part One: Contestation   173

Part Two: Decisive Position   187

Part Three: Nudity   199

Post-Scriptum 1953

Notes   209

Index of Names   291

Translator's Introduction

A Debauchery of Thought

Finally—what remained to be sacrificed? At long last, did one not have to sacrifice for once whatever is comforting, holy, healing; all hope, all faith in hidden harmony, in future blisses and justices; didn't one have to sacrifice God himself and, from cruelty against oneself, worship the stone, stupidity, gravity, fate, the nothing? To sacrifice God for the nothing—this paradoxical mystery of the final cruelty was reserved for the generation that is now coming up: all of us already know something of this.

—Friedrich Nietzsche, *Beyond Good and Evil* § 55.

In *Inner Experience*, I didn't fulfill the rules. I wrote what a philosopher never writes, a book without rigor, more an expression, a debauchery of thought.

—Georges Bataille, *The Unfinished System of Nonknowledge*, 174.

L'Expérience intérieure—rendered here as *Inner Experience*—was published in February 1943 by Éditions Gallimard, then as now the most prestigious publisher in France. That edition did not include *Method of Meditation*, which first appeared as a small book in 1947, or "Post-Scriptum 1953," which was written specifically for the second edition of *Inner Experience*, published in 1954. The second edition relocated *Inner Experience* and these other texts within a larger, projected multivolume textual assemblage under the general title *La Somme Athéologique*, the *Atheological Summa*, or, echoing and inverting its scholastic progenitor by St. Thomas Aquinas, the *Summa Atheologica*.

    Inner Experience was the first full-length book to carry the name of forty-four-year-old Georges Bataille on its cover. The author was nevertheless already well known in Parisian intellectual circles for his work organizing groups and lecture series, the Collège de Sociologie most notably, the secret society Acéphale most infamously, as well as for his contributions as an author and editor to influential journals like *Documents*, *La Critique Sociale*, the single issue of *Cahiers de Contre-Attaque*, and *Acéphale*. The disciplinary fields advertised in the subtitles of these journals speak to the diversity of Bataille's interests and to the reach of his restless but relentless mind: arche-ology, Beaux-Arts, demography, ethnography, history, literature, politics and political economy, philosophy, sociology, the Workers' Movement, and, not least of all, religion. He was also known to those in the know as the author of two pseudonymously published texts now recognized as classics of erotic literature: *L'Histoire de l'oeil* (Story of the Eye, 1928) and *Madame Edwarda* (1941). But, as noted, despite this range of inquiry and productivity—which takes up two of the twelve volumes of Bataille's *Oeuvres Complètes*—prior to *Inner Experience*, Bataille was not known as the author of books.

This is not to say that he had not written or at least attempted to write them. There was a novel "in the style of Marcel Proust" around 1922 and another abandoned literary effort, with the promisingly scabrous title *W.C.*, written just before *Story of the Eye*.[1] Notes for a work of topical, journalistic political theory projected under the title *Fascism in France* date to 1934 and an early version of the novel *Le Bleu du ciel* (Blue of Noon) to the following year, though it would not be published until 1957.[2] In the year immediately prior to writing *Inner Experience*, Bataille was working at least two book projects, an early draft of the material that would become *La Part Maudite* (The Accursed Share, 1949) and notebooks on eroticism and the sacred that would later be published as *Le Coupable* (Guilty, 1944).[3]

During the fall of 1941, however, as Bataille himself clarifies in notes and remarks included in this volume, his writing and writing life shifted directions somewhat abruptly: he abandoned the draft of *The Accursed Share* to write, in quick succession, the short erotic fiction *Madame Edwarda* and "Le Supplice" (Torture), the text that would become the germinal nucleus of *Inner Experience*. *Madame Edwarda* was published almost immediately, in December 1941, in a behind-the-counter edition bearing the pseudonym Pierre Angélique. And Bataille began work on the texts that encircle "Tor-ture"—like the labyrinth coiled around the minotaur—in *Inner Experience*. As he says in his foreword, he began writing these other parts of the text "with the laudable concern of writing a book." The book, if it is indeed a book, was completed the following summer while Bataille was away from Paris, in Boussy-Saint-Antoine, staying with the mother of his friend Marcel Moré.

The move away from Paris may have been motivated at least in part by health concerns: in April 1942, Bataille had been diagnosed with a resurgence of his previously contracted tuberculosis, taken medical leave from his job at the Bibliothèque Nationale, and undergone a pneumothorax treatment. *Inner Experience*, in other words, was written at least in part in wartime, under conditions of genuine physical solitude, not simply in response to abstract or disembodied morbid thoughts but under the actual threat of imminent death.

Significant as they may be, these were not the only factors motivating the work, certainly not at the moment of its inception. The list of books Bataille borrowed from the Bibliothèque Nationale offers a glimpse of the drift of his thoughts throughout 1941, from materials related to *The Accursed Share*—like Bernardino de Sahagun's *General History of the Things of New Spain*, borrowed in February, returned in June—to books closer to *Inner Experience* in the fall. In August, for example, Bataille borrowed Henry Corbin's translation of Martin Heidegger's *What Is Metaphysics?* (and extracts from *Being and Time*). In September, immediately prior to writing *Madame Edwarda*, he borrowed Søren Kierkegaard's *The Concept of Dread* and *Philosophical Fragments* along with Jean Wahl's *Études Kierkegaardiennes* and Karl Jaspers' three-volume *Philosophy*, among other related works. Over the winter and spring of 1941–42, his focus would shift to mysticism and psychology, with books by and about St. John of the Cross, St. Teresa of Avila, the Pseudo-Dionysius, and Janet's *De L'Angoisse à l'exstase* (From Anguish to Ecstasy). By late spring he would be reading in literature and poetics, most notably *Time Regained*, the final volume of Proust's *In Search of Lost Time*.[4]

These borrowings circumscribe the discursive background of *Inner Experience* fairly well: in disciplinary terms: philosophy, mysticism, and poetry. Other references within the book—and the book is very much a dialogue with other books—expand and clarify without changing the elements of this discursive space. Hegel and Nietzsche join Heidegger and Kierkegaard among philosophical references. Ignatius of Loyola, Angela of Foligno, and Meister Eckhart join St. John of the Cross and St. Teresa among the mystics. William Blake, Arthur Rimbaud, and the Comte de Lautréamont join Proust among the poets, all gathered in an extended critical engagement with—though mostly against—surrealism. Despite these influences and engagements, Bataille explicitly takes—or rather, more precisely, measures out and marks—his distance from each of these discourses. Bataille's writing in *Inner Experience* takes up the disciplines of religion, philosophy, and literature, but moves pointedly beyond all three. The band wrapping the first edition of *Inner Experience* was emblazoned "Beyond Poetry." And as he says decisively here, in *Method of Meditation*, "I am not a philosopher, but a *saint* perhaps a madman." Yet, if Bataille is a mystic saint, his experience of the sacred is the same as that of Nietzsche's madman, from *The Gay Science* § 125, which Bataille quotes and thereby reinscribes and mimics here, almost in full: his religious experience is that of a prophet of the death of god.

The shifts in Bataille's readings undoubtedly reflect changes in his significant relationships as well. Key interlocutors from the prewar years, like André Masson, Roger Caillois, and Pierre Klossowski, were no longer living in Paris, and new friendships had sprouted up in their place. Most notably among these was Bataille's friendship with the novelist and critic Maurice Blanchot (1907–2003). Pierre Prévost, a friend of both parties, introduced the two in December 1940 and the friendship that formed was profound and catalytic. In an autobiographical note written in the third person in 1957, Bataille understated the point somewhat laconically: "At the end of 1940 he meets Maurice Blanchot with whom links of admiration and agreement are immediately formed."[5] Blanchot made a similar remark: "I had the privilege, from 1940 onwards (more precisely from the end of that sinister year), of seeing Georges Bataille almost on a daily basis and discussing a whole range of subjects with him"[6] Blanchot evoked the paradoxical proximity and distance of this discussion in a memorial piece published at the time of Bataille's death and later included in *L'Entretien infini* (The Infinite Conversation, 1969): "Speaking with simplicity and with speech's light gravity, present through his speech not because he used it to express the pathos of a sensibility, but to affirm with reserve and caution the concern from which his interlocutors never heard him depart, Georges Bataille linked the detours of conversation to the unlimited play of thought."[7]

In a letter, Bataille expressed the proximity of their concerns: "*Fundamentally*, I think what Blanchot thinks."[8] And in both *Inner Experience* and *Guilty*, Bataille quotes Blanchot prominently on multiple occasions from both personal discussion and written discourse. In *Inner Experience*, he explains: "Outside of the notes in this volume, I only know of [Blanchot's 1941 novel] *Thomas the Obscure*, where the questions of the new theology (which has only the unknown as an object) are pressing, though there they remain hidden." Blanchot had completed *Thomas the Obscure*, his first novel, in May 1940, the month the Germans invaded France. The title carries echoes of Heraclitus, known as Heraclitus the Obscure, as well as Thomas Hardy's *Jude the Obscure*. Many passages of Blanchot's luminous but enigmatic narrative read as if they had been written by the author of *Madame Edwarda* and *Inner Experience*. In a footnote to "A New Mystic," his extended critical review of *Inner Experience*, Jean-Paul Sartre mentions that Albert Camus told him that *Inner Experience* is the "exact translation of, and commentary on Maurice Blanchot's *Thomas the Obscure*."[9]

The intriguing proximity of *Thomas the Obscure* and *Inner Experience* is not circumscribed by the initial or original texts of these books. In 1950, the year Bataille proposed a substantial revision of *Inner Experience* as volume one of a *Summa Atheologica*, Blanchot substantially revised *Thomas the Obscure*, cutting roughly one-quarter of the original text for its second edition. This revision of *Thomas the Obscure* refocused the text, changing it from a novel into what Blanchot called a *récit* or narrative. This revision thus also shifted the place of the text in the taxonomy of Blanchot's works: his first novel became his second narrative. Bataille's revision of *Inner Experience* would also propose a taxonomic reordering of his own work.

Nor does the proximity of these two first books circumscribe the relationship, textual or otherwise, between Bataille and Blanchot. Their friendship continued in correspondence when they were not living near enough to one another to speak face to face.[10] And they wrote about and under the influence of one another's work for the rest of their lives. The first six chapters of Blanchot's first collection of critical essays, *Faux Pas* (1943), reflect this enigmatically intertwined, public and private conversation by taking as their subject matter several major themes and materials significant in *Inner Experience*—Kiekegaard's journals, Meister Eckhart, William Blake, Hindu thought, the experience of Proust—as well as reprinting Blanchot's review of the book, originally published in the *Journal des Débats* (May 5, 1943).

Bataille and Blanchot also opened the space of their friendship to other interlocutors through organized conversations. In December 1941, they established an informal discussion group under the title the Collège Socratique (Socratic College) to develop "scholastic" propositions about inner experience. Bataille's "Socratic College" lecture was developed in the context of this group.[11] He undoubtedly also shared portions of *Inner Experience* while the book was in progress. The group first met at a restaurant on the rue de Pontieu, later at the offices of the cultural organization Jeune France, and finally at Bataille's apartment at 3 rue de Lille. Members included Pierre Prévost, who had introduced the two friends; Romain Petitot; Louis Ollivier; Georges Pelorson; and others. In early 1942, Bataille organized a second group with the same purpose, this one including Michel Leiris, Raymond Queneau, Raoul Ubac, Jean Lescure, and Michel Fardoulis-Lagrange, most of whom had been friends with Bataille for years and published in the literary journal *Messages*.

Other significant interlocutors are less easy to identify. In the notes to this volume, Bataille writes: "in the meantime those who were anticipating [inner experience] with me have disappeared, the answer that I gave [to the question of inner experience] is given to the desert—in a profound silence." Who are the "disappeared"? We can conjecture as we read, particularly the texts collected in part three as "Antecedents to the Torture," but we cannot be certain. "Antecedents to the Torture" traces the itinerary of inner experience through Bataille's previous life without fully revealing either that experience or that life. As the notes to this volume demonstrate, there are intentional omissions in the narrative. Bataille's closest friends and collaborators from the 1930s, those who participated in Contre-Attaque, the Collège de Sociologie, and Acéphale—including his lover Colette Peignot, who is better known by her middle name, Laure, and who is almost certainly the "second victim" mentioned in "Blue of Noon"—all go unnamed in the text, their identities either hidden or effaced. Bataille's prewar activities—interventions in art and anthropology, literature, politics, activism—faltered on their own. Their stories have been told elsewhere, their lessons sifted.[12] Herein Bataille writes poignantly and definitively: "The war put an end to my 'activity' and my life became all the less separated from the object of its search."

Bataille's writings from the war years are, like Nietzsche's later books, the works of a profoundly lonely and isolated man, a man whose experience and understanding of certain fundamental truths had put him beyond the company of the majority of his fellows, into the community, as he calls it herein, "of those who have no community." He writes: "there is such disquiet in the depths of the heart of man, that it is not in the power of any God—or any woman—to calm it." As he explains, the phrase "any God" can be taken to mean not only what it says most directly—any deity—but also any dogma, any science, or any aesthetic or experiential quest. The first and primary principle of inner experience is that it finds no other justification than itself, no justification *outside* of itself, certainly no salvation. Yet, despite his agonized disquiet, Bataille nevertheless insists that he is among the happiest of men: "No one is more gay that I," he writes, echoing Nietzsche's specific word for his own joyousness. Indeed, if this book has a central purpose, it is found in the phrase: "I teach the art of turning anguish into delight."

Inner experience is nothing if not paradox, contradiction. "Principle of inner experience: to get out through a project of the realm of the project." Elsewhere: "Inner experience is the opposite of action. Nothing more." If action is essentially the same as project, as in making plans for a future that never comes, inner experience is "existence without delay." "Existence," he writes, "is an exuberant tumult, where fever and laceration are linked to intoxication." In "Torture," he throws down this gauntlet: "every human being who does not go to the extremity is the *servant* or the *enemy* of man." To deny inner experience is to deny the very nature of human being, but this denial is common enough. Inner experience is a response to and recognition of radical contingency and fundamental freedom, but human beings all too often flee their own freedom, escape or compromise it in myriad ways: civilization itself is a bulwark against the chaos of contingency. Human cultures are networks of codes giving form to what would otherwise be formless, human being. Like Nietzsche, Bataille wonders why human beings need these codes, why we need truth, why we need our discourses of knowledge? "Why," he asks, "must there be *what I know?* Why is it a necessity? In this question is hidden—it does not initially appear—an extreme laceration, so profound that only the silence of ecstasy responds to it." Blanchot calls the experience of this laceration a limit-experience.[13]

The breakthrough that occasioned inner experience as a practice as well as *Inner Experience* as a text was Bataille's discovery of dramatic mimicry as a method of mystical meditation *and* of literary composition capable of communicating nonknowledge. Bataille's method of dramatic mimicry derives from many sources, most notably from the spiritual exercises of Ignatius of Loyola, but also from various practices associated with yoga, which Bataille had begun to practice in the late 1930s, as well as from the mode of modern poetics that involves deconstructing language and sense. In Loyola's spiritual exercises, the seeker identifies with the sufferings of Christ on the cross to the hyperbolic point of imaginary self-immolation. The central figure in Bataille's practice of dramatic meditation is not Christ on the cross but rather Fou-Tchou-Li, the Chinese murderer subjected to the torture known as the Leng T'che (cutting to pieces), pictured in photographs Bataille possessed.[14] As noted, Bataille's word here is "le supplice"—torture—a word that can refer to any form of torture, mental or physical, but that most often refers to the public torture and execution of criminals, like that of Damiens, detailed in Michel Foucault's *Surveiller et Punir* (in English as Discipline and Punish, 1975), the first part of which is titled "Torture." Torture is not mere torment, or discomfort: it is bodily laceration. The dismemberment of Fou-Tchou-Li recalls for Bataille the agony of Christ on the cross but also the dismemberment of Dionysus.

As a spiritual exercise, torture is tragic, resulting in the sacrificial loss of identity, the codes that support consciousness collapse; the self opens up to the opposite of self. As a literary exercise, its product is tragedy, a mode of discourse in which the structure and meaning of discourse itself is sacrificed, sense opens up to nonsense, knowledge to nonknowledge. And in a book wherein language is confounded with identity, life is literature and literature life. All literature is in some sense mimicry or imitation. Tragic literature uses the rhetoric of representation against itself to break the bonds of identity that ground our faith in imitation and vice versa. Toward these ends, Bataille tortures his text: he tears it apart. He interrupts his arguments with autobiographical reminiscences and flights of poetic language. He abandons his outlines, leaves things unfinished. He makes a mockery of rhetorical modes of persuasion: combines forms and registers, interjects quotations to the point of self-effacement, shifts between temporal moments—past and present—and personal and impersonal modes of discourse. He acknowledges even his limitations, incapacities, and awkwardness as an intellect and as a writer as part of his methodology: "My means: expression, my awkwardness."

The book that emerges, if it is a book, contains prose and poetry, argument and autobiography, analysis and exegesis, as well as the jargons of distinct discourses: religion, philosophy, and poetics most prominently. It is urgent and detached, digressive and determined, contingent and cohesive, suspended between chance and necessity. Almost no two pages pass without the book shifting in some significant way, slipping out from its own emergent but ultimately kaleidoscopic order. A thorough summary of the text would not reveal a systematically organized treatise but rather a catalog of strategies and effects. *Inner Experience* revels in its own rhetoric, not for persuasive effect but to provoke an experience for its author and for its reader. Experience here is primary: argument, persuasion, knowledge all secondary.

As Bataille both explains and demonstrates herein, poetry—language pushed to its limit—is a sacrifice in which words are the victims. From this comes Bataille's willingness to adopt the jargons of distinct and even contradictory disciplines and his willingness to change his terms, even his most significant ones—inner experience becomes "impalement" in *On Nietzsche*—when they lose their effectiveness. The point is not to develop a precise collection of personal technical terms, a jargon of his own, but rather to use language against itself to produce an effect, first for himself but also for his readers. If his terms are no longer effective in this way, he changes them, borrows words from different traditions, different discourses.

Bataille also overloads, overdetermines his language, after the fashion of tragic theater, with borrowings from other authors. "From one hour to the next," he writes, "I am sickened at the idea that I am writing, that I must pursue. I never have security, certainty. I hold continuity in horror. I persevere in disorder, faithful to passions that I truly know nothing about, that disturb me in every way." Here in a passage devoted to dramatization, the word "disturb" is *dérèglent*—an evocation of the famous dictate of French poet Arthur Rimbaud that the poet becomes a poet through a "long, immense, and reasoned disturbance [*dérèglement*] of all the senses" (letter to Paul Demeny, May 15, 1871). But Bataille's language and references are rarely singular in their sources. His repeated evocations of blindness in the text are literary and philosophical—tragic, Oedipal, Greek, via Nietzsche and Freud—but they are also biographical. His own father was blind as an effect of syphilis. One finds borrowed terms even at the climax of the text: in the final section of part four, where Bataille reinscribes § 125 of Nietzsche's *Gay Science*, the parable of the madman.[15] His rhetorical strategy here is dramatic, tragic stagecraft, playing with identities and the sacrifice of identity.

The book that emerges from all of these strategies is a dark corridor of distorting funhouse mirrors that never fix the images of the self they fleetingly capture. The book as a whole ultimately fails to cohere, falls apart. It is an exercise at the limits of representation that simultaneously demonstrates the collapse of representation. *Inner Experience* fails to express the extremity of inner experience. "Any expression whatsoever testifies to this: the extremity is distinct from it. It is never literature. If poetry expresses it, it is distinct from it: to the point of not being poetic, for if poetry has it as an object, it does not reach it. When the extremity is there, the means that serve to reach it are no longer there." This is what it means to be beyond poetry, but also beyond philosophy, beyond science, and beyond religion. Each of these words references a way of knowing, a perspective, that is also the principle that organizes a community. However respectfully, however politely, valorizing one *over* the others denies the final validity of the others. Valorizing one *and* the others, or rather *claiming* to do so, is, following Bataille, mere hypocrisy. Bataille writes to shatter the pretense to and vanity of any singular form of or approach to knowledge.

Can we take him seriously? Should we? His message is much the same, he claims, as Nietzsche's. His dramatic methods derive from and partake of several traditions: the theater of Dionysus, Christian mysticism, modern poetics. But dramatization is fundamentally deception, trickery, and Bataille is, first of all, fooling himself: playing language games, chasing shadows, playing conjurer's tricks on his own mind. Within a wider frame of ethnographic analysis, we might associate him with the tradition of the trickster found in so many cultures around the globe.[16]

Bataille's auditors and readers have been divided on this topic. During a public debate recorded as the "Discussion on Sin," Maurice de Gandillac remarked: "I wouldn't want to ask you [Bataille] an indiscrete question, but I feel more at ease with you now, because we've all been convinced by your tone. As [Arthur] Adamov was saying, if there were those among us who might occasionally doubt the profoundly authentic character of your experience and of your whole book, this suspicion has absolutely been dispelled by the tone even of our conversation."[17] Blanchot and others have left similar testimony without however dispelling doubts.

In the preface to the second edition of *Guilty*, Bataille remarks that the critics of *Inner Experience* "weren't lacking" but nevertheless "left [him] cold."[18] The apparent simplicity of the remark dissolves with consideration. Hardly numerous, what about these reviews might have been "not lacking"? Is it true that they "left him cold"? I have already mentioned Blanchot's sympathetic and accurate account for the *Journal des Débats*, reprinted in his book *Faux Pas*. Less sympathetically and less accurately, a group of Belgian surrealists penned a misguided pamphlet under the title *Nom de Dieu* that mistook Bataille's atheology for a new theology. As Bataille reported to his friend Jean Bruno, the piece was "without interest: except comical."[19]

Two other reviews however piqued Bataille for years. The existential theologian Gabriel Marcel published a challenging attack on *Inner Experience* titled "The Refusal of Salvation and the Exaltation of the Man of Absurdity" in *Revue de la Table Ronde* 3 (March 1944), reprinting it in his book *Homo Viator* (1945). Roughly the first half of the essay—the "refusal of salvation" part—considers *Inner Experience*, while the second half considers Albert Camus's *The Myth of Sisyphus*, then recently published as well. Marcel links Bataille and Blanchot together in the piece, so closely in fact that he reprints Blanchot's summaries of Bataille's thought. He also accurately associates Bataille with the traditions of both St. John of the Cross and Nietzsche, but he faults Bataille as essentially a failed mystic, one who revels in agony through self-complacency, through an unwillingness to push beyond the dark night of nonknowledge to the dawn of salvation. He presents Bataille as a kind of second-rate sequel to Nietzsche—one whom he cannot quite take seriously.[20] Bataille considered his response to Marcel carefully. Portions of that response are visible in "Le Dernier Instant" (The Last Moment), a review article on a work by Madeleine Deguy with a long essay-preface by Gabriel Marcel, published by Bataille in *Critique* in 1946.[21] But the notes for "Post-Scriptum 1953" are even more clear as a demonstration of Bataille's lingering pique, and not only because they were written eight years after Marcel's review. While Bataille was pleased that Marcel located him within the mystic tradition, he was persistently disappointed, as could be expected, that Marcel had been unable to take him seriously in the end and to understand the value of the infinite inquiry Bataille's experience proposed.

The most extensive and disappointing, if not in fact maddening, review of *Inner Experience* was, however, published by Jean-Paul Sartre in three successive issues of *Cahiers du Sud* in October, November, and December 1943 and reprinted in his first collection of essays, *Situations* (1947).[22] Sartre had just written *L'Être et Néant* (Being and Nothingness) and staged *Les Mouches* (The Flies): he was at the height of his powers, if not quite yet of his fame. He brought an exhaustive background in philosophy and French literary civilization as well as an obsessive and relentless rigor to bear on Bataille's text, which also, not surprisingly, served him as a vehicle for expressing his own thought and concerns at length, indeed almost ad nauseam. Cartesian, Hegelian, project driven, realist: Sartre's fundamental orientation could not have been more opposed to Bataille's. As could be expected, Sartre's reading was almost astonishingly sensitive and accurate, locating Bataille in the tradition of Pascal and Nietzsche, drawing his work into dialogue with Spinoza, distinguishing it from its own roots in Durkheim's sociology, and revealing Bataille's debts to Henry Corbin's translations of Heidegger and Jean Wahl's interpretations of Kierkegaard and Jaspers. Sartre also demonstrated his understanding of Bataille's rhetorical strategies, his mixed marshaling of analytical argument and evocative poetics, definite jargon, and indefinable terms. Unsurprisingly, as an academically trained professional philosopher, Sartre was impatient with Bataille's facile appropriation of figures from the tradition, Heidegger, Jaspers, Hegel, and Descartes in particular. Most significantly, though, Sartre found fault with Bataille's fundamental project, his conception of and quest for the communication of nonknowledge, the very thought of inner experience. His tone, at times, was that of a father scolding a petulant, rebellious child.

Bataille responded to Sartre in several ways over the next decade. Most directly, almost immediately, in fact, he asked his friend Marcel Moré to host a discussion between himself and a number of invited writers, philosophers, and theologians on the topic of sin (mentioned above). Bataille had finished writing *Inner Experience* at Marcel Moré's mother's house in Boussy-Saint-Antoine in the summer of 1942, and Moré had hosted other discussions at his home periodically through the war years, including a series of "Discussions on War" in which Bataille participated in November 1939. In some more or less direct ways these discussion groups, like Bataille's Collège Socratique, continued the efforts of the Collège de Sociologie.[23] The "Discussion on Sin," as the event has come to be known, included among its participants an unlikely who's who of the Parisian intelligentsia: Jean-Paul

Sartre, Simone de Beauvoir, Albert Camus, Maurice Merleau-Ponty, Jean
Hyppolite, Maurice de Gandillac, Jean Paulhan, Pierre Prévost, Gabriel Marcel, Arthur Adamov, Michel Leiris, Maurice Blanchot, and Reverend Fathers
Henri Dubarle, Augustin Maydieu, and Jean Daniélou, who responded to
Bataille's lecture with a prepared piece. Pierre Klossowski served as secretary
and facilitated the publication of the discussion in the journal *Dieu Vivant*.
The "Discussion" took place on March 5, 1944: three months after the third
part of Sartre's review of *Inner Experience* had been published and only three
or so weeks after the publication of *Guilty*. Bataille's lecture itself, titled
"Summit and Decline," would be printed as the central theoretical chapter
of *On Nietzsche* the following year.[24] *On Nietzsche* also includes an appendix
in which Bataille responds to Sartre even more directly, "Reply to Jean-
Paul Sartre (Defense of *Inner Experience*)." His response there is thorough,
patient, and if anything generous: he writes, for example: "Sartre, basing
himself on my book, aptly describes the workings of my mind, underscoring
the foolishness of its workings better from the outside than I could from
the inside (I was moved). He accurately analyzes my mental state and, as
I should point out, objectively and clearly dissects this state so as to bring
out (appropriate) comic effects."[25] Elsewhere in *On Nietzsche*, but more
obliquely, Bataille narrates, again to comic effect, a slightly drunken scene
at a party when he and Sartre danced together in a "potlatch of absurdity."[26]

This is not the place to attempt a thorough analysis of Sartre's reading
of *Inner Experience* or Bataille's responses to it. My purpose here is only
to situate *Inner Experience* and the texts that are most closely related to it.
Slightly afield from *Inner Experience*, though undoubtedly also more or less
directly related to the ongoing conversation, if not the quarrel, between
Bataille and Sartre, one should remember the series of review essays Bataille
devoted to several of Sartre's subsequent works: reviews of *Anti-Semite and
Jew* in 1946, *Baudelaire* and the general topic of "existentialism" in 1947,
"existentialism" again in 1950, and *Saint-Genet* in 1952. Bataille collected
his reviews of *Baudelaire* and *Saint-Genet* in *La Littérature et le Mal* (Literature and Evil, 1957).[27] Beyond all of this, Sartre would persist in Bataille's
notes and drafts through the early 1950s as *the* "philosopher," a figure of
scorn, against whom he would measure himself and his own work.[28] Sartre,
for his part, moved on: when he mentions Bataille at all, he does so with
derision and, what's worse, only in passing.[29]

In this context, *Method of Meditation* should of course also be read as
a response to and extension of some of the initial reviews and discussions of
Inner Experience, *Guilty*, and *On Nietzsche*, as a more or less direct attempt
to extend and clarify, to crystallize if not exactly codify—the concerns and

itineraries of those books and of that moment in Bataille's thought. The notes and drafts for *Method of Meditation* show that Bataille started work on the text in the spring of 1945, only a few months after the publication of *On Nietzsche* and essentially coincident with the publication of *Memorandum*, his extended collection of maxims, aphorisms, and fragments from Nietzsche, a book that begins: "I propose this book for long, slow meditations."[30] *Method of Meditation* and *Memorandum* are thus of a piece. They also both recall specific projects first conceived in the context of Acéphale in the late 1930s, elements of which are visible in various internal documents circulated among members of Acéphale and in essays like "The Practice of Joy before Death," with its famous "Heraclitean Meditation," first published in the final issue of *Acéphale* in 1939.[31]

But already in 1945, while still writing *Method of Meditation*, Bataille anticipated, in a note included in this edition, republishing that text as part of a much larger textual assemblage, as an additional concluding section of *La Haine de la poésie* (The Hatred of Poetry, 1947; reissued in 1962 as *L'Impossible*). The projected volume would thus have included *L'Oreste* (The Oresteia), *Histoire de Rats* (Story of Rats), *Dianus* (Dianus), and *Method of Meditation*, in that order.[32] But the same note also suggests gathering *Inner Experience*, *On Nietzsche*, and *The Hatred of Poetry* (perhaps meaning only *The Oresteia* and *Method of Meditation*) together under the general title *Beyond Poetry*, the phrase printed on the band wrapping the 1943 edition of *Inner Experience*. Another proposed gathering of texts would group *Guilty* with other writings under the general title *Nudity*, including *Allehuia, Story of Rats*, and a dialogue he anticipated writing. These notes suggest continuities and discontinuities between books like *Inner Experience*, *Guilty*, *On Nietzsche*, and *Method of Meditation* and writings that can be considered fictional, in a more traditional sense, like the texts collected in *The Impossible*. In this light, the heavily edited but *real* journals that constitute *Guilty* and large portions of *On Nietzsche* appear of a piece with the apparently *fictional* journals of *Story of Rats* and *Dianus*. In Bataille's dramatic method of meditation, fiction is a mode of experience.[33]

A year later, in 1946, Bataille wrote a letter to Raymond Queneau, his friend and editor at Gallimard, anticipating new editions of *Inner Experience* and *Guilty*, this time associating *Method of Meditation* with *Guilty* rather than with *Inner Experience*.[34] Bataille was in somewhat desperate straits at this point in his life: forty-nine years old, unemployed, and living in Vézelay with his second wife, Diana Kotchoubey de Beauharnois, on royalties and a small disability stipend from the Bibliothèque Nationale. Bataille's interest in this series of new editions was motivated at least in part by financial concerns. Other publications and projects nevertheless put the notion off for several years. It reappeared as a pressing agenda in 1950, when Bataille again discussed the matter in a letter to Raymond Queneau. This letter, sent on March 29, 1950, proposed a complex outline for the projected multivolume series and used the general title *La Somme Athéologique*, or *Summa Atheologica*, for the first time. In this outline, *Inner Experience* would appear under the volume title *L'Athéologie*, with *Method of Meditation* and unspecified "Studies in Atheology" (on existentialism, poetry, eroticism, and other topics). The second volume in the series would appear under the general title *L'Amitié* (Friendship) and be composed of *Guilty* and writings on a "secret society" (Acéphale presumably) and Maurice Blanchot. A third volume would have collected writings on and around Nietzsche: *On Nietzsche, Memorandum*, and others. A fourth volume would have collected various review essays, for the most part first published in *Critique*, on literary and other topics: Sade and Camus, Baudelaire, Michelet, Simone Weil, among others. This projected volume is at least partially visible in *Literature and Evil*.

Plans for the edition were delayed while Bataille struggled with other projects like the second volume of *The Accursed Share*, *L'Histoire de l'érotisme* (The History of Eroticism, 1950–51). In 1952, he began writing and organizing a mass of manuscript notes and drafts for the project while simultaneously delivering a series of loosely linked "Lectures of Nonknowledge" under the auspices of Jean Wahl's lecture series, the Collège Philosophique. Some of this material found its way into published articles like "The Sovereign" (1952) and "Nonknowledge" (1953) while other materials remained in draft form.[35] "Post-Scriptum 1953" condenses some of this material, while attempting to both summarize the key elements of *Inner Experience* and look back and relocate the book in relation to Bataille's then-current style and concerns, for he had by that point already abandoned the hyperbolic, dramatic style of the book. The notes also demonstrate the extent to which Bataille remained motivated to respond to his critics, Gabriel Marcel in particular. That motivation however was not strong enough to carry his response over into the published text, other than obliquely. He may on the other hand have been saving this material, along with the other writings he collected in a file labeled "Aphorisms for the 'System'" for another volume of the *Summa*.[36]

Along these lines, in 1954, when the new edition of *Inner Experience* finally appeared, a paratextual note listed the volumes of the *Summa Atheologica* as including *Inner Experience, Guilty,* and *On Nietzsche* as well as two other projected volumes, *Le Pur Bonheur* (Pure Happiness) and *Le Système inachevé du non-savoir* (The Unfinished System of Nonknowledge). Bataille drafted numerous outlines for these volumes over the next few years, shifting articles and topics into various juxtapositions. He also published an article under the title "Pure Happiness" in the journal *Botteghe oscure* in 1958 as well as other articles related to the project in other venues. Ultimately however neither of these volumes saw the light of day.[37] In 1961, when the second edition of *Guilty* finally appeared, it listed the books of the *Summa* as *Inner Experience, Guilty,* and *On Nietzsche.* Bataille did not live long enough to complete a second edition of *On Nietzsche,* but he did complete a second edition of *The Hatred of Poetry,* by then retitled *The Impossible* in 1962. This is undoubtedly significant in light of the previously mentioned association of that text with outlines for the *Summa.*

While this is not the place to attempt an exhaustive interpretation of Bataille's atheology or of his project for a *Summa Atheologica,* these facts are relevant to any attempt to locate and understand *Inner Experience,* whether the text is approached as the culmination of a long apprenticeship in the experience of the sacred, as the first book by one of this century's most influential writers, or, as "Post-Scriptum 1953" suggests, as one volume in an ultimately abortive multivolume work exploring the far-reaching effects of the disappearance of the discursive real in modern life. Cast between the disciplines of religion, philosophy, and poetics, the book is also suspended in these various conjunctions, as culmination, incipit, and cornerstone.

$\sim$

Translations—in my view, as undoubtedly might be intuited—are among the most shameless but also shamelessly sincere forms of interpretation, attempts to let a text speak for itself, circumscribed by the acknowledgement that this task is ultimately an illustration of and encounter with the impossible and therefore inevitably a betrayal. Historically contingent, a translation is never isolated: it always exists in relation to an original text and the space of a target language, a space defined and nuanced by the jargons of various communities, various disciplines. Bataille's original text—now seventy years old—activated and exploited tensions among the disciplines of religion, philosophy, and poetics that now live on the margins of those three disciplines, distinct as they are in their contemporary forms from the forms they assumed historically and in Bataille's day. Bataille's thought is still a scandal, but it is a scandal that has become, if possible, more hidden, more secret than it was at the point of its inception. The task of the translator necessarily extends Bataille's practice—his discursive and disciplinary shadow play, mimicry, and language games—across another border, into another language community, or rather into another conjunction of communities.

A book is also the sum of the translations it occasions. *Inner Experience* first appeared in English more than twenty years ago, in a translation by Leslie Anne Boldt that was marred by a number of small errors, omissions, and infelicities. It would be pedantic to detail them here. Working on this entirely new translation of *Inner Experience*, I have nevertheless come to hold Leslie Anne Boldt's version in greater esteem than I previously did for its numerous accurate and creative solutions to the many profound challenges posed by the original text. In this new version, nevertheless, in addition to other changes, small and large, occasional errors in line and page breaks were corrected through reference to early editions and printings of Bataille's text, wherein differences in pagination caused breaks to fall in different, more legible places. Most significantly, this new translation restores *Method of Meditation* and "Post-Scriptum 1953" to their places as addenda to *Inner Experience*, allowing Anglophone readers to experience the first volume of the *Summa Atheologica* as Bataille intended it. I previously co-translated *Method of Meditation* and "Post-Scriptum 1953" for inclusion in *The Unfinished System of Nonknowledge*. The translations of these texts included herein—like doubles redoubled with, I hope, greater fidelity—are nevertheless entirely new and my own.

The fundamental paradox of *Inner Experience*: a project against projects, it uses knowledge, disciplined discursive knowledge, language, against itself; as a book, it chatters on the alluring edge of silence. In one of the last lines of the notes to the text, Bataille acknowledges that an "author knows that he cannot be sovereign: to be sovereign he would have to silence himself, no longer be an author." The possibility of silencing oneself, however—of sacrificing authority within oneself, of letting the other speak, of speaking while remaining silent—is the very possibility that defines the task of translation. Inevitably though, and despite the silence of this speech, around every translator a mask is continually growing.

Notes to Translator's Introduction

1. See Georges Bataille, *Choix de lettres: 1917–62*, ed. Michel Surya (Paris: Gallimard, 1997) p. 28. On *W.C.*, see Bataille, *Louis XXX*, ed. and trans. Stuart Kendall (Prague: Equus, 2013).

2. For *Fascism in France*, see Bataille, *Oeuvres Complètes*, volume 2 (Paris: Gallimard, 1970), pp. 205ff.; for the 1935 version of *Le Bleu du Ciel*, see Bataille, *Romans et Récits* (Paris: Bibliothèque de la Pléiade, 2004) pp. 214–302.

3. See *La Limite de l'utile*, in Bataille, *Oeuvres Complètes*, volume 7, pp. 181–280 and *Guilty* (1944, 1961), trans. Stuart Kendall (Albany: State University of New York Press, 2011).

4. For all of this, see Jean-Pierre Le Bouler and Joëlle Bellec Martini, "Emprunts de Georges Bataille à la Bibliothèque Nationale (1922–1950)" in Bataille, *Oeuvres Complètes*, volume 12, pp. 616–18.

5. Georges Bataille, "Autobiographical Note" in *My Mother, Madame Edwarda, The Dead Man*, trans. Austryn Wainhouse (London: Marion Boyars, 1989) p. 221.

6. Maurice Blanchot, "Intellectuals Under Scrutiny" in *The Blanchot Reader* (Oxford: Blackwell, 1995) p. 226.

7. Maurice Blanchot, "The Play of Thought" in *The Infinite Conversation* (1969), trans. Susan Hanson (Minneapolis: University of Minnesota Press, 1993) p. 214.

8. Bataille, *Choix de lettres*, p. 283.

9. Jean-Paul Sartre, "A New Mystic" in *Critical Essays* (1947), trans. Christ Turner (London: Seagull Books, 2010) p. 293.

10. See Bataille, *Choix de lettres*, pp. 589–96, where, in the absence of existing letters from Bataille to Blanchot, one finds letters from Blanchot to Bataille.

11. See Bataille, "Socratic College" in *The Unfinished System of Nonknowledge*, ed. Stuart Kendall (Minneapolis: University of Minnesota Press, 2001) pp. 5–17.

12. See my *Georges Bataille* (Reaktion Books, Critical Lives, 2007).

13. See Blanchot, *The Infinite Conversation*, p. 203.

14. These photographs are reproduced in Georges Bataille, *The Tears of Eros* (1962), trans. Peter Connor (San Francisco: City Lights Books, 1989) pp. 204–7.

15. On this passage, see Denis Hollier, "From Beyond Hegel to Nietzsche's Absence" in Leslie Anne Boldt-Irons, ed., *On Bataille* (Albany: State University of New York Press, 1995) pp. 61–78.

16. On this tradition, see Lewis Hyde, *Trickster Makes the World: How Disruptive Imagination Creates Culture* (New York: Farrar, Straus, Giroux, 1998).

17. Bataille, "Discussion on Sin" (1944) in Bataille, *The Unfinished System of Nonknowledge*, p. 70.

18. See Bataille, *Guilty*, p. 3.

19. Bataille, *Choix de lettres*, p. 183.

20. See Gabriel Marcel, "The Refusal of Salvation and the Exaltation of the Man of Absurdity" in *Homo Viator: Introduction to the Metaphysic of Hope* (1945), trans. Emma Craufurd and Paul Seaton (South Bend, IN: St. Augustine's Press, 2010) pp. 178–204.

21. "Dernier Instant" *Critique* n° 5 (October 1946) pp. 448–57, reprinted in *Oeuvres Complètes,* volume 11, pp. 116–25; English translation by Thomas Walton, "The Ultimate Instant" *Transition* 48, n° 1 (January 1948) pp. 60–69. In a letter to Jean Bruno included herein, Bataille includes this article among those he intends to collect in later volumes of the proposed *Summa Atheologica*.

22. See Jean-Paul Sartre, "A New Mystic" in Sartre, *Critical Essays*, pp. 219–93.

23. For a transcription of the "Discussions sur la Guerre" see *Digraphe* 17 (1978) pp. 121–39.

24. For "Discussion on Sin," see Bataille, *The Unfinished System of Nonknowledge*, pp. 26–74. See also Michel Surya, "Éloge du péché," in Bataille, *Discussion sur le Péché* (Paris: Lignes, 2010) and Surya, *Sainteté de Bataille* (Paris: Éditions de l'éclat, 2012) pp. 127–54.

25. Bataille, *On Nietzsche* (1945), trans. Bruce Boone (New York: Paragon House, 1992) p. 180.

26. Bataille, *On Nietzsche*, p. 75.

27. See "Sartre" *Critique* n° 12 (May 1947) pp. 3–5; reprinted in Bataille, *Oeuvres Complètes*, volume 11, pp. 226–8. "Baudelaire" in *Literature and Evil*, pp. 35–61. "De l'existentialisme au primat de l'économie" *Critique* n° 19 and 21 (December 1947, pp. 515–26; February 1948, pp. 127–41); reprinted in Bataille, *Oeuvres Complètes*, volume 11, pp. 279–84; "Existentialisme" *Critique* n° 41 (October 1950) pp. 83–86; reprinted in Bataille, *Oeuvres Complètes*, volume 12, pp. 11–15. "Genet" in *Literature and Evil*, pp. 171–208.

28. See, for example, remarks in "Aphorisms for the 'System'" in Bataille, *The Unfinished System of Nonknowledge*, pp. 153–82. Bataille's conflict with Sartre can also be seen in his various writings in support of Albert Camus, whose work, like Bataille's own, had been attacked by both Sartre and André Breton.

29. See, for example, remarks in Jean-Paul Sartre, *What Is Literature? And Other Essays* (1948), trans. Jeffrey Mehlmann (Cambridge: Harvard University Press, 1988).

30. See Bataille, *Memorandum* (Paris: Gallimard, 1945); reprinted in Bataille, *Oeuvres Complètes*, volume 6, pp. 207–72.

31. See Bataille, "The Practice of Joy Before Death" in *Visions of Excess*, ed. and trans. Allan Stoekl (Minneapolis: University of Minnesota Press, 1985) pp. 235–9. For extensive documents related to Acéphale, see Marina Galletti, ed., *L'Apprenti Sorcier* (Paris: Éditions de la Différence, 1999).

32. The order of the texts in *The Hatred of Poetry* was changed when it was reissued as *The Impossible*, moving "The Oresteia" from first to last.

33. For more on this theme, see "Larvatus Prodeo," my post-face to Georges Bataille, *Louis XXX* (Prague: Equus, 2013).

34. Bataille, *Choix de lettres*, pp. 351–2.

35. See Bataille, *The Unfinished System of Nonknowledge*. This volume collects all of Bataille's essays, aphorisms, notes, and lectures related to the *Summa Atheologica* exclusive of those included in *Inner Experience, Guilty*, and *On Nietzsche*.

36. For "Aphorisms for the 'System.'" see Bataille, *The Unfinished System of Nonknowledge*, pp. 153–82.

37. Again, see Bataille, *The Unfinished System of Nonknowledge* for these materials.

Inner Experience

Night is also a sun.

—Zarathustra

Foreword[1]

How I would like to say of my book the same thing that Nietzsche did of The Gay Science: *"In almost every sentence profundity and passion go tenderly hand in hand."*[2]

Nietzsche wrote in Ecce Homo: *"Another ideal runs ahead of us, a strange, tempting dangerous ideal to which we should not wish to persuade anybody because we do not readily concede* the right to it *to anyone: the ideal of a spirit who plays naively—that is, not deliberately but from overflowing power and abundance—with all that was hitherto called holy, good, untouchable, divine; for whom those supreme things that the people naturally accept as their value standards, signify danger, decay, debasement, or at least recreation, blindness, and temporary self-oblivion; the ideal of a human, superhuman well-being and benevolence that will often appear* inhuman*—for example, when it confronts all earthly seriousness so far, all solemnity in gesture, word, tone, eye, morality, and task so far, as if it were their most incarnate and involuntary parody—and in spite of all of this, it is perhaps only with it that* the great seriousness *really begins, that the real question mark is posed for the first time, that the destiny of the soul changes, the hand of the clock moves forward, the tragedy begins."*[3]

I cite again these few words (note dating from 1882–84): "To see tragic natures sink and to be able to laugh at them, *despite the profound understanding, emotion, and sympathy that one feels, that is divine."*[4]

The only parts of this book written with necessity—in accordance with my life—are the second, Torture, *and the last. I wrote the others with the laudable concern of writing a book.*

3

Asking oneself before another: by what means will he calm within himself the desire to be everything? Sacrifice, conformism, trickery, poetry, moralism, snobbism, heroism, religion, vanity, money? Or several means together? Or all together? A wink of an eye with a glimmer of malice, a melancholic smile, a grimace of fatigue betray the disguised suffering that the astonishment at not being everything, at even having short limits, gives us. A suffering so hard to acknowledge leads us to inner hypocrisy, to distant solemn demands (such as Kant's morality).

On the other hand. To no longer want to be everything is to question everything. Anyone who, slyly, wants to avoid suffering confuses himself with the entirety of the universe, judges each thing as if he were it, in the same way that he imagines, at bottom, he will never die. We receive these hazy illusions with life like a narcotic necessary to bear it. But what happens to us when, disintoxicated, we learn what we are? Lost among babblers, in a night wherein we can only hate the appearance of light that comes from babbling. The self-acknowledged suffering of the disintoxicated is the object of this book.

We are not everything. We have only two certitudes in this world, that and that of dying. If we are aware of not being everything, as we are of being mortal, it is nothing. But if we have no narcotic, an unbreathable void reveals itself. I wanted to be everything: such that falling into this void, but gathering my courage, I tell myself: "I am ashamed of having wanted to be everything because I now see, that was to sleep." From there on begins a singular experience. The mind moves in a strange world where anguish and ecstasy take shape.

Such an experience is not ineffable, but I communicate it to those who are unaware of it: its tradition is difficult (the written tradition is hardly more than an introduction to the oral one); from others, it demands preliminary anguish and desire.

What characterizes such an experience, which does not proceed from a revelation, wherein nothing is revealed if not the unknown, is that it never provides anything calming. My book finished, I see its detestable sides, its insufficiency, and worse, in myself, the concern for sufficiency that I mixed into it, that I am still mixing into it. I detest at the same time the impotence and the share of intentionality.

⁵*This book is the narrative of a despair. This world is given to man as if it were an enigma to resolve. My entire life—its strange, disordered moments,*

as much as my weighty meditations—has passed in resolving this enigma. I actually went to the end of problems whose novelty and dimensions exalted me. Entering into unexpected regions, I saw what eyes have never seen. Nothing more intoxicating: reason and laughter, horror and light became penetrable . . . There was nothing that I did not know, that was not accessible to my fever. Like a marvelous madwoman, death opened endlessly or closed the doors of the possible. In this maze, I could lose myself at will, give myself over to ravishment, but I could discern the path at will, arrange a precise passage of intellectual steps. The analysis of laughter had opened a field of coincidences between the facts of a communal *and* rigorous *emotional understanding and those of a discursive understanding.* Losing themselves in one another, *the contents of diverse forms of expenditure (laughter, heroism, ecstasy, sacrifice, poetry, eroticism, or others) defined a law of* communication *in themselves organizing the play of the isolation and loss of beings. The possibility of uniting* in a precise point *two kinds of understanding that up to this point had been foreign to one another or roughly confused gave this ontology its un-hoped for consistency: the entire movement of thought was lost to itself, but completely rediscovered itself, in a point at which the unanimous crowd laughs. Here I experienced a feeling of triumph: perhaps illegitimate, premature? . . . To me it does not seem so.*[6] *I rapidly felt what came to me as a weight. What shook my nerves was having achieved my task: my ignorance turned to insignificant points, more enigmas to resolve! Everything collapsed! I awoke before a new enigma, and I quickly knew that one was unsolvable: that enigma was even so bitter, it left me in an impotence so overwhelming that I experienced it as God, if he exists, would have experienced it.*

Three quarters finished, I abandoned the work[7] *wherein the solved enigma could be found. I wrote* Torture, *wherein man attains the extremity of the possible.*[8]

Draft of an Introduction to Inner Experience

1

Critique of Dogmatic Servitude (and of Mysticism)[1]

By *inner experience*, I understand what one usually calls *mystical experience*: states of ecstasy, of ravishment, at least of meditated emotion. But I am thinking less of *confessional* experience, to which one has had to hold oneself hitherto, than of a bare experience, free of ties, even of an origin, to any confession whatsoever. This is why I don't like the word *mystical*.

Nor do I like narrow definitions. Inner experience responds to the necessity in which I exist—and human existence with me—to challenge (question) everything without acceptable rest. This necessity was in play despite religious beliefs, but its consequences are much more complete if one does not have these beliefs. Dogmatic presuppositions have given experience undue limits: someone who already knows cannot go beyond a known horizon.

I wanted experience to lead me where it was leading, not to some end given in advance. And I say at once that it does not lead to a harbor (but to a place of bewilderment, of nonsense). I wanted nonknowledge itself to be the principle—for this reason I have followed with a fierce rigor a method in which the Christians excelled (they engaged in this path as far as dogma permits). But this experience, born of nonknowledge, remains there decidedly. It is not ineffable, one does not betray it if one speaks of it, but to questions of knowledge, it steals from the mind the answers that it already had. Experience reveals nothing and cannot be the basis of belief or set out from it.

Experience is questioning (testing), in fever and anguish, what man knows of the facts of being. That in this fever, he has some apprehension, of whatever kind, he cannot say: "I have seen this, what I have seen is this"; he cannot say: "I have seen God, the absolute in the depths of the world";

he can only say, "what I have seen escapes understanding," and God, the absolute, the depths of the world are nothing if they are not categories of understanding.[2]

If I said decisively: "I have seen God," that which I have seen would change. In place of the inconceivable unknown—wildly free before me, leaving me wild and free before it—there would be a dead object and the thing of the theologian—to which the unknown would be subjugated, because, in the form of God, the obscure unknown that ecstasy reveals is *subjugated to serving me* (the fact that a theologian can leap out of the established order after the fact signifies simply that the order is useless; it is for experience only a presupposition to be rejected).

In any case, God is linked to the salvation of the soul—at the same time as to other *relations between the imperfect and the perfect*. Now, in experience, the feeling that I had of the unknown of which I have spoken is uneasily hostile to the idea of perfection (servitude itself, the "must be"[3]).

I read in Dionysius the Areopagite: "Since the union of divinized minds with the Light beyond all deity occurs in the cessation of all intelligent activity . . . [they] praise it most appropriately through the denial of all beings" (*Divine Names*, I, 5).[4] It is this way from the moment in which experience reveals or does not reveal the presupposition (to such a degree that, in the eyes of the Areopagite, the light is a "ray of darkness"; he would go so far as to say, according to Eckhart: "God is nothingness").[5] But positive theology—founded on the revelation of the Scriptures—is not in agreement with this negative experience. A few pages after having evoked this God that discourse only apprehends through negation, Dionysius writes: "He has dominion over all and all things revolve around him, for he is their cause, their source, and their destiny" (*Divine Names*, I, 7).[6]

On the subject of "visions," of "words," and of other "consolations" common in ecstasy, Saint John of the Cross witnesses if not hostility at least reserve. For him, experience only has meaning in the apprehension of a God without form and without mode.[7] In the end, Saint Teresa herself only valued "intellectual vision."[8] Similarly, I maintain that the apprehension of God, even without form or mode ("intellectual" vision and nontangible), is a stop in the movement that brings us to the most obscure apprehension of the *unknown*: of a presence that is no longer distinct in any way from an absence.

God differs from the unknown in that a profound emotion, coming from the depths of childhood, is initially linked in us to his evocation. The unknown on the contrary leaves us cold, does not make us love it before it overturns everything in us like a violent wind. In the same way, the upsetting images and middle terms to which poetic emotion has recourse touch us without difficulty. If poetry introduces the strange, it does so by way of the familiar. The poetic is the familiar dissolving into the strange and dissolving ourselves with it. It never dispossesses us entirely, because the words, the dissolved images, are charged with emotions already experienced, pinned to objects that link them to the known.

Divine or poetic apprehension is on the same level as the fruitless apparitions of the saints in that we can still, through it, appropriate that which surpasses us, and, without grasping it as a real possession, at least link it to ourselves, to what we have already touched. In this way, we do not die entirely: a thread, undoubtedly tenuous, but a thread links the apprehended to the self (having shattered the naive notion I had of Him, God remains the being whose role is set by the Church).

We are only totally laid bare by proceeding without trickery to the unknown. It is the share of the unknown that gives the experience of God—or the poetic—its great authority. But in the end the unknown demands an empire without shares.[9]

2

Experience, Sole Authority, Sole Value

Opposition to the idea of project—which takes up an essential part of this book—is so necessary for me that, having written a detailed outline of this introduction, I cannot hold myself to it. Having abandoned for a time its execution, having passed to the post-scriptum (which was unforeseen), I can only change it. I hold myself to the project in secondary things: in what is important to me, it quickly appears to be what it is: contrary to myself being project.

I have to explain myself on this point, interrupting the account: I must do it, being unable to guarantee the homogeneity of the whole. Perhaps this is sloppy. Nevertheless, I want to say it, I don't in any way oppose project with a negative mood (a sickly spinelessness), but the spirit of decision.

The expression of inner experience must in some way respond to its movement, cannot be a dry verbal translation, executed on command.[10]

From the outline that I stopped, I give the chapter titles, which were:

—Critique of dogmatic servitude (sole written)
—Critique of the scientific attitude
—Critique of the experimental attitude
—Position of experience itself as value and authority
—Principle of a method
—Principle of a community.
I will now try to extract a movement that was to emerge from the whole.

Inner experience cannot have its principle in a dogma (a moral attitude), in a science (knowledge cannot be either its goal or its origin), or in a search for enriching states (the aesthetic, experimental attitude), it cannot have any other concern or other goal than itself. Opening myself to inner experience, I have placed all value, all authority in it. I cannot henceforth have another value or another authority.* Value, authority imply the rigor of a method, the existence of a community.

I call experience a journey to the end of the possible of man. Not everyone can take this journey, but, if one does, this supposes the negation of authorities, of existing values, that limit the possible. From the fact that it is the negation of other values, of other authorities, experience having positive existence itself becomes value *and authority* positively.**

Inner experience has always had other goals than itself, wherein one placed value, authority. God in Islam or the Christian Church; in the Buddhist Church this negative end: the suppression of pain (it was also possible to subordinate it to knowledge, as does Heidegger's ontology†). But that God, knowledge, the suppression of pain cease to be in my eyes convincing goals, if the pleasure to be drawn from a ravishment disturbs me, shocks me even, must inner experience suddenly seem empty to me, henceforth impossible, without justification?

The question is in no way pointless. The absence of a formal response (which I passed over until now) leaves me with great uneasiness. Experience itself tore me to shreds, and these shreds, my impotence to respond tore them apart. I received the answer from others: it demands a solidity that at this moment I had lost. I posed the question to several friends, letting them see a part of my disarray: one of them†† stated simply this principle, that experience itself is the authority (but that authority expiates itself).[11]

From the moment that answer calmed me, barely leaving me (like a scar slowly closing over a wound) a residue of anguish. I measured its significance the day I worked out the project for an introduction. I saw then that it brought the entire debate about religious existence to an end, that it even had the Galilean significance of a reversal in the exercise of thought, that it substituted itself at once for the traditions of the Church and philosophy.

---

*Understood in the realm of the mind, as one says of the authority of science, of the Church, of the Scriptures.

**The paradox in the authority of experience: founded on questioning, it questions authority: questioned positively, man's authority defines itself as questioning itself.

†At least in the way that he exposes his thought, before a community of men, of knowledge.

††Maurice Blanchot. Later on I refer to this conversation on two occasions.

For some time already, the only living philosophy, that of the German school, tended to make knowledge the final extension of inner experience. But this *phenomenology* gives knowledge the value of a goal that one reaches through experience. This is a brittle alloy: the share given to experience here is at once too much and not great enough. Those who provide this place for it must feel that it overflows, through an immense possibility, the use to which they limit themselves. What preserves the appearance of philosophy is the lack of acuity of the experiences from which the phenomenologists set out. This absence of equilibrium does not survive the play of experience going to the end of the possible. When going to the end means at least this: that the limit that is knowledge as a goal be crossed.

From the philosophical perspective, it is a question of ending the analytic division of operations, thereby escaping to the empty feeling of intelligent questions. From the religious perspective, the solved problem is weightier. The traditional authorities, values, have for a long time no longer had meaning for a great number of people. And those whose interest is the extremity of the possible cannot be indifferent to the critique to which the tradition has succumbed. It is linked to movements of intelligence wanting to exceed its limits. But—it is undeniable—the advance of that intelligence has had the secondary effect of diminishing the possible into a realm that appears foreign to intelligence: *that of inner experience.*

Again, to say diminished is to say too little. The development of intelligence leads to a drying up of life that, in return, has shrunken intelligence. It is only if I state this principle: "inner experience itself is authority," that I get out of this impotence. Intelligence destroyed the authority necessary for experience: by this means of decision, man arranges once again his possibility and it is no longer the old, the limited, but the extremity of the possible.

These statements have an obscure theoretical appearance and I see no remedy to this other than to say: "one must grasp the meaning from within." They are not logically demonstrable. One must *live* the experience, it is not easily accessible, and even, considered from outside by the intelligence, it would be necessary to see in it a sum of distinct operations, some intellectual, others aesthetic, others still ultimately moral and the whole problem must be taken up again. It is only from within, lived to the point of a trance, that it appears to unify what discursive thought must separate. But it does not unify any less than these forms—aesthetic, intellectual, moral—the diverse contents of past experience (like God and His Passion) in a fusion leaving outside only the discourse by which one attempted to separate these objects (making them answers to moral difficulties).

In the end experience attains the fusion of the object and the subject, being as subject nonknowledge, as object the unknown. It can let the agitation of the intelligence be shattered there: repeated failures serve it no less than the final docility that one can anticipate.

Attaining this as an extremity of the possible, it goes without saying that philosophy properly speaking is absorbed, that, being already separated from the simple attempt at the cohesion of knowledge that is the philosophy of the sciences, it dissolves. And dissolving in this new way of thinking, it finds itself to be no more than the heir to a fabulous mystical theology, but mutilated by a God and wiping the slate clean.

The separation of the trance from realms of knowledge, of feeling, of morality obligates one to *construct* values reuniting *from the outside* the elements of these realms in the forms of authoritative entities, when one must not look far, must return to oneself on the contrary to find what was missing on the day when one contested the constructions. "Oneself" is not the subject isolating itself from the world, but a place of communication, of fusion of subject and object.

Principles of a Method and of a Community[12]

When the ravages of the intelligence had dismantled the edifices about which I have spoken, human life felt a lack (but not right away a total failure). This communication going far, the fusion that it had effected up to then through a meditation on objects having a history (pathetic and dramatic), like God, it seemed that one could no longer attain it. One therefore had to choose to remain faithful, obstinately, to dogmas fallen in a realm of critique—or to renounce the only form of passionate life, fusion.

Love, poetry, in a romantic form, were ways in which we attempted to escape isolation, into the diminishment of a life shortly deprived of its most visible outlet. But when these new outlets were of a kind that created no regrets for the old ones, the old ones became inaccessible, or so those affected by the critique believed: thereby their life was deprived of a share of its possibility.

In other words, one attained states of ecstasy or ravishment only by *dramatizing* existence in general. Belief in a betrayed God, who loves us (to the point that he dies for us), redeems us and saves us, played this role for a long time. But one can say that, this belief failing, the dramatization is impossible: ultimately, other peoples have known it—and through it, ecstasy—not being informed of the Gospel.

One can say only this: that dramatization necessarily has a key, in the form of an uncontested (decisive) element, of value without which there could be no drama, only indifference. Thus, from the moment when the drama reaches us, or at least if it is felt to be touching mankind generally in us, we attain authority, which causes the drama. (Similarly, if there is an authority, a value in us, there is drama, for if it is so, it must be taken seriously, totally).

In every religion dramatization is essential, but if it is purely exterior and mythic, it can have several independent forms at the same time. Sacrifices with different sources and intentions are combined. But each of them, from the moment the victim is sacrificed, marks the point of intensity of a dramatization. If we didn't know how to dramatize, we would not be able to get out of ourselves. We would live isolated and boxed in. But a kind of rupture—in anguish—leaves us at the limit of tears: then we lose ourselves, we forget ourselves and communicate with the ungraspable beyond.

From this way of dramatizing—often forced—comes an element of comedy, of foolishness, that turns into laughter. If we didn't know how to dramatize, we would not know how to laugh, but in us laughter is always ready, which makes us burst into a renewed fusion, once again shattering us in the play of errors committed in wanting to shatter ourselves, but this time without authority.[13]

Dramatization becomes entirely general only by making itself inner, but it cannot exist without means commensurate with naive aspirations— like that of never dying. When it became inner and general, it fell into an exclusive authority, jealous (out of the question to laugh from then on, it became that much more forced). All this so that the being not shrink into itself too much, not end up a greedy shopkeeper, a debauched old man.

Between the shopkeeper, the rich debauchee, and the devotee, secluded in anticipation of salvation, there are also many affinities, even the possibility of being united in a single person.

Another equivocation: stemming from the compromise between the positive authority of God and the negative authority of the suppression of pain. In the will to suppress pain, we are driven to action, in place of limiting ourselves to dramatization. Action guided by the suppression of pain ultimately leads in the opposite direction from the possibility of dramatization in its name: we no longer tend toward the extremity of the possible, we remedy pain (without great effect), but the possibility that awaits no longer has any meaning, we live on projects, forming a world rather unified (under the pretense of inexpiable hostilities) with that of the debauchee, the shopkeeper, and the egotistical devotee.

In these ways of dramatizing at the extremity, within traditions, we can separate ourselves from them. Recourse to a desire not to die and even, save for the humiliation before God, the habitual means are almost a failing in Saint John of the Cross, who, falling into the night of nonknowledge, touches the extremity of the possible: among a few others in a less striking way, perhaps no less profound.

Kierkegaard, by dint of going to the end of the possible, and in some way of the absurd, having received the authority of each element of the drama from tradition, displaces himself in a world wherein it becomes impossible to rely on anything, where irony is free.

I have come to what is most important:[14] *external means must be rejected.* The dramatic is not being in these conditions or those conditions, which are positive conditions (like being half-lost, the power to be saved). It is simply to be. To perceive this is, without anything else, to contest with enough persistence the subterfuges through which we usually capitulate. No longer a question of salvation: this is the most odious of subterfuges. The difficulty—that contestation must be done in the name of an authority—is thus resolved: I contest in the name of contestation what experience itself is (the will to go to the end of the possible). Experience, its authority, its method cannot be distinguished from contestation.*

I could have told myself: value, authority is ecstasy; inner experience is ecstasy, ecstasy is, it seems, communication, opposing itself to the diminishment about which I have spoken. I would have in this way *known* and *found* (there was a time when I believed I knew, had found). But we reach ecstasy through a contestation of knowledge. Were I to arrest myself in ecstasy and grasp it, in the end I would define it. But nothing resists the contestation of knowledge and I have seen in the end that the idea of communication itself leaves bare, knowing nothing. Whatever it may be, failing a positive revelation in myself present at the extremity, I can offer it neither justification nor end. I remain in intolerable nonknowledge, which has no other outlet than ecstasy itself.

State of nudity, of supplication without response wherein I nevertheless perceive this: that it is a matter of evading subterfuges. Such that,

---

*As I say in the fourth part, the principle of contestation is one of those upon which Maurice Blanchot insists as a foundation.

specific knowledge remaining as such, only the ground, the foundation, giving way, I grasp in sinking that the only truth of man, finally glimpsed, is to be a supplication without response.

Taken with belated simplicity, the ostrich, in the end, leaves an eye, free of the sand, strangely open . . . But when one reads me, with great attention and goodwill, should one arrive at the ultimate degree of conviction, one will not be laid bare for all that. Because nudity, sinking, supplication are first notions added to others. Though linked to the evasion of subterfuges, in that they themselves extend realms of knowledge, they are themselves reduced to the state of subterfuges. This is the work of discourse within us. And this difficulty is expressed in this way: *the word silence is still a sound*, to speak is in itself to imagine knowing, and to no longer know, it would be necessary to no longer speak. The sand let me open my eyes, I spoke: words, *which serve only to flee*, when I ceased fleeing, return me to flight. My eyes are open, its true, but it would have been necessary not to say it, to remain frozen like an animal. I wanted to speak, and as if the words carried the weight of a thousand slumbers, gently, as if appearing not to see, my eyes closed.[15]

It is through an "intimate cessation of every intellectual operation" that the mind is laid bare. If not, *discourse* maintains itself in its little box. Discourse, if it wants, can blow up a storm, whatever effort I make, the wind cannot chill by the fireside. The difference between inner experience and philosophy resides principally in that, in experience, the statement is nothing, if not a means and even, as much as a means, an obstacle; what counts is not the statement of the wind, it's the wind.

At this point we see the second meaning of the word dramatize: it is the will, added to discourse, not to limit oneself to the statement, to oblige one to feel the chill of the wind, to be laid bare. Hence dramatic art utilizing nondiscursive sensation, forcing a blow, toward that end imitating the sound of the wind and attempting to chill—as by contagion: it makes a character tremble on-stage (rather than resorting to these rough means, the philosopher surrounds himself with narcotic signs). On this subject, it is a classic error to assign Saint Ignatius's *Exercises* to discursive method: they rely on discourse, which regulates everything but in the dramatic mode.[16] Discourse exhorts: represent yourself, it says, the place, the characters in the drama, and remain there as one among them; dissipate—extend your will for that reason—the stupor, the absence toward which the words incline. The truth is that the *Exercises*, completely horrified by discourse (by absence), attempt to alleviate that through the tension of discourse, and that often artifice fails (on the other hand, the object of contemplation that they propose is no doubt drama, but engaged in the historical categories of discourse, far from the God without form or mode of the Carmelites, more thirsty than the Jesuits for inner experience).

The weakness of the dramatic method is that it always forces one to go beyond what is naturally felt. But this weakness is less that of the method than our own. And it is not the voluntary side of the process (to which here is added sarcasm: the comical appears not as an authority, but as that which, desiring it, never comes through its efforts to submit to it) that stops me: it is its impotence.

In fact, the contestation would remain impotent in us if it limited itself to discourse and to dramatic exhortation. That sand into which we bury ourselves so as not to see, is formed from words, and contestation, before making use of them, occasions thoughts—if I pass from one image to another different image—of the stuck, struggling man and of his efforts that bury him for sure: and it is true that words, their mazes, the exhausting immensity of their possibilities, in short their treachery, are something like quicksand.

We would not get out of these sands without some sort of cord extended toward us. Even though words drain almost all of our life from us—of this life there almost isn't a single twig that hasn't been seized, dragged, piled up by this restless, busy crowd of ants (the words)—it remains in us a silent, elusive, ungraspable part. In the region of words, of discourse, this part is unknown. It also usually eludes us. Only under certain conditions can we attain it or use it. These are vague inner movements, which do not depend on any object and have no purpose, states that, similar to others linked to the purity of the sky, to the fragrance of a room, are not motivated by anything definable, such that the language that, with respect to the others, has the sky, the room, to which it can refer—and which in this case directs attention toward what it grasps—is dispossessed, cannot say anything, limits itself to stealing these states away from attention (profiting from their lack of precision, it draws attention elsewhere right away).

If we live without contestation under the law of language, these states are in us as if they did not exist. But if we throw ourselves against this law, we can in passing fix our consciousness on one of them and, silencing discourse within ourselves, linger over the surprise that it gives us. It is better to shut oneself in, to make it night, to remain suspended in this silence in which we sneak up on the sleep of a child. With a little luck, in such a state we perceive what favors the return, increases the intensity. And undoubtedly, there is no more for this than the sick passion with which, for a long moment in the night, a mother stays close to a cradle.

But the difficulty is that one does not easily and completely come to silence oneself, that one must struggle against oneself, with precisely a mother's patience: we seek to grasp in ourselves what subsists in the shelter of verbal servilities and, what we grasp is ourselves fighting the campaign, stringing sentences together, perhaps on the subject of our effort (then of its failure), but sentences, and impotent to grasp anything else. We must persist—making ourselves familiar, cruelly, with an impotent foolishness, usually concealed, but falling in full light: the intensity of the states builds quickly and from that moment they absorb, even enrapture. The moment comes when we can reflect, once again no longer silencing ourselves, linking words: this time, it is off-stage (in the background) and, without worrying us any longer, we let their sound fade away.[17]

This mastery of our innermost movements, which we can eventually acquire, is well known: it is *yoga*.[18] But *yoga* comes to us in the form of rough recipes, embellished with pedantism and strange statements. And *yoga*, practiced for its own sake, advances no further than an aesthetics or a hygiene, while I have recourse to the same means (laid bare) *in despair*.

Christians passed over these means, but for them experience was only the final stage of a long ascesis (Hindus gave themselves up to asceticism, which lends their experience an equivalent of the religious drama that it lacks). But being unable and not wanting recourse to an ascesis, I must link contestation to the *liberation of the power of words* that is mastery. And if, as opposed to the Hindus, I reduced these means to what they are, then affirmed that inspiration must create a part of them, I can also not fail to say that one cannot reinvent them. Their practice, heavy with tradition, is analogous to common culture, which the freest of the poets have not been able to surpass (no great poet who hasn't done secondary studies).

What I have taken on is as far as I can be from the scholastic atmosphere of *yoga*. The means in question are double: one must find: *words* that serve as food for habit, but turn us away from those objects the whole of which enclose us; *objects* that cause us to slip from the external (objective) level to the interiority of the subject.

I will only give one example of a slipping *word*. I say *word*: it could also be the phrase in which one inserts the word, but I limit myself to the word *silence*. As a word it is already, as I have said, the abolition of the sound that is a word; among all words it is the most perverse, or the most poetic: it is itself proof of its own death.

Silence is given in the sick delectation of the heart. When the fragrance of a flower is charged with reminiscences, we linger alone in breathing in the flower, questioning it, in the anguish of the secret that its sweetness will in a moment deliver to us: this secret is only the inner presence, silent, unfathomable, and bare, that an attention always given to words (to objects) steals from us, which if necessary returns to us if we give it to those most transparent among objects. But it only returns fully if we know how to detach it, in the end, even from these discrete objects: which we can do by choosing for them as a resting place wherein they will complete their dissipation the silence that is no longer anything.

The resting place that the Hindus chose is no less interior: it is breath. And even as a slipping word has the virtue of capturing the attention offered in advance to words, so breath, attention disposed toward gestures, movements directed toward objects: but of these movements only breath leads to interiority. So that Hindus breathing gently—and perhaps in silence—deeply, have not wrongly given breath a power that is not the one that they thought, that nonetheless opens the secrets of the heart.[19]

Silence is a word that is not a word and breath an object that is not an object . . .

I interrupt once again the course of the account. I do not give the reasons for this (which are several, coinciding). I limit myself now to notes from which the essential emerges and in a form answering better to the intent than to continuity.

The Hindus have other means; which in my eyes have only one value, to show that only impoverished means (the most impoverished) have the virtue of effecting rupture (rich means have too much meaning, come between us and the unknown, like objects sought for themselves). Intensity alone matters. Now—

We have just barely directed attention toward an inner presence: what was up to now concealed assumes the fullness not of a storm—it concerns slow movements—but of an invading flood. Now the sensibility is exalted: it suffices that we detach it from the neutral objects that we usually give it.

A sensibility having become through detachment from that which reaches the senses so internal that every return to the outside, the drop of a pin, a cracking, has an immense and distant resonance . . . The Hindus have noted this strangeness. I imagine it arrives as in a vision, sharpened by a dilation of the pupil in the darkness.[20] *Here obscurity is not an absence of light (or of noise) but the absorption of the outside. In a simple night, our attention is entirely given to the world of objects by way of words, which persist. True silence takes place in the absence of words; that a pin should then drop: like the blow of a hammer, I jump up . . . In this silence made from within, there is no longer one organ, it is the entire sensibility, the heart, which is dilated.*

Various means of the Hindus.

They pronounce in a cavernous way, prolonged as in the resonance of a cathedral, the syllable OM. They hold this syllable sacred. They thus create for themselves a religious torpor, full of unclear, even majestic divinity, whose prolongation is purely internal. But here one must have the naivety—the purity—of the Hindu, must have the sickly taste of the European for exotic color.

Others, on occasion, use intoxicants.

The Tantrics *have recourse to sexual pleasure: they don't sink into it; it serves as a springboard.*

Games of virtuosity, of deliquescence merge and nothing is far from the will to lay bare.

But I know little, at bottom, about India . . . The few judgments I hold—more of distancing than of reception—are linked to my ignorance. I have no hesitation on two points: the books of the Hindus are, if not clumsy, uneven; these Hindus have friends in Europe that I don't like.

The tendency among Hindus—mixed with contempt—to flatter the Occident, its religion, its science, its morality, to justify their appearance of backwardness; one is in the presence of a system in itself remarkable, that measures itself, does not develop a bad conscience from this starting point; the intellectual pretension causes naiveties to come out without being touching or indifferent; when it comes to morality, modern Hindus attenuate to their detriment an audacity that perhaps they have maintained (the tradition of "advaita" in the Vedanta, in which Nietzsche saw precursors[21]), do not rid themselves of a concern borrowed from reverence to principles. They are what they are and I hardly doubt that in all respects they raise themselves high enough to see from on high; but they explain themselves in an Occidental way, hence the reduction to a common measure.

I don't doubt that Hindus go far into the impossible, but to the highest degree, *they are missing that which counts for me, the faculty of expressing it. From the little I know, I believe I can gather that ascesis plays a decisive role among them. (The opposite disorders—eroticism, intoxicants—seem rare, are rejected by a great number. The disorders themselves do not exclude asceticism, they even demand it by virtue of a principle of equilibrium.) The key is the search for salvation.*

The poverty of these people is that they are concerned with a salvation, however different from Christian salvation. We know that they imagine a succession of rebirths—up to deliverance: no longer being reborn.[22]

What I find striking on this topic, what seems convincing (although the conviction does not come from reasoning, but only from the feelings that it defines):

Assume X is dead, that I was (in another life) A life, and Z, what I will be. I can in A life discern AY that I was yesterday, AT that I will be tomorrow (in that life). A knows that AY was itself yesterday, which no one else was. He can even isolate AB among all the men who will exist tomorrow. But A cannot do this of X dead. He does not know who X was, has no memory of him. In the same way, X cannot imagine A. In the same way, A knows nothing of Z, who has no memory of A. If between X, A, and Z none of the relationships that I perceive between AY, A, and AT exist, one can only introduce inconceivable relationships among them, as if they had not existed. Even if it is true from some unintelligible point of view that X, A, and Z were but one, I can only be indifferent to this truth in that, by definition, X, A, and Z are necessarily indifferent to one another. It is comical on the part of A to be concerned about Z forever unknown to him, for whom he will always be unknown, as comical as being concerned in particular with what might happen tomorrow to one or another of the passersby opposite us. Assume K is passing by, between A, X, and Z there is, there will always be, the same absence of relationship of the AY, A, AT type (which is to say of graspable relationships) as between A and K.

From that point on: if it is proven that I have a soul, that it is immortal, I can assume relationships of the A, AT type between this soul and myself after my death (my soul remembering me as A *remembers* AY*). Nothing is simpler, but if I introduce between them the same relationships of the* A, AT *type, these relationships remain arbitrary, they will not have the same clear consistency as those that characterize* A, AT. *Assume* AD, *my soul after death, I can have in regard to this* AD *the same indifference that I have with regard to* K, *which it is impossible for me to have in regard to* AT *(if I say I can, impossible, I speak strictly for myself, but the same reaction would be obtained from each straightforward and lucid man).*

The truth—the most comical truth—is that one never pays attention to these problems. One discusses the strong or weak foundation of beliefs without perceiving an insignificance that makes the discussion useless. Nevertheless I can only offer a precise form to the feeling of each person of some intellect, believer or not. There was a time when the relationships between A and AD *actually existed (in uncultivated minds) in the* A, AT *type of relationship, wherein one had a real, inevitable concern for the afterlife: human beings initially imagined a terrifying survival, not necessarily long but charged with harmfulness and the cruelty of death. Then the links between the self and the soul were unreasoned (as are the relationships between A and* AT*). But these relationships between A and* AD, *still unreasoned, were in the end dissolved through the exercise of reason (in which they were entirely different from the relationship of* A *to* AT, *sometimes fragile in appearance, yet remaining very resistant when put to the test). Reasoned relationships, linked to ever more elevated moral ideas, were eventually substituted for these relationships, bound to dreams. In the confusion, human beings can continue to say: "I am concerned with* AD *(elsewhere about* Z*) as much as about* AT*"; tell themselves not to be really concerned. The uncultivated images dissipated, the comical truth slowly emerges; no matter what he says, A is hardly any more interested in* AD *than in* K; *he lives lightly in view of hell. A cultivated Christian is no longer, at bottom, unaware that* AD *is another and mocks this as he does* K *with only, superimposed, the principle: "I must be concerned about* AD *not* AT*." At the moment of death, there is added to this the pious wishes of his loved ones, the terror of the dying who can no longer imagine himself dead, and speechless, continuing to live as* AD.

"What makes me shudder with love is not the heaven that you have promised me, the horrible hell does not make me shudder . . . if there were no heaven I would love you and if there were no hell I would fear you" (St. Teresa of Avila). *In Christian faith, the rest is pure convenience.*

When I was a Christian, I had so little interest in AD, *it seemed so fruitless to concern myself with it more than with* K, *that, in the Scriptures, no phrase pleased me more than these words from* Psalm 38: *"* . . . ut refrigerer* pruisquam abeam et amplius non ero" (. . . that I may be refreshed before I die and am no more).[23] Today would someone prove to me by some absurd means that AM will boil in hell, I wouldn't be concerned about it, saying: "it doesn't matter, him or someone else." What would affect me—and from which I would boil while alive—would be that hell exists. But no one ever did believe it. One day Christ spoke of the grinding teeth of the damned; he was God and required them, being himself the requirement, nevertheless he did not break in two and his unfortunate pieces were not thrown against one another: he wasn't thinking about what he was saying but about the impression that he wanted to make.

On this point, many Christians resemble me (but the convenience of a project that one is not really forced to believe remains). A lot of artifice already enters in with the concern of A for AT (the identity A, AY, AT is reduced to the thread linking the moments of a being alternating, becoming estranged from itself from one hour to another). Death breaks the thread: we can only grasp a continuity because of a threshold that interrupts it. But a movement of freedom, of moving brusquely, suffices; AD and K appear equivalent.[24]

This immense interest in K through the ages is moreover neither purely comical nor purely sordid. To be so interested in K, without knowing that it was him!

"All of my laborious fervor and all of my nonchalance, all of my self-mastery and all of my natural inclination, all my bravery and all my trembling, my sun and my lightning burst from a black sky, my whole soul and mind, all of the solemn and heavy granite of my 'Self,' all this has the right to be repeated ceaselessly: 'What does it matter what I am?'" (Nietzsche, fragment, 1880–81).[25]

To imagine oneself effaced, abolished by death, missing from the universe . . . On the contrary, if I continue to exist, with me the crowd of the dead, the universe would grow old, all of these dead would leave a bad taste in its mouth.

I can only bear the weight of the future on one condition: that others, always others, live there—and that death washes us, then washes these others without end.[26]

What is most hostile about the morality of salvation: it assumes a truth and a multitude that, without seeing it, lives in error. To be juvenile, gener-

ous, laughing—and, what goes along with this, loving that which seduces, girls, dancing, flowers, is to err: if she were not foolish, the pretty girl would want to be repulsive (salvation alone matters). Worse undoubtedly: happy defiance of death, the feeling of glory that inebriates and makes air breathed in invigorating, so many vanities that cause the sage to mutter under his breath: "if they knew . . ."

There is on the contrary an affinity between, on the one hand, the absence of care, generosity, the need to defy death, tumultuous love, nervous sensitivity, and, on the other, the will to become the prey of the unknown. In both cases, the same need for unlimited *adventure, the same horror of calculation, of* project *(the withered, prematurely old faces of the "bourgeois" and their prudence).*

Against asceticism.

That a bloodless, non-laughing particle of life, grumbling in front of excesses of joy, lacking freedom, *should attain—or claim to have attained—the extremity, is a deception. One attains the extremity in the fullness of means: it demands fulfilled beings, that know every audacity. My principle against asceticism is that the extremity is accessible through excess, not through lack.*

Even the asceticism of successful beings takes on in my eyes the sense of a sin, of an impotent poverty.

I do not deny that asceticism is conducive to experience. I even insist on it. Asceticism is a sure means to detach oneself from objects: it is to kill the desire that links one to the object. But it is at the same time to make experience an object (one has not killed the desire for objects, only proposed a new object for desire).

Through asceticism, experience is condemned to take on the value of a positive object. Asceticism postulates deliverance, salvation, the possession of the most desirable object. In asceticism, the value cannot be experience alone, independent of pleasure or suffering; it is always a beatitude, a deliverance, that we work to procure for ourselves.

Experience at the extremity of the possible nevertheless demands a renunciation: to cease to want to be everything. While asceticism understood in the ordinary sense is rightly the sign of a pretension to become everything, by possession of God, etc. St. John of the Cross himself wrote: "Para venir a serlo todo . . ." *(to arrive at being all).*[27]

It is doubtful in each case if salvation is the object of true faith or if it is only a convenience permitting one to give "spiritual" life the form of a project (ecstasy is not sought for its own sake, it is the path of a deliverance, a means). Salvation is not necessarily the value that the end of suffering is for the Buddhists; God for the Christians, Muslims, non-Buddhist Hindus. It is the perspective of value perceived from the point of view of personal life. Besides, in both cases, the value is totality, completion, and, for the faithful, salvation is "to become everything," divinity directly for the majority, nonindividuality for the Buddhists (suffering is, according to Buddha, the individual). The project of salvation formed, asceticism is possible.

Now imagine a different, even opposed will, wherein the will to "become everything" would be regarded as an obstacle to that of losing oneself (of escaping isolation, to the diminishment of the individual). Wherein "becoming everything" would be considered not only as the sin of man but of every possibility and even of God!

To lose oneself in this case would be to lose oneself and in no way save oneself. (Further on one will see the passion that a man brings to contesting each slip in the meaning of the whole, of salvation, of the possibility of a project.) But then the possibility of asceticism disappears!

Nonetheless inner experience is project, no matter what.
It is project, man being entirely project through language that in essence, with the exception of its poetic perversion, is project. But the project is no longer in this case that, positive, of salvation, but that, negative, of abolishing the power of words, therefore of project.

The problem is then the following. Asceticism is not a cause, without support, with a purpose that makes it possible. If asceticism is a sacrifice, it is a sacrifice of a part of oneself that one loses so that one may save another part. But if one wants to lose oneself entirely: this is possible beginning with a bacchanal movement, not calm in any way. Calmness is on the contrary necessary for asceticism. One must choose.

Roughly, I can show that in principle the means are always double. On the one hand, one appeals to the excess of forces, to movements of drunkenness, of desire. And on the other hand, in order to have at one's disposal a quantity of forces, one mutilates oneself (through asceticism, like a plant, without seeing that the experience is domesticated *in this way—like a flower—thereby ceasing to respond to the hidden demand. If it is a question of salvation, what one mutilates . . . But the journey to the end of the possible demands freedom of temperament, that of a horse that has never been mounted).*

In itself asceticism has, for many, something attractive, satisfying; like an accomplished mastery, but more difficult, the domination of the self, of all its instincts. Asceticism can look from on high at what is below (in any case, human nature, through the contempt that it has for itself). It imagines no means of living outside of the form of a project. (I don't look at anyone from on high, but at ascetics and pleasure seekers laughingly, like a child.)

One says naturally: no other way out. Everyone agrees on one point: no sexual excess. And almost everyone: absolute chastity. I dare to dismiss these pretensions. And if chastity, like every asceticism, is in a sense easy, wildness, accumulating contrary circumstances, is more favorable than asceticism in that it returns the old maid—and whoever resembles her—to their domestic *poverty.*

The man who knows nothing of eroticism is no less foreign to the end of the possible than he is without inner experience. One must choose the arduous, stormy path—that of the "whole man" nonmutilated.

I have come to the point of saying with precision: the Hindu is a stranger to drama, the Christian cannot attain within himself bare silence. The one and the other have recourse to asceticism. The first two means alone are burning (not demanding any project): no one has yet brought them together into play, but only one and the other with asceticism. If I had access to one of the two, for want of a strained exercise, like asceticism, I would not have had any inner experience, but only that of everyone, linked to the exteriority of objects (in a calm exercise of inner movements, one makes of interiority itself an object; one seeks a "result"). But access to the world of the inside, of silence, having been linked in me to extreme interrogation, I escaped verbal flight at the same time as the empty and peaceful curiosity of states. Interrogation encountered the answer that changed the logical operation into vertigo (like an excitation taking form in the apprehension of nudity[28]).

Something sovereignly attractive in the fact of being discourse itself as much as the driest Occidental and at the same time having at one's disposal a brief means of silence: it is the silence of the tomb and existence ruins itself in the full movement of its force.

A phrase from Was ist Metaphysik? *struck me: "Our existence* [unseres Dasein]," *says Heidegger, "—in the community of researchers, teachers, and students—is determined by knowledge."*[29] *Undoubtedly in this way stumbles a philosophy whose meaning should be linked to a human existence determined by inner experience (life in play beyond separated operations). This less to indicate the limit of my interest in Heidegger than to introduce a principle: there can be no knowledge without a community of researchers, nor any inner experience without a community of those who live it. Community is understood in a different sense than Church or order. The* Sannyasin *of India have among them less formal links than Heidegger's "researchers."*[30] *The human existence that* yoga *determines in them is no less that of a community: communication is a fact that is in no way added to human existence, but constitutes it.*

Now I must shift direction. The communication of a given "human existence" assumes among those who communicate not formal links but general conditions. Historical, current conditions, but at risk in a certain sense. I speak of them here concerned with reaching what is decisive. When elsewhere I have wounded, then opened the wound.

At the extremity of knowledge, what is forever missing is what revelation alone offered:
An arbitrary answer, saying: "you now know what you must know, what you don't know is what you have no need to know: it suffices that someone else knows it and that you depend upon him, you can join him."
Without that answer, man is dispossessed of the means to be everything, is a lost madman, a question without a way out.[31]

What one has not grasped in doubting revelation is that no one having ever spoken to us, no one would speak to us any longer: we are henceforth alone, the sun set forever.
One believed in reason's answers without seeing that they only stand up by giving themselves an authority like divine authority, by mimicking revelation (with a foolish pretension to say everything*).*

What one couldn't know: that only revelation permits man to be everything, this is not reason, but one has the habit of being everything, hence reason's fruitless effort to answer as God did, and to give satisfaction. Now the die is thrown, the game a thousand times lost, man definitively alone—not being about to say anything (at least until he acts: decides*).*

The great derision: a multitude of little, contradictory "everythings," intelligence surpassing itself, culminating in multivocal, discordant, indiscrete idiocy.

The most strange: to no longer want to be everything is for man the highest ambition, it is to want to be man (or, if you will, to rise above man—to be what he would be, released from the need to ogle the perfect, acting its opposite).

And now: before a declaration of Kantian morality (act as if . . .[32]), before a reproach formulated in the name of that declaration, even an act, a desire, a bad conscience, we can, far from venerating, look at the mouse in the cat's paws: "You wanted to be everything, the fraud discovered, you will serve as a toy for us."

In my eyes, the night of nonknowledge that follows the decision: "To no longer wish to be everything, therefore to be man rising above the need that he had to turn away from himself," neither adds nor takes away anything from Nietzsche's teaching. The entire morality of laughter, of risk, of the exaltation of virtues and of forces is the spirit of decision.

Man ceasing—at the limit of laughter—to want to be everything and wanting in the end to be what he is, imperfect, incomplete, good—if he can be, up to moments of cruelty; and lucid . . . to the point of dying blind.

A paradoxical movement demands that I introduce in the conditions of a community what I refused in the principles of inner experience themselves. But in these principles, I separated the possible dogmas *and I have only now stated the facts, those at least that I see.*

Without the night, no one would have to decide, but in a false light, to undergo. The decision is what is born before the worst and rises above. It is the essence of courage, of the heart, of the being itself. And it is the inverse of project (it demands that one reject delay, that one decide on the spot, everything at stake: what follows matters second).

There is a secret in the decision, the most intimate, that is found at last in the night, in anguish (which the decision brings to an end). But neither the night nor the decision is a means; *in no way is the night a* means *for the decision: the night exists for itself or it does not exist.*

What I say about the decision or about the fate of the man to come is at stake, is included in each real decision, each time a tragic disorder demands a decision without delay.

This engages me to the maximum of effacement (without concern), as opposed to comical romanticism (and to the extent that I distance myself in this way—decidedly—from romantic appearances—that I have had to take on—it is what someone who is lazy engages to see poorly . . .). The deep meaning of Ecce homo*: to leave nothing in the shadows, to dismantle pride in the light.*

I have spoken of community as existing: Nietzsche related his affirmations about it but remained alone.[33]

In relation to him, I burn, as through a shirt of Nessus, with a feeling of anxious fidelity.[34] *That he only advanced on the path of inner experience through indecisive inspiration does not stop me: if it is true that as a philosopher he had as a goal not knowledge but, without separating the operations, life, its* extremity, *in a word experience itself,* Dionysos philosophos. *The desire to communicate was born in me from a feeling of community linking me to Nietzsche, not from an isolated originality.*

Undoubtedly I have tended more than Nietzsche toward the night of nonknowledge.[35] *He does not linger in these swamps where, as if bogged down, I spend time. But I hesitate no longer: Nietzsche himself would be misunderstood if one did not go to this depth. He has had, up till now, superficial consequences, as imposing as they may be.*

Loyal—not without the dazed lucidity, even in regard to myself, that makes me find myself as if absent. I imagine that Nietzsche had the experience of the eternal return in a mystical form, properly speaking, confused with discursive representations. Nietzsche was only a burning solitary man, without relief from too much force, with a rare equilibrium between intelligence and unreasoned life. Equilibrium is hardly favorable to the developed exercise of intellectual faculties (which demand calm, hence the existence of Kant, of Hegel). He proceeded by insights, putting into play forces of all kinds, not linked to anything, starting again, not building stone by stone. Speaking after a catastrophe of the intelligence (if one wants to see it that way). Being aware first. Unconcerned with contradictions. In love only with freedom. Gaining access first to the abyss and succumbing from having dominated it.

"Nietzsche was only a man . . ."
On the other hand.
Not to see Nietzsche exactly as a "man."
He said: "But where do those waves of everything that is great and sublime
in man finally flow? Is there not an ocean for these torrents? Be that ocean:
there will be one" (Fragment, 1881–82).[36]

Better than the image of Dionysos philosophos, *the one who is lost in
this ocean and this bare demand: "be that ocean" designates experience and the
extremity to which it leads.*

*In experience, existence is no longer limited. A man cannot distinguish
himself from others here in any way: in him what is torrential in others is lost.
Such a simple commandment: "be that ocean," linked to the* extremity, *makes
man at once a multitude and a desert. It is an expression that summarizes and
makes precise the sense of a community. I know how to respond to Nietzsche's
desire speaking of a community having no object but experience (but designating
that community, I speak of a "desert").*

*In order to give the distance from contemporary man to the "desert," from
man to a thousand cacaphonic stupidities (pseudo-scientific, ideological, happy
jokes, progress, touching sentimentality, faith in machines, in big words, and, in
the end, discordance with and total ignorance of the unknown), I will say of the
"desert" that it is the most complete abandonment of the concerns of "contemporary man," being the continuation of the "ancient man," that regulated the
organization of festivals. He is not a return to the past: he has undergone the
rot of "contemporary man," and nothing has a greater place in him than the
ravages left by that rot—they give the "desert" its "desert-like" truth, behind him
extends, like a field of ashes, the memory of Plato, of Christianity, and above
all, most hideous, of modern ideas. But between the unknown and himself the
chirping of ideas has been silenced, and through that he is similar to "ancient
man": he is no longer the rational (alleged) master of the universe, but the dream.*

The alacrity of the "desert" and of the dream created by the "desert."
"How wonderful and new and yet how fearful and ironic my new insight
makes me feel toward all of existence! I have discovered for myself that the
ancient humanity and animality, indeed the whole prehistory and past of all
sentient being continues within me to invent, to love, to hate, and to infer—I
suddenly awoke in the midst of this dream, but only to the consciousness that
I am dreaming and that I must go on dreaming lest I perish." (Nietzsche, The
Gay Science)[37]

Between the world and the "desert," there is an agreement of all instincts, of numerous possibilities of the irrational gift of the self, a vitality of dance.

The idea of being the dream of the unknown (of God, of the universe) is, it seems, the extreme point that Nietzsche reached.* The happiness of being, of affirmation, the refusal to be everything, cruelty, natural fecundity are at play in it: man a bacchant philosopher.[38]
It is difficult to make it understood how distant the "desert" is, where my voice would ultimately carry, with this bit of sense: the sense of a dream.

A continual questioning of everything takes away the power to proceed through separated operations, obligates expression through rapid flashes, to free as much as one can the expression of one's thought from a project, to include everything in a few sentences: anguish, decision, and right up to the poetic perversion of words without which a domination seemed to be undergone.

Poetry is despite all the restrained part—linked to the realm of words. The realm of experience is the entirety of the possible. And in the expression that it is, in the end, necessarily, it is no less silence than language. Not through impotence. All language is given to it and has the force to engage it. But silence intended not to hide, to express at a higher degree of detachment. Experience cannot be communicated if the bonds of silence, effacement, distance, do not change those that it puts at risk.[39]

---

*As Friedrich Würzbach says in the preface to his edition of *The Will to Power*.

Part Two

Torture

1

There is in divine things a transparency so great that one slips to the illuminated depths of laughter starting from even opaque intentions.

I live by tangible experience and not by logical explanation. I have of the divine an experience so mad that one will laugh at me if I speak of it.

I enter into a cul-du-sac. There every possibility is exhausted, the possible slips away, and the impossible reigns. To face the impossible—exorbitant, indubitable—when nothing is possible any longer is in my eyes to have an experience of the divine; it is analogous to torture.

There are hours in which Ariadne's thread is broken: I am only an empty irritation, I no longer know what I am; I'm hungry, cold, and thirsty. In such moments, resorting to will would make no sense. What counts is disgust for a viable attitude, disgust for what I have been able to say, write, for what could bind me: I feel my loyalty as an insipidity. There is no way out of the contradictory impulses that agitate me and it is in this that they satisfy me. I doubt: I see nothing more in myself than cracks, impotence, empty agitation. I feel myself to be rotten, everything that I touch is rotten.

A singular courage is required in order not to succumb to depression and to continue—in the name of what? Nevertheless, I continue, in my darkness: man continues in me, passes through there. When I utter in myself: *what is it?* When I am there without a conceivable answer, I believe that within me, at last, this *man* should kill what I am, become *himself* to the point that my stupidity ceases to make me laughable. As for . . . (rare and furtive witnesses will perhaps discover me) I ask them to hesitate: for condemned to become man (or more), I must now die (to myself), give birth to myself. Things could no longer remain in their state; man's possibility could not limit itself to this constant disgust for itself, to the repeated denials of the dying. We cannot endlessly be what we are: words canceling each other out, at the same time unwavering joists, believing ourselves the foundation of the world. Am I awake? I doubt it and I could cry. Would I be the first on earth to feel human impotence drive me mad?

Glimpses where I perceive the path traveled. —Fifteen years ago (perhaps a little more), I returned from I don't know where, late at night. The rue de Rennes was deserted. Coming from Saint-Germain, I crossed the rue du Four (the post office side). I held in my hand an open umbrella and I believe it wasn't raining. (But I hadn't been drinking: I say it, I'm sure.) I had this umbrella open without needing it (if not for what I will speak about later). I was very young then, chaotic and full of empty drunkenness: a round of indecent, dizzying ideas, but already full of anxieties, rigor, and crucifying, running their course . . . In this shipwreck of reason, anguish, solitary degradation, baseness, worthlessness came due: a little later the festivity started again. What is certain is that this ease, simultaneously a collision with the "impossible," burst in my head. A space constellated with laughter opened its dark abyss before me. Crossing the rue du Four, I became in this unknown "nothingness," suddenly . . . I negated these gray walls that enclosed me, I rushed into a kind of rapture. I laughed divinely: the umbrella came down on my head covering me (I covered myself expressly with this black shroud). I laughed as perhaps no one had ever laughed, the final depth of each thing opened, laid bare, as if I were dead.

I don't know if I stopped, in the middle of the street, masking my delirium under an umbrella. Perhaps I jumped (no doubt it's illusory): I was convulsively illuminated, I laughed, I imagine, while running.

Doubt fills me with anguish without respite. What does illumination mean? Of whatever nature it should be? Even if the flash of sunlight blinded me internally and set me on fire? A little more, a little less light changes nothing; in any case, solar or not, man is only man: being only man, not getting out of it; it's suffocation, weighty ignorance, the intolerable.

"I teach the art of turning anguish into delight," "to glorify": the entire meaning of this book. The bitterness in me, the "unhappiness," is only the condition. But anguish that turns into delight is still anguish: it is not delight, not hope, it's anguish that is painful and perhaps decomposes. He who does not "die" from being only a man will forever be only a man.

Anguish, obviously, is not learned. Would one provoke it? It's possible. I hardly think so. One can stir up the dregs of it . . . If someone admits anguish, it is necessary to show the nothingness of his reasons. He imagines an escape from his torments: if he had more money, a wife, another life . . . The foolishness of anguish is infinite. In place of going to the depths of his anguish, the anxious one babbles, degrades himself, and flees. Anguish however was his chance: he was *chosen* by the extent of his *forebodings*. But what a waste if he evades them: he suffers as much and humiliates himself, he becomes stupid, false, superficial. Evaded anguish makes a man an agitated Jesuit, but empty.

Trembling. Remaining immobile, standing, in a solitary darkness, in an attitude without the gesture of the supplicant: supplication, but without gesture and certainly without hope. Lost and supplicating, blind, half dead. Like Job on the dung heap, imagining nothing, night fallen, defenseless, knowing that all is lost.

The meaning of supplication.—I express it in this way, in the form of a prayer: "Oh God our Father, You who, in a night of despair, crucified Your son, who in this night of butchery, to the extent that agony became *impossible*—to proclaim—became the *Impossible* Yourself and felt *impossibility* to the point of horror, God of despair, give me this heart, Your heart, which fails, which exceeds and no longer tolerates Your existence!"

One does not grasp the way in which we should speak of God. My despair is nothing, but that of God! I cannot live through or know anything without imagining it lived, known by God. We retreat, from possible to possible, in us everything starts over and is never *risked*, but in God: in this "leap" of being that He is, in his "once and for all"? No one would go to the end of supplication without placing himself in the exhausting solitude of God.

But in me everything begins again, nothing is ever risked. I destroy myself in the infinite possibility of my fellows: it annihilates the meaning of this *self*. If I attain, an instant, the extremity of the possible, a little later, I will flee, I will be *elsewhere*. And what sense is there in the ultimate absurdity: to add to God the limitless repetition of possibles and this torture of being forsaken, drop by drop, in the multitude of the misfortunes of man? Like a herd chased by an infinite shepherd, the bleating sheep that we are would flee, would ceaselessly flee the horror of a reduction of Being to totality.

God speaks to me, the idiot, mouth to mouth: a voice like fire comes from the darkness and speaks—cold flame, burning sadness—to . . . the man with the umbrella. When I weaken, God responds to supplication (How? At whom should I laugh in my room? . . .) *Myself, I* am standing, on diverse summits, so sadly ascended, my different nights of terror collide, they multiply, stand beside themselves, and these summits, these nights . . . unspeakable joy! . . . I stop myself. I am? A cry—overcome, I collapse.

Philosophy is never supplication, but without supplication, there is no conceivable answer: no answer ever preceded the question: and what does the question mean without anguish, without torture. At the moment of going mad, the answer suddenly appears: how would one hear it without that?

The essential is the extremity of the possible, where God himself no longer knows, despairs and kills.

Forgetting everything. Deep descent into the night of existence. The infinite supplication of ignorance, drowning in anguish. Slipping over the abyss and into the completed darkness, experiencing its horror. To tremble, to despair, in the cold of solitude, in the eternal silence of man (the foolishness of every phrase, the illusory answers of sentences, only the insane silence of the night responds). The word *God*, to have used it to reach the depth of solitude, but no longer knowing, to hear his voice. To be unaware of it. God: final word meaning that every word, later on will fail: to perceive its own eloquence (it is unavoidable), to laugh at it to the point of an unknowing daze (laughter no longer needs to laugh, sobbing to sob). Further on the head bursts: man is not contemplation (he only has peace in flight); he is supplication, war, anguish, madness.

The voices of the good apostles: they have an answer for everything, indicating the limits, discretely, the steps to follow, as does, at a burial, the master of ceremonies.

Feeling of complicity in: despair, madness, love, supplication. Inhuman, disheveled joy, of *communication*, since despair, madness, love, not a point in empty space that is not despair, madness, love, and more: laughter, dizziness, nausea, loss of self to the point of death.

2

Derision! That one should call me pantheist, atheist, theist! . . . But I cry out to the sky:[1] "I know nothing." And I repeat in a *comical* voice (I cry to the sky, sometimes, in this way): "Nothing, absolutely."

The extremity of the possible—In the end here we are. But so late? . . . How, without knowing it, did we come here?—(in fact, nothing has changed) by a detour: one laughs (in bursts), another is caught and beats his wife, one becomes dead drunk, one tortures others to death.

Absurdity of reading what should tear one apart to the point of dying and, to begin with, to prepare one's lamp, a drink, one's bed, to wind one's watch. I laugh at this, but what can be said of "poets" who imagine themselves above intended attitudes without admitting that they have, like me, empty heads: to show this one day, with rigor—coldly—up to the point where one is shattered, supplicant, where one ceases to dissimulate, to be absent. Is this a question of exercises? Concerted? Intended? It is a question, effectively, of exercises, of *constraints*. The joke of wanting to be a man going with the flow, without ever hunting oneself down, forcing final retrenchments: this is to become an accomplice of inertia. What is strange is that by avoiding this one does not see the responsibility that one assumes: none can be more overwhelming, it is *inexpiable sin*, the possibility glimpsed for once of abandoning it for the seeds of any life whatsoever. The possibility is silent, it neither threatens nor condemns, but one who, fearing death, lets it die, is like a cloud disappointing the expectation of the sun.

I no longer imagine man *laughing*, laughing at the ultimate possibility itself—laughing, turning his back without a word to give himself to the enchantment of life, without ever, not even once, avoiding it. But that failure, one day, should seize him, that he refuse, in failure, to go to the end (along the path of failure, then the possibility itself reclaims him, lets him know that it is waiting for him), he avoids it and that's it for his innocence: in him begins the ungraspable play of sin, of remorse, of the simulation of remorse, then of total forgetting and the mundane.

Should one look at last at the history of men, over the long term, man by man, on the whole as a flight, first facing life, it is sin; then facing sin, it is the long night crossed by stupid laughter, with an inner depth of anguish alone.

Each man, to conclude, has conquered the right to absence, to certitude; each street is the limited face of this conquest.

From the firmness of despair, to experience slow pleasure, decisive rigor, to be hard and more the guarantor of death than its victim. The difficulty, in despair, is to be whole: however, the words, as I write, fail me . . . The egoism inherent in despair: indifference to communication is born in it. "Born" at least, because . . . I write. Besides, the words poorly designate what human beings experience: I say, "despair," one must understand me: here I am defeated, in the depths of the cold, breathing an odor of death, at the same time heavy, *dedicated* to my destiny, loving it—like a beast its babies—desiring nothing more. The height of joy is not joy, since, in joy, I feel the moment coming when it will end, while, in despair, I sense only death coming: I have of it only an anguished desire, but a desire and no other desire. Despair is simple: it is the absence of hope, of every *delusion*. It is the state of deserted expanses and—I can imagine—of the sun.

I fail, no matter what I write, in this: that I would have to link the infinite richness—insane—of possibilities to the precision of meaning. I am compelled to this Danaïdean task—gaily? Perhaps, since I cannot conceive of my life henceforth, if not nailed to the *extremity of the possible*. (This assumes, first, a superhuman intelligence, while I have often had to rely upon the more skillful intelligence of others. . . . But what can be done? Forget? Immediately, I feel it, I would go *mad*: we still poorly comprehend the misery of a *divested* mind.) Undoubtedly, it is sufficient that a single individual reach the extremity: still there must remain, between him and the others—who avoid him—a link. Without this there would only be a strangeness, not the extremity of the possible. Noises of all kinds, cries, chatter, laughter, everything must be lost in him, be emptied of meaning in his despair. Intelligence, communication, supplicating misery, *sacrifice* (what is hardest is undoubtedly to *open oneself* to an infinite foolishness: in order to escape it—the extremity is the only point through which man escapes his limited stupidity—but at the same time so as to sink into it), there is nothing that should not go to the rendezvous. What is most strange is despair, which paralyzes the rest and absorbs it into itself. And "my everything"? "My everything" is only a naive being, hostile toward jokes: when it is there, my night becomes colder, the desert where I am most empty, there is no longer any limit: beyond the known possibilities, such a great anguish inhabits the gray skies, in the same way that a monk inhabits the darkness of a tomb.

My effort will be vain if it does not compel conviction. But it shatters itself in me at every hour! From the *extremity*, I descend into the most stupefied state, admitting that, in rare moments, I have touched the *extremity*. In these conditions, how can it be believed that the *extremity* must one day be a human *possibility*, that one day men (be it in infinitesimal numbers) should have access to the extremity? And, moreover, without the extremity, life is only a long deception, a series of defeats without struggle followed by impotent retreat; it's degradation.

By definition, the extremity of the possible is this point at which, despite the unintelligible position that he has within being, a man, having stripped himself of delusion and fear, advances so far that one cannot conceive of a possibility of going further. Useless to say the extent to which it is vain (even though philosophy closes itself in this impasse), of imagining a pure play of intelligence without anguish. Anguish is no less than intelligence the means of knowing and, besides, the extremity of the possible is no less life than knowledge. Communication still is, like anguish, to live and to know. The extremity of the possible assumes laughter, ecstasy, terrified approach to death; assumes error, nausea, incessant agitation of the possible and of the impossible, and, in the end, however, shattered, by degrees, slowly wanted, the state of supplication, its absorption in despair. Nothing that a man can *know*, to this end, could be eluded without degradation, without sin (I think, making matters worse, the stakes being the ultimate stakes, of the worst of disgraces, of desertion: for he who has felt himself to be called once, there is no further reason, no excuse, he can only hold his place). Every human being who does not go to the extremity is the *servant* or the *enemy* of man. To the extent that he does not, through some servile task, attend to the common subsistence, his desertion contributes to giving man a contemptible destiny.

Common knowledge or knowledge found in laughter, anguish, or any other analogous experience is subordinated—this arises from the rules it follows—to the extremity of the possible. All knowledge is valuable in its limits; still it is necessary to know what it is worth if the extremity is there, to know what an ultimate experience of it adds. First, in the extremity of the possible, everything breaks down: the edifice itself of reason, a moment of insane courage, its majesty is dissipated; what remains at worst, like a piece of shaking wall, increases, does not calm the dizzying feeling. Useless impudence of recriminations: it was required, nothing resists the necessity of going further. If needed, dementia would have been the payment.

A contemptible fate . . . Everything has solidarity with man. There was always some bitter will—however diffuse—in some people to go further than man could. But if man ceased *to wish to be himself* with so much bitterness? That would only happen with the weakening of every desire—in whatever way that this desire is exerted (enchantment, struggle, conquest).

In order to go to the end of man, it is necessary, at a certain point, to no longer submit, but to force fate. The contrary, poetic nonchalance, the passive attitude, the disgust of a virile reaction, that decides: this is literary degradation (beautiful pessimism). The damnation of Rimbaud, who had to turn his back on the possible that he had attained, to rediscover the decisive force intact within him. Access to extremity has as a condition the hatred not of poetry but of poetic femininity (the absence of decisiveness, the poet is woman, invention, words rape him). I oppose the experience of the possible to poetry. It is less a question of contemplation than of laceration. It is however of "mystical experience" that I am speaking. (Rimbaud practiced it, but without the tenacity that he later brought to trying his fortune. To his experience, he gave a poetic outlet; in general, he ignored the simplicity that affirms—futureless inclinations in his letters—he chose feminine evasiveness, aesthetics, uncertain, involuntary expression.)

A feeling of impotence: to the apparent disorder of my ideas, I have the key, but I do not have the time to use it. Enclosed distress, solitary, the ambition I formed is so great that . . . I would like, even I, to lie down, to cry, to go to sleep. I remain there, several moments longer, wanting to force fate, *and shattered.*

Last hope: to forget, to return to innocence, to the playfulness of despair.

Praying to lie down: "God, who sees my efforts, give me the night of your blind eyes."

Provoked, God responds, I extend myself to the point of collapse and *I see Him,* then I forget. As much disorder as in dreams.

3

Relaxation. Crossed the church of Saint-Roch. Before the giant, golden, hazy image of the sun, a movement of gaity, of childish humor and rapture. Further on, I looked at a wooden balustrade and I saw that the room was unkempt. I touched, on a whim, one of the banisters: the finger left a mark in the dust.

The end of a discussion on a train. Those who don't know that the foundation is lacking, who cling to wise maxims, when they would be suddenly reduced, if they knew, to the absurd, to supplication. I waste my time in wanting to warn. Tranquility, good-naturedness, a nice discussion, as if the war . . . and when I say war. Decidedly, no one looks squarely: the sun, the human eye flees it . . . God's skull bursts . . . and no one hears.

My friends avoid me. I frighten, not because of my cries but I cannot leave anyone in peace. I simplify: haven't I often given good pretexts?

To grasp the bearing of knowledge, I go back to its origin. First, a small child, in every way similar to madmen (the absent), with whom I'm playing today. The miniscule "absents" are not in contact with the world, *if not through the channel of grown-ups*: the result of the intervention of grown-ups is *childishness*, a fabrication. Grown-ups *obviously* reduce the being that comes into the world, which we are at first, to trinkets. This seems important to me: that the passage from the state of nature (of birth) to our state of reason necessarily takes place along the path of *childishness*. It is strange on our part to attribute to the child himself the responsibility for childishness, which would be the expression of the proper character of children. Childishness is the state wherein *we put* the naive being, from the fact that we must lead it there, even without precisely willing it, we lead it toward the point where we are. When we laugh at childish absurdity, the laugh disguises the shame that we feel, seeing to what we reduce life emerging from nothingness.

Assume that the universe engenders the stars, the stars the earth . . . the earth the animals and children, children men. The error of children: to hold onto the adults' truths. Each truth possesses a convincing force—why doubt it—but it has a counterpart of errors as a consequence. It is a fact that our truths, first of all, introduce the child into a series of errors that constitute childishness. But we speak of childishness when it is *visible* communally: no one laughs at a scholar, for to see childishness in him it would be necessary to surpass him—as much as an adult surpasses a child (this is never completely true—if he is not inherently ridiculous—and, in a word, it almost never happens).

My conduct with my friends is motivated: each being is, I think, incapable on his own, of going to the end of being. If he tries, he sinks into a "particular" that only has meaning for himself. Now there is no meaning for one alone: the lone being would reject on his own the "particular" if he saw it as such (if I want my life to have a meaning for me, it must have meaning *for others*; no one would dare give life a meaning that he alone would perceive, to which life in its entirety, except in him, would escape). At the extremity of the possible, it's true, it's nonsense . . . but only of that which had a meaning until then, since *supplication*—born of the absence of meaning—fixes a definitive meaning, a final meaning: it is fulguration, even the "apotheosis" of nonsense. But I do not attain the extremity on my own and really I cannot believe the extremity has been attained, since I never remain there. If I had to be alone in having attained it (admitting that . . .), it would be as if it had not been attained. For if a satisfaction subsisted, as small as I imagine it to be, it would distance me as much from the extremity. I cannot for a moment cease to incite myself toward the extremity and cannot create a difference between myself and those others with whom I desire to communicate.

I can only, I suppose, touch the extremity through repetition, in that I am never sure of having attained it, that I will never be sure. And even supposing the extremity attained, it would still not be the extremity, if I fell asleep. The extremity implies "one must not fall asleep during that time" (up to the moment of death), but Pascal accepted sleeplessness in view of the beatitude to come (at least he gave himself that reason). I refuse to be *happy* (to be saved).

The desire to be happy signifies: suffering and the desire to escape. When I suffer (for example, yesterday, rheumatism, cold, and certainly anguish having read passages of the *120 Days*[2]), I become attached to little pleasures. Nostalgia for salvation perhaps responds to the increase in suffering (or rather to the incapacity to bear it). The idea of salvation, I think, comes to one who *breaks apart* suffering. Someone who dominates it, on the contrary, needs to be shattered, to engage himself in being torn apart.

A little comic summary. Hegel, I imagine, touched the extremity. He was still young and thought he was going mad. I even imagine that he elaborated the system to escape (each kind of conquest, undoubtedly, is made by a man fleeing a threat). In the end, Hegel arrives at *satisfaction*, turns his back on extremity. *Supplication is dead in him.* When one seeks salvation, in any case, one continues to live, one cannot be certain, one must continue to supplicate. While living, Hegel won salvation, killed supplication, *mutilated himself.* All that remained of him was the handle of a shovel, a modern man. But before mutilating himself, he undoubtedly touched the extremity, knew supplication: his memory brought him back to the perceived abyss, *to annul it*! The system is annulment.

The end of the summary. Modern man, the annulled (but without cost), enjoys salvation on earth. Kierkegaard is the extremity of Christianity. Dostoevsky (in *Underground*) that of shame.[3] In the *120 Days*, we attain the summit of voluptuous terror.

In Dostoevsky, the extremity is the effect of a breaking apart; but it is a breaking apart like a winter flood: it overflows. Nothing is more painful, sickly, pale religious complication. The *Underground* attributes the extremity to misery. Trickery, as in Hegel, but Dostoevsky withdraws himself from it in other ways. In Christianity, this does not count to debase supplication, to sink man entirely into shame. One says: "forget that . . ." but no, since (except for the ambiguity) it is a matter of humiliation, of the deprivation of value. For all that, I didn't moan: that extremity passes through shame is not bad, but limiting it to shame! Dazzled in the depths, pushing the extremity back into the demonic—at all costs—is betrayal.

My means: expression, my awkwardness. The ordinary condition of life: rivalry between diverse beings, which will be the most. Caesar: ". . . rather than second in Rome."[4] Men are such that—so poor—and everything seems worthless, unless it surpasses. I am often so sad that measuring my insufficiency of means without despairing wears me out. The problems worth being considered only have meaning on the condition that, posing them, one comes to the summit: mad pride necessary to be torn apart. And sometimes—our nature slips into dissolution for nothing—one tears oneself apart for the sole goal of satisfying this pride: everything is ruined in a sticky vanity. It would be better to be nothing more than a village shopkeeper, to look at the sun with a sickly eye, rather than . . .

Returning from extremity to vanity, then vanity to extremity. Childishness, knowing itself as such, is deliverance, but taking itself seriously, it is bogged down. The search for the extremity can become a habit in its turn, dependent upon childishness: one must laugh at it, unless, by chance, one has a heavy heart: then ecstasy and madness are near.

Once again childishness recognized as such is the glory, not the shame of man. On the other hand, if one says, with Hobbes, that laughter is degrading, one attains the depths of degradation: nothing is more puerile, nor further from knowing itself to be.[5] All seriousness eluding the extremity is the degradation of man: through this his slavish nature is rendered tangible. Once again, I appeal to childishness, to glory; the extremity is at the end, only at the end, like death.

At the elusive extremity of myself, I am already dead, and *I* in this nascent state of death speak to the living: of death, of extremity. The most serious seem to be children to me, who do not know that they are: they separate me from true children, who know they are children and laugh at being children. But to be a child, one must know that seriousness exists— elsewhere and insignificant—if not the child could no longer laugh or know anguish.

It is the extremity, the mad tragedy, not the seriousness of statistics, which children need to play and to become afraid.

The extremity is a window: fear of extremity commits one to the darkness of a prison, with a will void of "penal administration."

4

In the infinite horror of war, man has access en masse to the extreme point that terrifies him. But man is far from wanting horror (and extremity): his fate is in part to attempt to avoid the unavoidable. His eyes, although greedy for light, obstinately avoid the sun, and the gentleness of his gaze, in advance, betrays the shadows, quickly arrived, of sleep: if I envision the mass of humanity, in its opaque consistency, it is already as if sleeping, elusive and withdrawn in stupor. The fatality of a blind movement nevertheless throws them back toward extremity, where one day they hastily gain access.

The horror of the war is greater than that of inner experience. The desolation of a battlefield, in principle, has something more grave than the "dark night."[6] But in battle, one approaches horror with a movement that overcomes it: action, project linked to action permit the *surpassing* of horror. This surpassing gives action, project, a captivating grandeur, but horror in itself is negated.

I have understood that I was avoiding the project of an inner experience and I contented myself with being at its mercy. I had a thirsty desire for it, its necessity imposed itself on me, without me having *decided* anything. In fact, no one can, the nature of experience is, apart from derision, not to be able to exist as project.

I live and everything becomes as though life with extremity was conceivable. And what's more, desire persists in me, but it is weak. Still more, the dark perspectives of extremity are inscribed in my memory, but I am no longer horrified by them and I remain an imbecile, anxious about laughable miseries, about cold, about the sentence that I will write, about my projects: the "night" in which I know I am thrown, into which I fall during this time, and with me everything that exists, this truth that I know, which I cannot doubt, I am like a child before it, it flees from me, I remain blind. I belong for a moment to the realm of objects that I use and remain foreign to what I write. To be in the night, to sink into the night, without even having enough force to *see it*, to know oneself in this closed darkness, and despite it *to see clearly*, I can still bear this test while laughing, eyes closed, at my "childishness."

I come to this position: inner experience is the opposite of action. Nothing more.

"Action" is entirely dependent upon project. And, what is oppressive, discursive thought is itself engaged in the mode of existence of project. Discursive thought is the fact of a being engaged in action, it takes place in him starting with his projects, on the level of reflection upon projects. The project is not only the mode of existence implicated by action, necessary to action, it is a paradoxical way of being in time: *it is putting existence off until later.*

One who, now, discovers pity for the multitudes losing life (to the extent that projects dominate them) could have the simplicity of the Gospel: the beauty of tears, anguish would introduce transparency into his words. I say it as simply as I can (although a hard irony agitates me): impossible for me to go before others. Besides, the news is not good. And this is not "news"; in one sense, it is a secret.

Therefore, to speak, to think, at least to joke or . . . is to evade existence: it is not to die but to be dead. It is to go into the extinguished and calm world wherein we normally drag along: there everything is suspended, life is put off till later, put off and put off . . . The little displacement of projects suffices, the flame is extinguished, a respite follows the storm of the passions. What is most strange is that on its own the exercise of thought introduces in the mind the same suspension, the same peace as activity in place of work. Descartes's little affirmation is the most subtle of escapes. (Descartes's motto: *Larvatus prodeo*;[7] what moves forward is masked: I am in anguish and I think, the thought in me *suspends* anguish, I am the being gifted with the power to *suspend* within him being itself. Following Descartes:

the world of "progress," in other terms of project, is our world. War disturbs it, it's true: the world of project remains, but in doubt and anguish.)

Inner experience is the denunciation of the truce, it is existence without delay.

Principle of inner experience: to get out through a project of the realm of the project.

Inner experience is driven by discursive reason. Reason alone has the power to undo its work, to throw down what it has built up. Madness has no effect, leaving debris to subsist, deranging the faculty of communication with reason (perhaps it is before every rupture of inner communication). Natural exaltation or drunkenness has the virtue of a flash in the pan. Without the application of reason, we don't reach the "dark incandescence."

Until now, almost every inner experience has depended upon the obsession with salvation. Salvation is the summit of every possible project and peak in matters of project. From the fact itself that salvation is a peak, it is also the negation of projects of momentary interest. At the extremity, the desire for salvation turns into the hatred of all project (of the putting off of existence until later): of salvation itself, suspected of having a vulgar motive. If I exhaust, in anguish, distant prospects and intimate depths, I see this: salvation *was* the only means of disassociating eroticism (the Bacchic consummation of bodies) and nostalgia for existing without delay. A vulgar means undoubtedly, but eroticism . . .

Against pride. My privilege is to be humiliated by my profound stupidity and undoubtedly, through others, I perceive an even greater stupidity. To this degree of thickness, it is vain to linger over differences. What I have more than others; to see in myself immense storage closets, dressing rooms; I have not succumbed to the dread that ordinarily averts its gaze; I did not flee the feeling that I have of an inner collapse, I only weakly attempted to mislead myself and I certainly did not succeed. What I perceived is the entire destitution of man, the key to his thickness, the condition of his self-satisfaction.

The imitation of Jesus: according to Saint John of the Cross, we must imitate in God (Jesus) the fall, the agony, the moment of "nonknowledge" of the *lama sabachthani*; drunk to the lees, Christianity is the absence of salvation, the despair of God. It fails in that it reaches its goals out of breath. The agony of God in the person of man is fatal; it is the abyss in which vertigo tempted him to fall. The agony of a God can only explicate sin. It not only justifies heaven (the dark incandescence of the heart), but hell (childishness, flowers, Aphrodite, laughter).

Despite contrary appearances, concern for misery is the dead part of Christianity. It is anguish reducible to project: indefinitely variable formula, each day a little thicker, an increased state of death. Existence and anguish losing themselves, on the scale of the human masses, in project, life put off infinitely. Of course ambiguity is mixed in: life is condemned in Christianity and the men of progress sanctify it; Christians have limited it to ecstasy and sin (this was a positive attitude); progress negates ecstasy, sin, confuses life with project, sanctifies project (work): in the world of progress, life is only licit childishness, once project is recognized as what is serious in existence (anguish, which misery substantiates, is necessary for authority, but project occupies the mind).

Where the intimate character of the project is revealed. The mode of existence of project transposed in the idleness of rich women and, in general, of the worldly. If polite, calm manners and the emptiness of project prevail, life no longer supports idleness. Similarly, the boulevards on a Sunday afternoon. Worldly life and bourgeois Sundays bring out the character of an ancient festival, forgetting every project, unlimited consummation.

And above all "nothing," I know "nothing," I moan nothing like a sick child, whose attentive mother holds his forehead (mouth open over the bowl). But I have no mother, man has no mother, the bowl is the starry sky (in my poor nausea, it's this way).

A few lines read in a recent brochure:
"I have often thought of the day when the birth of a man who would have his eyes very sincerely *on the inside* would finally be consecrated. His life would be like a long tunnel of phosphorescent furs and he would only have to stretch out in order to plunge into everything which he has in common with the rest of the world and which is atrociously incommunicable to us. I would like it if each of us, at the thought that the birth of such a man were to be rendered possible, tomorrow, through a common accord between his fellow beings and the world, could, like me, shed tears of joy."* This

---

*Jean-François Chabrun, "La Transfusion du Verbe" in *Naissance de l'Homme-objet* (1941) [recently reprinted in *La Main à Plume: Anthologie du Surréalisme sous l'Occupation*, ed. Anne Vernay and Richard Walter (Paris: Syllepse, 2008).]

is accompanied by four pages that express an intention principally turned toward the outside. The possibility of the envisioned birth leaves me, alas, with dry eyes, I have *fever* and no more tears.

What can this "Golden Age" mean, this vain concern for the "best possible conditions" and the sick will of unanimous man? In fact, a will to *exhausting* experience always begins in euphoria. Impossible to grasp what one is engaged in, to divine the price that one will pay—but later one will pay *without tiring of paying*; no one anticipated the degree to which he would be ruined or the shame that he would have for not being ruined enough. That said, if I see that one cannot bear *living*, that one is suffocating, that in any case, one flees anguish and resorts to project, my anguish grows from the anguish that turbulence evades.

Poetic idleness, poetry as a project, that which an André Breton could not tolerate laid bare, which the intended abandon of his sentences was to veil. And for me, anguish without escape, the feeling of complicity, of being harassed, hunted. Never however more complete! One cannot offend me: I wanted the desert, the place (the condition) that was necessary for a clear and interminable death.

What I see: poetic facility, diffuse appearance, verbal project, ostentation, and the fall into the worst: vulgarity, literature. One trumpets that one is going to revive man: one commits him a little more in the old rut. Vanity! It's quickly said (the vanity is not what it seems to be, it is only the condition of a project, of a putting off of existence until later). One only satisfies one's vanity in a project: the satisfaction escapes as soon as one realizes it, one quickly returns to the plan of the project; one falls in this way into flight, like a beast in an endless trap, one day or another, one dies idiotically. In the anguish in which I enclose myself, as much as I can my gaiety justifies human vanity, the immense desert of vanities, its dark horizon where pain and night are hiding—a dead, divine gaiety.

And vanity in myself!
Assuredly.

"What I write: an appeal! The most insane, the best destined for the deaf. I address a prayer to my fellows (to some of them at least): the vanity of this cry from a man of the desert! You are such that if you perceived yourselves as I do, you could no longer be this way. So (here, I fall to the earth) have pity on me! I have seen what you are."

Man and his possible. Sordid being, stupid (to the point of crying out in the cold), has laid his *possible* on the ground. The gentle (flattering) idea arises: he follows it, catches it. But, this *possible*, posed, for a moment, on the floor?

He forgets it!

Decidedly, he forgets!

That's it: it's gone.

Speaking of the extremity reached, here and there, I have spoken of writers, even of a "man of letters" (Dostoevsky). At the thought of easy confusions, I will specify. One can know nothing of man that has not taken the form of a sentence and, on the other hand, the infatuation for poetry makes untranslatable series of words a summit. The extremity is elsewhere. It is only entirely reached if communicated (man is several, solitude is the void, uselessness, lies). Any expression whatsoever testifies to this: the extremity is distinct from it. It is never literature. If poetry expresses it, it is distinct from it: to the point of not being poetic, for if poetry has it as an object, it does not reach it. When the extremity is there, the means that serve to reach it are no longer there.

The last known poem by Rimbaud is not the extremity. If Rimbaud attained the extremity, he only attained the communication of it by means of his despair: he suppressed possible communication, he no longer wrote poems.

The refusal to communicate is a more hostile means of communication, but the most powerful; if it was possible, it is because Rimbaud turned away from it. So as to no longer communicate, he renounced it. If not, it was for having renounced it that he ceased to communicate. No one will know if the horror (the weakness) or modesty commanded Rimbaud's renunciation. It might be that the limits of horror were pushed back (further than God). In any case, to speak of weakness makes little sense: Rimbaud maintained his will to extremity on other levels (above all that of renunciation). It might be that he gave up without having attained it (extremity is not disorder or luxuriance), too demanding to bear, too lucid not to see. It might be that after having attained it, but doubting that this had a meaning or even that it had a place—as the state of one who attains it does not last—he could not bear the doubt. A longer search would be useless, when the will to extremity stops at nothing (we cannot really attain it).

The self in no way matters. For a reader, I am any being whatsoever: name, identity, history change nothing. He (the reader) is anyone
and I (author) am anyone. Nameless, he and I came out of . . . nameless,
so that . . . nameless as are two grains of sand in the desert, or rather
two waves lost in neighboring waves in the sea. The . . . without name to
which belongs the "known personality" of the world of the etc., to which
it belongs so totally that it is not aware of it. Oh death infinitely blessed
without which a "personality" would belong to the world of etc. Misery
of living men, disputing to death the possibilities of the world of the etc.
Joy of the dying, wave among waves. Inert joy of the dying, of the desert,
fall into the impossible, cry without resonance, silence of a fatal accident.

The Christian dramatizes life easily: he lives before Christ and for
Christ he is more than himself. Christ is the totality of being, and yet he
is, like the "lover," personal, like the "lover," desirable: and suddenly torture,
agony, death. The follower of Christ is led to torture. Has led himself to
torture: not to some insignificant torture, but to divine agony. He not only
has the means of attaining torture, but he could not avoid it, and it is the
torture of more than himself, of God himself, who, God, is not less man
and torturable than him.

It does not suffice to recognize, this only puts the mind in play;
the recognition must also take place in the heart (half-blind, intimate
movements . . .). This is no longer philosophy, but sacrifice (communication). Strange coincidence between the naive philosophy of sacrifice (in
ancient India) and the philosophy of supplicating nonknowledge: sacrifice,
the movement of the heart, transposed into knowledge (there has been an
inversion from the origin to now, the ancient path leading from the heart
to the intelligence, the present contrary).

What is most strange is that nonknowledge has a sanction. As if, from
the outside, it was said to us: "At last here you are." The path of nonknowledge is the most empty of nonsense. I could say: "Everything is completed."
No. Yet supposing that I say it, I immediately perceive the same closed
horizon as the moment before. The more I advance in knowledge, even on
the path of nonknowledge, the more the last nonknowledge becomes heavy,
agonizing. In fact, I give myself to nonknowledge, this is communication,
and as there is communication with the darkened world, rendered abyssal
by nonknowledge, I dare say God: and it is in this way that there is new
knowledge (mystical), but I cannot stop myself (I can't—but I must catch
my breath): "God, if he knew." And further on, always further on. God as

the lamb substituted for Isaac. This is no longer sacrifice. Further on is the naked sacrifice, without the lamb, without Isaac. The sacrifice is madness, the renunciation of all knowledge, the fall into the void, and nothing, neither in the fall nor in the void is revealed, since the revelation of the void is only a means of falling further into absence.

NONKNOWLEDGE LAYS BARE.

This proposition is the summit, but should be understood in this way: lays bare, therefore *I see* what knowledge was hiding up to there, but if I see *I know*. In effect, I know, but what I knew, nonknowledge again lays bare. If nonsense is sense, the sense that is nonsense loses itself, becomes nonsense once again (without possible end).

If the proposition (nonknowledge lays bare) possesses a meaning—appearing, disappearing immediately—it is that it means to say NON-KNOWLEDGE COMMUNICATES ECSTASY. Nonknowledge is first of all ANGUISH. In anguish appears nudity, which leads to ecstasy. But ecstasy itself (nudity, communication) slips away if anguish slips away. Thus ecstasy only remains possible in the anguish of ecstasy, in the fact that it cannot be satisfaction, *grasped knowledge*. Evidently, ecstasy is first of all *grasped knowledge*, in particular in the extreme destitution and the extreme construction of the destitution that, myself, my life and my written work represent (this I know, no one has taken knowledge as far, no one has been able to, but for me, it was easy—obligatory). But when the extremity of knowledge is there (and the extremity of knowledge that I just understood is beyond absolute knowledge); it is the same as in absolute knowledge, everything is overturned. I have hardly known—entirely known—that destitution on the level of knowledge (where knowledge leaves me) reveals itself and anguish begins again. But anguish is the horror of destitution and the moment comes when, in audacity, destitution is loved, when I give myself to destitution: it is then nudity that leads to ecstasy. Then knowledge returns, satisfaction, anguish again, I start over redoubling it up to the point of exhaustion (just as, in mad laughter, anguish born of what it has displaced from laughter redoubles the laughter).

In ecstasy, one can *let oneself go*, this is satisfaction, happiness, platitude. Saint John of the Cross contests the seductive image and rapture, but calms himself in the theopathic state. I have followed his method of hardening right to the end.

Suppression of the subject and of the object, sole means not leading to the possession of the object by the subject, which is to say of avoiding the absurd rush of the *ipse* wanting to become everything.[8]

Conversation with Blanchot. I say to him: inner experience has neither goal nor authority that justifies it. If I leap, burst the concern for a goal, for an authority, at least a void subsists. Blanchot reminds me that goal, authority are requirements of discursive thought; I insist, describing the experience in the form given in its final place, asking him how he believes this is possible without authority or anything. He adds on the subject of this authority that it must be expiated.

Once again I'd like to offer the sketch of the experience that I call pure experience. First of all I reach the extremity of knowledge (for example, I mimic absolute knowledge, the method hardly matters, but this supposes an infinite effort of the mind wanting knowledge). I know then that I know nothing. *Ipse*, I wanted to be everything (through knowledge) and I fall into anguish: the occasion of this anguish is my nonknowledge, nonsense without remedy (here nonknowledge does not do away with particular knowledge, but its meaning, lifts all meaning from it). After the fact, I can know the anguish about which I spoke. Anguish assumes the desire to communicate, which is to say to lose myself, but not complete resolve: anguish testifies to my fear of communication, of losing myself. Anguish is given in the theme of knowledge itself: as *ipse*, I would like to be everything through knowledge, therefore to communicate, lose myself, yet to remain *ipse*. For communication, before it has taken place, presents itself with the subject (self, *ipse*) and object (in part undefined, insofar as it is not entirely grasped). The subject wants to take hold of the object to possess it (this will comes from the being engaged in the play of compositions, see the *Labyrinth*), but it can only lose itself: the nonsense of the will to knowledge arises, nonsense of every possible, making the *ipse* know that it is going to lose itself and knowledge along with it. Insofar as *ipse* perseveres in its will to know and to be *ipse* anguish lasts, but if the *ipse* abandons itself and knowledge with it, if it gives itself to nonknowledge in this abandonment, rapture begins. In rapture, my existence recovers a meaning, but the meaning immediately refers to the *ipse*, becomes *my* rapture, a rapture that I *ipse* possess, giving satisfaction to my will to be everything. As soon as I return there, communication, the loss of my self ceases, I have ceased to abandon myself, I remain there, but with a new knowledge.

The movement starts again from there; I can develop the new knowledge (I have just done so). I arrive at this notion: that the subject, object are perspectives of being at the moment of inertia, that the intended object is the projection of the subject *ipse* wanting to become everything, that all representation of the object is phantasmagoria resulting from this foolish and necessary will (that one postulates the object as thing or as existing, hardly matters), that one necessarily comes to speak of communication by grasping that communication pulls the rug out from under the object as from under the subject (this is what becomes clear at the summit of communication, when there is communication between subject and object of the same nature, between two cells, between two individuals). I can develop this representation of the world and regard it at first as the solution to all enigmas. Suddenly I perceive the same thing as with the first form of knowledge, that this supreme knowledge leaves one like a child in the night, naked in the depths of the woods. This time, what is more serious, the meaning of the communication is at stake. But when the communication itself, in a moment wherein it has disappeared, inaccessible, appears to me as nonsense, I attain the height of anguish, in a desperate surge, I abandon myself and communication once again is given to me, rapture and joy.

At this moment, development is no longer necessary, it is done: it is immediate and from the rapture itself I enter once again into the night of the lost child, in anguish, to return further on to rapture and thus without any other end than exhaustion, without possibility of stopping other than a collapse.

This is supplicating joy.

The maladies of inner experience. In it the mystic has the power to animate what pleases him; the intensity suffocates, eliminates doubt and one perceives what one was expecting. As if we disposed of a powerful breath of life: each presupposition of the mind is animated. Rapture is not a window on the outside, on the beyond, but a mirror. This is the first malady. The second is putting experience into a project. No one can lucidly have experience without having had the project for it. This less serious malady is unavoidable: the project must even be maintained. Now experience is the contrary of the project: I attain experience contrary to the project I have of having it. Between experience and project a relationship between pain and the voice of reason is established: reason represents the inanity of a moral pain (saying: time will erase pain—as when a lover must be renounced). The wound is there, present, horrible, and contesting reason, recognizing its own validity, but only seeing in this more horror. I don't suffer any less from a wound, if I sense that it will soon be healed. It is necessary to make *use* of the project as of the guarantee of a coming cure. The project can, like a guarantee, be a mocking servant, ignoring nothing, skeptical and aware of being a servant, withdrawing as soon as the experience truly takes place, in the way the pain (of torture) demands solitude, bitterly cries: "leave me."

The servant, if everything takes place as he intends, must make himself forgotten. But he can trick. The first malady, the mirror, is evidence of a crude servant, who escapes the profound servitude to which he is bound.

The servant of experience is discursive thought. Here, the nobility of the servant rests upon the rigor of servitude.

Nonknowledge attained, absolute knowledge is no more than one knowledge among others.

5

One must. Is this to moan? I no longer know. Where am I going? Where is this insipid cloud of thoughts directed, I imagine it resembles sudden blood in a wounded throat. Insipid, not at all bitter (even in the lowest disarray, I remain gay, open, generous. And rich, too rich, this throat rich with blood . . .).

My difficulty: total loss of certainty, the difference between a sculpted object and fog (usually we imagine that it is horrible). If I expressed joy, I would fail myself: the joy that I experience differs from other joys. I am faithful to it in speaking of a fiasco, endless collapse, an absence of hope. Yet . . . fiasco, collapse, despair are in my eyes light, laying bare, glory. On the other hand: deadly indifference—to what is important to me, succession of characters without continuity, dissonances, chaos. If I still speak of equilibrium, euphoria, power, one will only grasp this on the condition of resembling me (already). To be less obscure: I crucify myself in my time, drag myself to the question, but without any right (without the authority to do so). If I had authority at my disposal, everything in me would be servitude, I would confess myself to be "guilty." There is nothing to this: I am not bitter. Here a deceptive inconsequentiality unveils itself, inescapably *sovereign*.

The concern for harmony is a great servitude. We cannot escape by refusal: in wanting to avoid the false window, we introduce an aggravated lie: the *false* at least admitted it was!

Harmony is a means of "realizing" the project. Harmony (measure) makes good the project: passion, puerile desire prevent waiting. Harmony is a fact of man in project, he has found calm, eliminated the impatience of desire.

The harmony of the fine arts realizes project in another sense. In the fine arts, man makes "real" the harmonious mode of existence inherent in the project. Art creates a world in the image of the man of project, reflecting this image in all its forms. However art is less harmony than the passage (or the return) of harmony to dissonance (in its history and in each work).

Harmony, like project, rejects time from outside; its principle is the repetition by which every possibility is made eternal. The ideal is architecture, or sculpture, immobilizing harmony, guaranteeing the duration of motifs whose essence is the annulment of time. Art has moreover borrowed repetition, the tranquil investment of time through a renewed theme, from project.

In art, desire returns, but, first of all, it is the desire to annul time (to annul desire), while, in project, there was simply the rejection of desire. Project is expressly a fact of the slave, it is work and work executed by one who does not enjoy its fruits. In art, man returns to sovereignty (to the expiration of desire) and, if it is first a desire to annul desire, it has hardly arrived at its goals and it is the desire to rekindle desire.

Of the successive characters that I am, I do not speak. They are not interesting or I must silence them. I am my words—evoking an inner experience—without having to challenge them. These characters, in principle, are neutral, a bit comical (in my eyes). In relation to the inner experience about which I spoke, they are deprived of sense, save in this: that they complete my disharmony.

> *I don't want more, I moan*
> *I cannot suffer more*
> *My prison.*
> *I say this*
> *Bitterly:*
> *Words that suffocate me,*
> *Leave me,*
> *Release me,*
> *I am thirsty*
> *For something else.*

I want death
Don't admit
This reign of words,
Enchaining
Without dread
Such that dread
Should be desirable;
It's nothing,
This self that I am,
If not
Cowardly acceptance
Of what is.
I hate
This instrumental life,
I seek a crack,
My crack,
To be shattered.
I love the rain
Lightning
Mud
A vast expanse of water
The depths of the earth
But not me.
In the depths of the earth,
O my tomb,
Deliver me from myself,
I no longer want to be.

Almost every time, if I attempted to write a book, fatigue would come before the end. I slowly became a stranger to the project that I formed. I would forget what enflamed me the day before, changing from one hour to the next with a drowsy slowness. I escape myself and my book escapes me; it becomes almost completely like a forgotten name: I am too lazy to seek it, but the obscure feeling of forgetting agonizes me.

And if this book resembles me? If the conclusion eludes the beginning: is unaware of it or indifferent to it? Strange rhetoric! Strange means of invading the impossible! Denial, forgetting, formless existence, equivocal weapons . . . Laziness itself used as unbreakable energy.

At nightfall, suddenly, I remembered, in the street, Quarr Abbey, a French monastery on the Isle of Wight, where in 1920, I spent two or three days—remembered as a house surrounded by pines, under a moonlit softness, beside the sea; the light of the moon linked to the medieval beauty of the services—everything which made me hostile to a monastic life disappeared—I experienced only exclusion, in this place, from the rest of the world. I imagined myself in the walls of the cloister, withdrawn from agitation, an instant imagining myself as a monk and safe from jagged, discursive life: on the street itself, with the help of the darkness, my heart streaming with blood caught fire, I knew a sudden rapture. With the help as well of my indifference to logic, to the spirit of consequence.

Within the walls, the sky a spectral gray, dusk, the damp uncertainty of the space at that precise time: divinity then had a mad, deaf presence, illuminating to the point of intoxication. My body had not interrupted its rapid step, but ecstasy slightly twisted its muscles. No uncertainty this time, but an indifference to certainty. I write divinity not wanting to know anything, not knowing anything. At other times, my ignorance was the abyss over which I was suspended.

What I must *execrate* today: voluntary ignorance, the methodical ignorance through which I came to seek ecstasy. Not that ignorance opens, in fact, the heart to rapture. But I put the *impossible* to the bitter test. All profound life is heavy with the *impossible*. Intention, project destroy it. Yet *I have known* that I know nothing and this, my secret: "nonknowledge communicates ecstasy." Existence has since begun again, banal and based on the appearance of knowledge. I wanted to escape it, saying to myself: this knowledge is false, I know nothing, absolutely nothing. But I know: "nonknowledge communicates ecstasy." I no longer had *anguish*. I lived enclosed (miserably). At the beginning of this night, the precise image of myself in monastic harmony communicated ecstasy to me: undoubtedly through the foolishness to which I abandoned myself in this way. Nonviability, the impossible! In the disharmony to which *I must* honestly adhere, harmony alone, because of the *I must*, represents a possibility of disharmony; necessary dishonesty, but one cannot become dishonest through a concern for honesty.

And ecstasy is the way out! Harmony! Perhaps, but lacerating. The way out? It suffices for me to seek it: I fall back again, inert, pitiful: the way out from project, out of the will for a way out! For project is the prison

from which I want to escape (project, discursive existence): I formulated
the project of escaping from project! And I know that it is sufficient to
shatter discourse in me, from then on ecstasy is there, from which only
discourse distances me, the ecstasy that discursive thought betrays by offering it as a way out and betrays by offering it as the absence of a way out.
Impotence cries out in me (I recall) a long, anguished inner cry: having
known, knowing no longer.

That through which discourse is nonsense in its rage as well, but (I
moan) not *enough* (in me *not enough*).

Not enough! Not enough anguish, suffering . . . I say it, I, child of
joy, whom a wild, happy laughter—never ceased to carry (it released me
sometimes: its infinite lightness, *distant*, remained temptation in collapse,
in tears, and even in the blows that I at times gave my head against walls).
But! . . . holding a finger in boiling water . . . and I cry "not enough"!

I forget—once again: suffering, laughter, that finger. Infinite surpassing
in oblivion, ecstasy, indifference, to myself, to this book: I see, what discourse never attained. I am *open*, breach gapping before the unintelligible sky
and everything in me hurled forward in accordance with the final discord,
rupture of every possibility, violent kiss, abduction, lost in the complete
absence of the possible, in the opaque, dead night, nevertheless light, no
less unknowable, blinding, than the depths of the heart.

And above all *no more object*. Ecstasy is not love: love is possession
for which the object is necessary, at once possessing and possessed by the
subject. There is no longer subject=object, but "gapping breach" between
one and the other and, in the breach, subject and object are dissolved, there
is a passage, communication, but not from one to the other: *one* and the
other have lost their distinct existence. The questions of the subject, its will
to know are suppressed: the subject is no longer there, its interrogation no
longer has any meaning or principle which introduces it. In the same way,
no response remains possible. The response should be "such is the object,"
when there is not longer any distinct object.

The subject preserves on the margin of its ecstasy the role of a child
in a drama: surpassed, its presence persists, incapable of more than vaguely—and distractedly—sensing—profoundly absent presence; it remains in
the wings, occupied as with toys. Ecstasy has no meaning for him, if not
that *being new* it captivates; but that it endures and the subject becomes

bored: ecstasy decidedly no longer has meaning. And as there is in it no desire to persevere in being (this desire is a fact of distinct beings), it has no consistency and dissipates. As foreign to *man*, ecstasy arises in man, ignorant of the concern that occasioned it, as of the intellectual scaffolding leaning on it (that it lets fall down): for concern, it is nonsense; for thirst for knowledge, it is nonknowledge.

The subject—weary of itself, the necessity of going to extremes—seeks ecstasy, it's true; it never has the *will* for its ecstasy. There is an irreducible discord of the subject seeking ecstasy and ecstasy itself. However, the subject knows ecstasy and senses it: not as a voluntary direction coming from himself, as the sensation of an effect coming from outside. I can go before it, instinctively, driven by the disgust for stagnation that I am: ecstasy is thus born of disequilibrium. I attain it better by external means, from the fact that it cannot exist in me from necessary moods. The place where I previously knew ecstasy, the memory bewitched by physical sensations, the banal ambiance of which I have kept an exact memory, had an evocative power greater than the voluntary repetition of a describable movement of the mind.

I carry within me like a burden the concern for writing this book. In fact, I am *acted*. Even if nothing, absolutely, responded to my idea of necessary interlocutors (or readers), the idea alone would act in me. I create with it to such a degree that one could lift one of my limbs more easily.

The *third*, the companion, the reader who acts upon me, is discourse. Or again, the reader is discourse, it is he who speaks in me, who maintains in me the living discourse of his address. And undoubtedly, discourse is project, but it is nevertheless still this *other*, the reader, who animates me and who already forgets me (kills me), without whose present insistence I could do nothing, would have no inner experience. Not that in moments of violence—of misfortune—I don't forget him, as he himself forgets me—but I tolerate in myself the action of the project in that it is a link with this obscure *other*, sharing my anguish, my torture, desiring my torture as much as I desire his.

Blanchot asked me: why not pursue my inner experience as if I were the *last man*?[9] In a certain sense . . . However, I know myself to be the reflection of the multitude and the sum of its anguish. In another sense, if I were the last man, the anguish would be the most insane imaginable! I could in no way escape, I would remain before infinite annihilation, thrown back into myself, or again: empty, indifferent. But inner experience is conquest and as such *for others*! The subject in experience is lost, loses itself in the object, which itself is dissolved. It could not however dissolve itself to this extent if its nature did not permit this change; the subject in the experience in spite of everything remains: to the extent that it is not a child in a drama, a fly on a nose, it is *consciousness of others* (I neglected this the other time). Being the fly, the child, it is no longer exactly the subject (it is laughable, laughable in its own eyes); making itself *consciousness of others*, and like the ancient chorus, the witness, the popularizer of the drama, it loses itself in human communication, insofar as the subject throws itself outside of itself, it ruins itself in an indefinite crowd of possible existences. But if this crowd were absent, if the possible were dead, if I were . . . the last? Would I have to renounce leaving myself, remaining enclosed in this self as in the depths of a tomb? Would I from today onward moan at the idea of not being, at not being able to hope to be the last one; from today, a monster, weeping the *misfortune* that overcomes me—since it's possible, the *last* without chorus, I imagine, dying dead to himself, in the infinite twilight where he would be, would feel the walls (the depths even) of the tomb open. I can imagine again . . . (I only do it for others!): it is possible that already alive, I am enshrouded in his tomb—the tomb of the *last one*, of this being in distress, unleashing being in himself. Laughter, dreams, and, in sleep, rooftops falling in a rain of gravel . . . knowing nothing, to this degree (not of ecstasy, of sleep): to strangle myself in this way, unsolvable enigma, to accept sleep, the starry universe my tomb, glorified, glory constellated with deaf stars, unintelligible and further than death, terrifying (nonsense: the taste of garlic from the roasted lamb).

Part Three

Antecedents to the Torture
(or the Comedy)

. . . old Nobodaddy aloft
Farted & Belchd & coughd
Then swore a great oath that made heavn quake
And calld aloud to English Blake
Blake was giving his body ease
At Lambeth beneath the poplar trees
From his seat then started he
And turnd himself round three times three
The Moon at that sight blushd scarlet red
The stars threw down their cups & fled . . .

—William Blake[1]

I will now provide the narrative of the antecedents to my "inner experience" (the result of which is "torture"). Toward this end, I will take up what I have written that has been equal to it, at least what I still have of it (most often I have written in an obscure, stilted, and overloaded way: I have changed the form, cut down, sometimes explained, which changes nothing at bottom).

I limit the narrative to what leaves me merged with human being (in itself), rejecting what would unveil this lie and make of my person an "error": I show straightforwardly that inner experience asks someone who engages in it to begin by placing himself on a pinnacle (the Christians know this, feeling themselves held to "pay for" their sufficiency, it hurls them into humility: at the very instant of the disgrace, however, the most bitter saint knows himself to be chosen).

*Every man is unaware of the pinnacle upon which he lives perched. Unaware or pretends to be (difficult to judge the share of ignorance or of feigned ignorance). Few cases of honest insolence (*Ecce homo, *the passage from Blake).*

[I take myself back twenty years: at first I laughed, my life had dissolved upon leaving a long Christian piety, in laughter, with a spring-like bad faith. Of this laughter, I have already described the point of ecstasy, but, from the first day, I no longer had any doubts: laughter was revelation, opened the depths of things. I will speak of the occasion in which this laughter emerged:

69

I was in London (in 1920) and I was to have dinner with Bergson; I had at that time read nothing by him (nor for that matter and for what it's worth by other philosophers); I had this curiosity, finding myself at the British Museum I asked for Laughter *(the shortest of his books); reading it irritated me, the theory seemed to fall short (thereto the public figure disappointed me: this little careful man, philosopher!) but the question, the meaning of laughter remaining hidden, was from then on in my eyes the key question (linked to happy, intimate laughter, by which I suddenly saw that I was possessed), the enigma that I had to resolve at all costs (which, resolved, would itself resolve everything).[2] For a long time I had only known a chaotic euphoria. Only after several years, I felt the chaos—faithful image of an incoherence of diverse being—by degrees, become suffocating. I was shattered, dissolved by having laughed too much, such that, depressed, I found myself: the inconsistent monster that I was, void of meaning and of will, frightened me.]*

I Want to Carry My Person to the Pinnacle

If the cashier falsifies the accounts, the director is perhaps hidden behind a piece of furniture, to unmask the dishonest employee. To write: to falsify accounts? I don't know about this, but I know that a *director* is possible, and that if he appeared unexpectedly, I would have no other recourse than shame. There are no readers, nevertheless, who have in them anything to cause this disarray. The most perspicacious of them accusing me, I would laugh: it is of myself that I am afraid.

Why think: "I am a lost man" or "I seek nothing"? Does it suffice to admit: "I cannot die without playing this role, and, to keep silent, one must not die." And any other excuse! The stale smell of silence—or: silence, imaginary attitude, the most "literary" of all. So many excuses: I think, I write, to know no way of being better than a tattered rag.

I would like very much to no longer hear anything, but to speak, to cry out: why do I fear hearing my own voice as well? And I am not speaking of fear, but of terror, of horror. That someone should silence me (if they dare)! Sew my lips together like those of a wound!

I know that I am descending alive, not even into a tomb but into a common pit, without grandeur or intelligence, truly naked (as a woman of pleasure is naked). Would I dare to affirm: "I will not yield, in no case

will my confidence give way and leave me to be buried like a dead man?"
If someone had pity and wanted to pull me out of this, I would, on the
contrary, accept: I would have for his intentions a cowardly distaste. It
would be better to let me see that nothing can be done (save, perhaps,
involuntarily, to overwhelm me), that my silence is expected.

What is *ridiculous?* The ridiculous as pain? Absolute? The adjective,
ridiculous, is its own negation. But the ridiculous is what I don't have the
heart to bear. Things are like this: what is ridiculous is never entirely ridiculous, that would be bearable; thus the analysis of the elements of the ridiculous (which would be the easy way of getting out of this), once formulated,
remains useless. The ridiculous—these are the other men—innumerable; in
the middle: myself, inevitably, like a wave in the sea.

Excessive joy, which the mind does not avoid, obscures the intelligence. Sometimes one uses it in order to arrange—in one's own eyes—the
illusion of a personal possibility—the compensation of an excessive horror; sometimes one imagines regulating things, precisely by passing into
obscurity.

I play the role of the jester in saying in the name of intelligence that
it definitively refuses to formulate anything whatsoever; that it lets loose
not only the one who speaks but the one who thinks.

The procedure that consists of endlessly finding some novelty in order
to escape the preceding results is offered to agitation, but nothing is more
stupid.

If I find a thought ridiculous, I dismiss it. And, to push this further,
if all thought is ridiculous and if it is ridiculous to think . . .
If I say: "*One man is the mirror of another*," I express my thought, but
not if I say, "*The blue of noon is an illusion.*" If I say: "*The blue of noon is an
illusion,*" in the tone of one who expresses his thought, I am ridiculous. *To
express my thought*, a personal idea is necessary. I betray myself in this way:
the idea matters little, *I want to carry my person to the pinnacle.* Besides, I
could not avoid it in any way. If I had to equate myself to others, I would
have for myself the contempt that ridiculous beings inspire. In general, we
turn ourselves away, terrified, from those truths without a way out: any
escape is good (philosophical, utilitarian, messianic). I will perhaps find a
new way out. One procedure consisted of grinding one's teeth, becoming

the prey of nightmares and great suffering. Even this affectation was better, at times, than to catch oneself in the act of climbing a pinnacle.

These judgments should lead to silence, and I write. This is in no way paradoxical. Silence is itself a pinnacle and, better, the holy of holies. The contempt implied in all silence means that one no longer cares to verify it (as one does by ascending to an ordinary pinnacle). Now I know: I don't have the means to silence myself (it would be necessary to perch myself at such a height, to deliver me, with the hope of distraction, to a ridiculousness so visionary . . .). I am ashamed of it and can say the extent to which my shame is insignificant.

[*The time came when, in a carefree movement, I abandoned myself without constraint to myself. My infinite vanity received belated and, moreover, miserable, confirmations from outside. I ceased to greedily exploit possibilities for unhealthy contestation. My disorder started again, less carefree, more adept. If I recalled what I said of the "pinnacle," I saw in it the sickest aspect of my vanity (but not a true refusal). I had had the desire, when writing, to be read, esteemed: this memory had the same stench of comedy as my whole life. It was linked, moreover—quite distantly but linked—to the literary fashion of the time (to the inquiry in* Litté-rature, *to the question posed one day: "why do you write?"). My "response," several years later, was not published, was absurd.[3] It seemed to me nevertheless to come from the same spirit as the inquiry: from a decision to approach life from the outside. I had trouble seeing a way out of such a state of mind. But I no longer doubted finding the necessary values, so clear and at the same time so profound, that they eluded the answers destined to fool others or oneself.*

In what follows—written in 1933—I could only glimpse ecstasy. It was a path without discipline and at most an obsession.

These few pages are linked:
—to the first phrases that seemed to me to have a lacerating simplicity, the overture of Leonora; *I never really go to concerts and went to one only to hear Beethoven; a feeling of divine intoxication invaded me that I neither could nor can describe straightforwardly, that I attempted to follow by evoking the suspended nature—and bringing me to tears—of the depths of being;*
—to a separation that was a little cruel: I was sick, in bed—I remember a beautiful afternoon sun—I suddenly glimpsed the identity of my pain—that a departure had just caused—with an ecstasy, a sudden rapture.]

Death Is in a Sense a Deception[4]

1

I demand—around me extends the void, the darkness of the *real* world—I exist, I remain blind, in anguish: each of the others is entirely different from me, I feel nothing of what they feel. If I envisage my coming to the world—linked to birth then to the union of a man and a woman, and even, to the moment of union—a unique chance decided the possibility of this *self* that I am: in the end, the mad improbability of a sole being without whom, *for me*, nothing would exist. The smallest difference in the continuity of which I am the result: in place of *me*, avid to be me, there would be with respect to *me* only nothingness, as if I were dead.

This infinite improbability from which I come is under me like a void: my presence, above this void, is like the exercise of a fragile power, as if this void demanded the challenge that I *myself* bring to it, me, which is to say the infinite, painful improbability, of an irreplaceable being that I am.

In the abandonment in which I am lost, empirical knowledge of my similitude with others is indifferent, for the essence of my self arises from this, that nothing will ever be able to replace it: the feeling of my fundamental improbability situates me in the world where I remain like it, being foreign, absolutely foreign.

More rightly, the historical origin of the *self* (regarded by this *self* itself as a part of everything that is an object of knowledge), or even the explanatory study of its ways of being, are only so many insignificant traps. The misery of every explanation before an inexhaustible demand. Even in the cell of a condemned man, this *self* that my anguish opposes to all that remains would perceive what preceded it and what surrounds it as a void subordinated to its power. [*Such a way of seeing renders the distress of the condemned man suffocating: he mocks it, must nevertheless suffer, for he cannot abandon it.*]

In these conditions, why would I concern myself with other points of view, as reasonable as they may be? The experience of the *self*, of its improbability, of its mad demands, nonetheless exists.

2

I should, it seems, choose between two opposed ways of seeing. But this necessity of a choice presents itself linked to the position of the fundamental problem: what exists? What is profound existence cleared of illusory forms? Most often the response is given as if the question "*what is imperative?*" (what is the moral value?) and not "*what exists?*" were posed. In other cases, the answer is a way out (uncomprehending evasion of, not destruction of the problem) if the matter is given as profound existence.

I escape confusion by turning away from the problem. I have defined the *self* as a value, but refused to confuse it with profound existence.

In every honest (matter-of-fact) search, this *self*, entirely other to its fellows, is rejected as nothingness (practically ignored); but it is precisely as nothingness (as *illusion*—to the extent that it is) that it answers to my demand. What is dissipated in it (what seems futile, shameful even) as soon as one poses the question of substantial existence, is precisely what it wants to be: what is necessary for it is really an empty vanity, improbable to the limit of terror and without a real, true relationship to the world (the explained, known world is the contrary of the improbable: it is a foundation, that which one cannot withdraw, whatever one does).

If the consciousness that I have of my *self* escapes the world, if, trembling, I abandon all hope of logical harmony and dedicate myself to *improbability*—first to my own and, finally, to that of all things [*this is to play the drunk, staggering man, who, following the thread, takes himself for a candle, blows it out, and, crying out with fear, finally, takes himself for the night*]—I can grasp the *self* in tears, in anguish (I can even prolong my vertigo to the vanishing point and only find myself in the desire for another—for a woman—unique, irreplaceable, dying, in all things similar to me), but only when death approaches will I know without fail what it is about.

It is by dying that, without possible flight, I will perceive the laceration that constitutes my nature and in which I have transcended "what exists." As long as I live, I content myself with comings and goings, with a compromise. Whatever I say about it, I know myself to be an individual of a species and, roughly, I remain in accordance with a common reality; I take part in what, by all necessity, exists, in what nothing can withdraw. The self-that-dies abandons this accord: it truly perceives what surrounds it as a void and itself as a challenge to this void; the self-that-lives limits itself to intuiting the vertigo in which everything will end (much later).

And still, it's true: the self-that-dies, if it has not arrived at the state of "moral sovereignty," in the very arms of death, maintains with things a kind of harmony in ruin (wherein idiocy and blindness are mixed). It challenges the world no doubt, but weakly, it evades its own challenge, hides what it was from itself right until the end. Seduction, power, *sovereignty*, are necessary for the self-that-dies: one must be a god in order to die.

Death is in a sense vulgar, inevitable, but in a sense deep, inaccessible. The animal is unaware of it even though it throws man into animality. The ideal man incarnating reason remains foreign to it: the animality of a god is essential to its nature; at the same time dirty (malodorous) and sacred.

Disgust, feverish seduction unite; exasperated in death: it is no longer a question of banal cancelation, but of the point itself where the final greed and extreme horror collide. The passion that commands so many frightful games and dreams is no less the desperate desire to be my *self* than that of no longer being anything.

In the halo of death, and there only, the *self* founds its empires; there the purity of a hopeless demand comes to light; there the hope of the self-that-dies is realized (vertiginous hope, burning with fever, where the limit of the dream is pushed back).

At the same time, the carnally inconsistent presence of God is distanced, not as a vain appearance, but insofar as it depends on the world thrown back into oblivion (that which founds the interdependence of the parts).

There is no longer a God in the "inaccessible death," no longer a God in the closed night; one no longer hears anything but *lama sabachthani*, the little sentence that, of all sentences, men have charged with a sacred horror.[5]

In the ideally dark void, chaos, to the point of revealing the absence of chaos (there everything is deserted, cold, in the closed night, even though at the same time of a fever-inducing, painful brilliance), life opens itself to death, the *self* grows until it reaches the pure imperative: this imperative, in the hostile part of being, is formulated "die like a dog"; it has no application in a world from which it turns away.

But, in the distant possibility, this purity of "dies-like-a-dog" responds to the demands of passion—not of the slave for the master: life devoting itself to death is the passion of the lover for the beloved; the angry jealousy of the beloved is in play, but never "authority."

And, to conclude, the fall into death is dirty; in a solitude heavy in a different way than that in which lovers are laid bare, the approach of rot links the self-that-dies to the nudity of absence.

3

[In the preceding I have said nothing of the suffering *that, ordinarily, accompanies death. But suffering is united to death in a deep way and its horror reemerges in every line. I imagine that suffering is always this same game of the final shipwreck. A pain means very little and is not clearly different from a sensation of pleasure, before nausea, the intimate cold in which I succumb. A pain is perhaps only a sensation incompatible with the tranquil utility of the* self*: some action, external or internal, challenges the fragile ordering of the composite existence, decomposes me, and the horror of that menacing action makes me grow pale. Not that a pain is necessarily a threat of death: it unveils the existence of possible actions that the* self *would not know how to survive, it evokes* death, *without introducing a real threat.]*

If I now represent the opposite view: how little importance death has, I have reason on my side. *[In suffering, it's true, reason reveals its weakness and there are moments it cannot dominate; the degree of intensity to which pain reaches shows how little weight reason has; even more, the excessive virulence of the self, evident despite reason.]* Death is in a sense a deception. The self, dying as I said a dreadful death, no less inattentive to reason than a dog, encloses itself in horror of its own free will. Should it escape for an instant the illusion that founds it, it will welcome death like a child falling asleep (it is the same way with an old man whose youthful illusion was slowly extinguished or a young man living the life of the masses: the work of reason, destroying illusion, realizes itself roughly in them).

The agonizing character of death signifies the human need for anguish. Without this need, death would seem easy. Man, dying *poorly*, distances himself from nature, engenders an illusory, human world, fashioned for *art*: we live in a tragic world, in the false atmosphere of which "tragedy" is its completed form. Nothing is tragic for the animal, which does not fall into the trap of the *self*.

Ecstasy is born in this tragic, artificial world. Without any doubt, every object of ecstasy is created by art. All "mystical knowledge" is founded on the belief in the revelatory value of ecstasy: on the contrary, it must necessarily be regarded as a fiction, as analogous, in a certain sense, to the intuitions of art.

However, if I say that, in "mystical knowledge," existence is the work of man, I mean that it is the daughter of the *self* and of its essential illusion: the ecstatic vision has no less of this than some inevitable object.

The passion of the *self*, the love burning within it, seeks an object. The *self* is only liberated *outside itself*. I can know that I created the object of my passion, that it does not exist on its own: it is no less there. My disillusion undoubtedly changes it: it is not God—*I created it*—but for the same reason it is not nothingness.

This object, chaos of light and shadow, is *catastrophe*. I perceive it as an object, my thought, however, forms itself in its image, at the same time that it is its reflection. Perceiving it, my thought sinks in annihilation as in a fall wherein one cries out. Something immense, exorbitant, is liberated in every sense with a noise of catastrophe; this surges from an unreal, infinite void, at the same time that it is lost there, in a shock with a blinding flash. In a crash of telescoping trains, a window shattering while causing death is the expression of this imperative, all-powerful, and already annihilated occurrence.

In ordinary conditions, time is annulled, enclosed in the permanence of forms or foreseen changes. Movements inscribed in the interior of an order *stop* time, which they freeze in a system of measures and equivalences. The "catastrophe" is the most profound revolution—it is time "unhinged": the skeleton is the sign of this, at the outcome of rot, from which its illusory existence emerges.

4

Thus as the object of its ecstasy, time responds to the ecstatic fever of the self-that-dies: for in the same way as time, the self-that-dies is pure change and neither the one nor the other has real existence.

But if the initial interrogation subsists, if in the disorder of the self-that-dies the little question persists: "what exists?"

Time only signifies the flight of objects that seemed real. The substantial existence of things moreover has for the *self* only a lugubrious meaning: their insistence is for it comparable to the preparations for its execution.

Lastly this emerges: whatever it is, the existence of things can only enclose the death that it brings to me, it is itself projected in my death that encloses it.

If I affirm the illusory existence of the self-that-dies or of time, I don't think that the illusion should be submitted to the judgment of things whose existence would be substantial: I project their existence on the contrary in an illusion that encloses it.

By the very reason of its improbability, under its "name," the man that I am—whose coming into the world was what could be thought of as most improbable—encloses however the group of things. Death, delivering me from a world that kills me, effectively encloses this real world in the unreality of a self-that-dies.

July 1933

[In 1933, I was sick a first time; at the beginning of the following year, I was sick once more, and only got out of bed to limp, crippled with rheumatism (I only recovered in the month of May—since which time I have enjoyed normal health).* Believing myself better, wanting to recover in the sun, I went to Italy, but it rained (this was in the month of April). On certain days, I walked with great difficulty, sometimes crossing the street made me moan: I was alone and recall (I was so ridiculous) having wept the entire length of the road around Lake Albano (where I tried in vain to stay). I resolved to return to Paris, but in two days: I left early from Rome and slept in Stresa. The next day was very beautiful and I stayed. This was the end of a paltry odyssey: afternoons of the trip spent lying on hotel beds were there followed by delicious relaxation in the sun. The large lake surrounded by spring mountains sparkled before my eyes like a mirage: it was hot, I remained seated under palm trees, in gardens of flowers. I already suffered less: I tried to walk, it was again possible. I went up

---

*At least up until the moment I wrote this page: a few days later, I fell gravely sick and I have still not recovered (1942).

to the pontoon bridge to check the time. Voices of an infinite majesty, at the same time lively, sure of themselves, crying to the sky, were raised in a chorus of incredible strength. I remained gripped, on the spot, not knowing what those voices were: a moment of transport passed before I understood that a loudspeaker was broadcasting mass. I found a bench on the bridge where I could enjoy the immense landscape, to which the luminosity of the morning lent its transparency. I remained there to hear the mass sung. The chorus was the purest, the richest in the world, the music achingly beautiful (I know nothing of the conductor or the composer of the mass—on the subject of music, my knowledge is haphazard, lazy). The voices were raised as though by successive and varied waves, slowly attaining intensity, rapidity, mad richness, but what came out of the miracle was a bursting forth as from a shattering crystal, which they reached at the very moment when everything seemed at its end. The secular power of the basses was sustained, ceaselessly, and brought to the burning point (to the point of a cry, of blinding incandescence) the high flames of the children's voices (just as in a hearth, abundant coals, release an intense heat, tenfold the delirious force of the flames, playing with their fragility, rendering them more insane). What must be said in any case of these melodies is the consent that nothing could have withdrawn from the mind, which had nothing to do with points of dogma (I distinguished some Latin phrases from the Credo . . . from others, it didn't matter) but with the glory of the torrent, the triumph that human strength had attained. It seemed to me, on this pontoon bridge, before Lake Maggiore, that other melodies could never consecrate with such power the accomplishment of cultivated, refined, yet torrential and joyous, man that I am, that we are. No Christian pain, but an exaltation of the gifts with which man has made light of countless difficulties (in particular—this took on a lot of meaning—in the technique of song and chorus). The sacred character of the incantation could only affirm a feeling of strength, cry out even more to the sky and to the point of laceration the presence of a being exultant in its certitude and as though assured of infinite chance. (It mattered little that this comes from the ambiguity of Christian humanism, nothing mattered any more, the chorus cried out with superhuman strength.)

It is vain to want to liberate life from the lies of art (we come to have contempt for art in order to escape, to trick). It was that year that the storm raised up above me, but as simple and shattering as it was, I know not to betray anything by speaking, not of the things themselves, but, to express myself with greater strength, of liturgical melodies or opera.

I came back to Paris, restored my health: this was to enter suddenly into horror.

I encountered horror, not death. To the one it weds, as to the spectator, whom it invites, tragedy incidentally dispenses anguish, intoxication, and rapture. I returned to Italy, and although this was "like a madman," chased from place to place, I lived the life of a god (flasks of black wine, lightning, omens). However, I can barely speak of it.

Terrified, religious silence that took place in me is undoubtedly expressed in this new silence. And, as I said, this was not about my life.

It was strange to gain access to power, to strengthen an authority, even in paradox, and to settle into *a glory of complete rest. The triumph grasped on the pontoon bridge at Stresa only attained full meaning at the moment of expiation (moment of anguish, of sweat, of doubt).*

Not that there was sin, for one could not have, one should *not have committed sin, whereas triumph was necessary, one* had *to* assume it *(tragedy consists essentially in this—in that it is irremediable).*

To express the movement that proceeds from exaltation (from its happy, dazzling irony) to the instant of laceration, I will resort once again to music.
Mozart's Don Juan *(which I evoke after Kierkegaard and which I heard—one time at least—as if the skies had opened—but the first time only, for after the fact, I expected it: the miracle no longer functioned[6]) presents two decisive moments. In the first, anguish—for us—is already there (the Commandatore is invited to supper), but Don Juan sings:*
"Vivan le femmine—viva il buon vino—sostegno e gloria d'umanità . . ."[7]
In the second, the hero holding the stone hand of the Commandatore—which chills him—and pressed into repenting—answers (this is before he falls thunderstruck, the final reply):
"No vecchio infatuato!"[8]
(The useless—psychological—chatter about "Don Juanism" surprises me, repulses me. Don Juan is, in my eyes—more naive—only a personal incarnation of the festival, of the carefree orgy, which negates and divinely overturns obstacles.)]

The Blue of Noon[9]

When I solicit gently, at the very heart of anguish, a strange absurdity, an eye opens at the summit, in the middle of my skull.

This eye that, in order to contemplate the sun, in its nudity, face to face, opens up to it in all its glory, does not derive from my reason: it is a cry that escapes me. At the moment when the fulguration blinds me, I am the flash of a shattered life, and this life—anguish and vertigo—opening itself up to an infinite void, is lacerated and exhausted at once in this void.

The earth bristles with plants carried by a continuous movement, day by day, to the celestial void; its innumerable surfaces reflect the collectivity of men, laughing and lacerated, to the shining immensity of space. In this free movement, independent of all consciousness, the elevated bodies extend themselves toward a breathtaking absence of limits; but even though the agitation and the inner hilarity lose themselves ceaselessly in such a beautiful sky, but no less illusory than death, my eyes continue to subjugate me through a vulgar link to the things that surround me, in the middle of which my steps are limited by the habitual necessities of life.

It is only by means of a sickly representation—an eye opening at the summit of my own head—at the very place where ingenuous metaphysics placed the seat of the soul—that human beings, forgotten on the Earth—such as today I reveal myself to myself, fallen, without hope, in oblivion—suddenly gain access to the lacerating fall into the void of the sky.[10]

This fall presumes as an impetus the attitude of a command to stand at attention. The erection, however, does not have the sense of a military stiffness; the human bodies erect themselves from the ground like a challenge to the Earth, to the mud that engenders them and that they are happy to send back to nothingness.
Nature giving birth to man was a dying mother: she gave "being" to the one whose coming into the world was her own death.

But as in the reduction of Nature to a void, the destruction of the one who has destroyed is engaged in this insolent movement. The negation of Nature accomplished by man—raising himself above a nothingness that is his work—returns him without delay to vertigo, to the fall into the void of the sky.

To the extent that it is not enclosed in useful objects that surround it, existence initially escapes the servitude of nudity only by projecting into the sky an inverted image of its destitution. In this formation of the moral image, it seems that, from the Earth to the Sky, the fall is reversed from the Sky to the dark depths of the ground (from sin); his true nature (man victim of the shining Sky) remains veiled in mythological exuberance.

The very movement in which man denies Mother Earth who gave birth to him opens the path of servitude. The human being abandons himself to a paltry despair. Human life is represented thereafter as insufficient, overwhelmed by sufferings or privations that reduce it to ugly vanities. The Earth is at its feet like scraps. Above, the Sky is empty. Due to a pride large enough to stand up to this void, it prostrates itself, face to the earth, eyes riveted to the ground. And, in fear of the fatal freedom of the sky, it affirms between itself and the infinite void the relationship of a slave to a master; desperately, like a blind man, it seeks a terrified consolation in a laughable renunciation.

Beneath the elevated immensity, become oppressive from fatal emptiness, existence, which destitution removes from all possibility, follows once more a movement of arrogance, but the arrogance this time opposes it to the flash of the sky: profound movements of liberated anger support it. And it is no longer the Earth, of which it is a scrap, that its challenge provokes, it is the reflection in the sky of its fears—divine oppression—that becomes the object of its hate.

In opposing itself to Nature, human life had become transcendent and returned to the void everything that it is not: in contrast, if this life rejects the authority that maintained it in oppression and becomes sovereign itself, it detaches itself from the links that paralyze a vertiginous movement toward the void.

The limit is crossed with a weary horror: hope seems a respect that fatigue grants to the necessity of the world.[11]

The ground will give way beneath my feet.

I will die in hideous conditions.

I take pleasure today from being the object of disgust for the sole being to whom destiny links my life.

I solicit everything bad that a laughing man can receive.

The exhausted head in which "I" am has become so timid, so greedy that death alone could satisfy it.

Several days ago, I arrived—really, not in a dream—in a town evoking the décor of a tragedy.[12] One evening, I only say it to laugh in a more unhappy way, I was not alone, drunk, watching two old man turning while dancing—really, not in a dream. During the night, the Commandatore came into my room; in the afternoon (I was passing in front of his tomb), pride and irony incited me to invite him. The appearance of the ghost struck me with terror, I was a wreck; a second victim was recumbent beside me: a foam uglier than blood flowed from lips that disgust rendered similar to those of a dead woman. And now I am condemned to this solitude that I do not accept, that I don't have the heart to bear. Yet I have only a cry to repeat the invitation and, if I believe my anger, it would no longer be me, it would be the shadow of the old man who would go away.

Beginning with an abject suffering, the insolence that slyly persists grows again, first slowly, then, in a flash, reaches the wave of a happiness affirmed against all reason.[13]

Today, beneath the dazzling light of the Sky, justice aside, this sickly existence, close to death, and yet real, abandons itself to the "lack" that reveals its coming into the world.

Completed "being," from rupture to rupture, after a growing nausea had delivered it to the void of the sky, has become no longer "being" but wound, and even "agony" of all that it is.

August 1934

[Going back, if I again follow the path that man followed in search of himself (of his glory), I cannot but be seized by a strong and overflowing movement—that is exuberant. I get angry at myself sometimes for permitting the feeling of sickly existence. Laceration is the expression of richness. The insipid and weak man is incapable of it.

That everything should be in suspense, impossible, unlivable . . . I don't care! Would I be breathless at this point?

To summon all the tendencies of man into a point, all the possibilities that he is, to draw from them at the same time agreements and violent oppositions, no longer to leave outside laughter tearing apart the thread (the fabric) of which man is made, on the contrary to know oneself assured of insignificance so long as thought is not itself this profound tearing of the fabric and its object—being itself—the torn fabric (Nietzsche had said: "Regard as false that which has not made you laugh at least once."—Zarathustra, On Old and New Tablets[14]*). In this my efforts recommence and undo Hegel's* Phenomenology. *Hegel's construction is a philosophy of work, of "project." Hegelian man—Being and God—is* *accomplished, completed in the appropriateness of project. Ipse before becoming everything does not fail, does not become comic, insufficient, but the private individual, the slave engaged in the paths of work, gains, after many detours, the summit of the universal. The only obstacle to this way of seeing (of a profound inequality, moreover, in some ways inaccessible) is what, in man, is irreducible to project: nondiscursive existence, laughter, ecstasy, that link—in the end—man to the negation of the project that he nevertheless is—ultimately, man ruins himself in a total effacement of what he is, of all human affirmation. Such would be the easy passage from the philosophy of work—Hegelian and profane—to the philosophy of the sacred, which "torture" expresses, but which assumes a more accessible philosophy of communication.*

I have trouble conceiving that "wisdom"—science—is linked to inert existence. Existence is an exuberant tumult, where fever and laceration are linked to intoxication. Hegelian collapse, the finished, profane character of a philosophy whose movement was its principle, comes from the rejection, in Hegel's life, of everything that could seem to be sacred intoxication. Not that Hegel was "wrong" to avoid the limp concessions to which vague minds had recourse during his times. But to confuse existence and work (discursive thought, project), he reduces the world to the profane world: he negates the sacred world (communication).

When the storm that I mentioned was calmed, my life knew a time of slight depression. I don't know if this crisis completed itself by fixing my steps forward, but since then they have had a primary object. With a clear conscience, I devoted myself to the conquest of an inaccessible good, a "grail," a mirror in which would be reflected, to the extremity of the light, the vertigos that I have had.

I didn't give it a name initially. Besides, I stupidly went astray (it hardly matters). What counts in my eyes: to justify my foolishness (and no less that of others), my immense vanity . . . If I have prophesied, better still, I indict myself slightly for that. Among the rights that man claims, he forgets that of being stupid; he is necessarily so, but without the right, and sees himself constrained to dissimulate. I wouldn't in any way want to hide.

At first my search had a double object: the sacred, then ecstasy. I wrote what follows as a prelude to this search and really only carried it out later. I insist on this point, that a feeling of unbearable vanity is the foundation of all of this (as humility is of the Christian experience).]

The Labyrinth (or the Composition of Beings)[15]

There exists a principle of insufficiency at the base of human life. In isolation, each man imagines the others incapable or unworthy of "being." A free, slanderous conversation expresses a certitude of the vanity of my fellows; apparently petty chatter reveals a blind straining of life toward an indefinable summit.

The sufficiency of each being is contested ceaselessly by his neighbors. Even a look expressing admiration is attached to me like a doubt. [*"Genius" lowers as much as it lifts up; the idea of "genius" prevents one from being simple, commits one to showing what is essential, to dissimulating what is disappointing: "genius" is inconceivable without "art." I would like to simplify, to brave the feeling of insufficiency. I am not myself sufficient and only maintain my "pretense" thanks to the shadow in which I exist.*] A burst of laughter, an expression of repugnance greets gestures, sentences, failings in which my deep insufficiency is betrayed.

The disquiet of many mounts and is multiplied to the extent that they perceive, at every turn, the solitude of man in an empty night. Without human presence, the night in which everything is found—or rather is lost— would seem like existence for nothing, nonsense equivalent to the absence of being. But this night stops being empty and charged with anguish when I grasp that in it men are nothing and add their discordance to it in vain. If the demand persists in me that, in the world, there should be "being," "being" and not only my obvious "insufficiency," or the simpler insufficiency of things, I will one day be tempted to respond to this by introducing divine sufficiency into my night—even though this is the reflection of the sickness of "being" in me. [*I see today the essential link between this "sickness" and what we hold to be divine—sickness is divine—but in these conditions divinity is not "sufficient," which is to say that no "completion" is conceivable starting from the anguish that the sensation of incompletion introduces in us.*]

Being is in the world so *uncertain* that I can project it where I wish— outside myself. It is a kind of clumsy man—who did not know how to evade the essential intrigue—who limited being in me. In fact, being is precisely *nowhere* and it was a game to grasp it as *divine* at the summit of the pyramid of individual beings. [*Being is "ungraspable," it is only ever "grasped" by mistake; the mistake is not only easy, in this case, it is the condition of thought.*]

Being is *nowhere*.

Man can enclose being in a simple, indivisible element. But there is no being without "ipseity." *Without "ipseity," a simple element (an electron) enclos- es nothing.* The atom, despite its name, is a composite, but only possesses an elementary complexity: the atom itself, because of its relative simplicity, can only be determined through "ipseity."* Thus the number of particles that compose a being intervenes in the constitution of its "ipseity": if the knife of which one successively replaces the handle then the blade loses the shadow of its ipseity, it is not the same as a machine, in which would have disappeared, replaced piece by piece, each of the *numerous* elements that made it new: still less a man whose constituent parts die incessantly (such that nothing of these elements that we *were* subsists after a certain number of years). I can, if necessary, admit that from an extreme complexity, being imposes upon reflection *more* than an elusive appearance, but complexity, raised degree by degree, is for this *more* a labyrinth in which it wanders endlessly, loses itself once and for all.

A sponge reduced by pounding to a dust of cells, the living dust formed by a multitude of isolated beings is lost in the new sponge that it reconstitutes. A fragment of siphonophore is on its own an autonomous being, however the whole siphonophore, in which the fragment partici- pates, is itself not very different from a being possessing its unity. It is only beginning with linear animals (worms, insects, fish, reptiles, birds, or mammals) that the living individuals definitively lose the faculty of con- stituting, severally, groups linked in a single body. Nonlinear animals (like the siphonophore, coral) aggregate in *colonies* whose elements are cemented, but they do not form *societies*. On the contrary, superior animals assemble without having bodily attachments among them: bees, human beings, which form stable societies, still have autonomous bodies. Bees and human beings have, without a single doubt, an autonomous body, but for all that are they autonomous beings?

With regard to human beings, their existence is linked to language. Each person imagines, knows, his existence with the help of words. Words come to him in his head charged with the multitude of human—or nonhu- man—existences in relation to which his individual existence exists. Being is in man mediated by words, which can only give themselves arbitrarily as "autonomous being" and profoundly as "being in relation to." It suf-

---

*See Paul Langevin, *La notion de corpuscules et d'atomes* (Hermann, 1934) pp. 35ff.

fices to follow for a short time the trace, the repeated course of words, to perceive, in a kind of vision, the labyrinthine construction of being. What one vulgarly calls *knowledge* when a fellow man *knows* a fellow woman—and names her—is only ever the existence of a composed moment (in the sense in which all existence is composed—thus the atom composes its unity from simple elements) that once made of these beings an ensemble as real as its parts. The exchange of a limited number of sentences suffices for a banal and durable connection: two existences are henceforth both at least partially penetrable. The knowledge that the man has of the woman is no less distanced from a meeting of strangers than life is from death. *Knowledge* appears in this way like an unstable biological link, no less real, however, than that of the cells of a tissue. The exchange between two people possesses in effect the power to survive momentary separation. [*This way of seeing has the defect of offering knowledge as a foundation of the social bond: it is even more difficult and even, in a sense, it isn't like this at all. Knowledge of a being by another is only a residue, a mode of banal liaison that the essential facts of communication have rendered possible (I am thinking of the intimate operations of religious activity, of sacrifice, of the sacred: from these operations, language, which knowledge uses, remains intensely charged). I have done well to speak of* knowledge, *not of the sacred, in the sense that it is better to begin with a familiar reality. I am nevertheless more annoyed to have given in to a confused mass of scholarly ideas: but this earlier explanation introduces the theory of communication that one will see sketched further on. It is undoubtedly pitiful, but man only gains access to the notion that is most charged with burning possibilities by opposing common sense, by opposing the facts of science to common sense. I do not see how, without the facts of science, one would have been able to return to the obscure feeling, to the instinct of the man still deprived of "common sense."*]

A MAN IS A PARTICLE INSERTED INTO UNSTABLE AND TAN-GLED ENSEMBLES. These ensembles are composed with personal life, to which they bring multiple possibilities (society offers the individual the easy life). Beginning with *knowledge*, the existence of a person is only isolated from the ensemble from a narrow and negligible point of view. Only the instability of the liaisons (this banal fact: however intimate a bond might be, separation is easy, is multiplied and can be prolonged) permits the illusion of an isolated being, folded back on itself and possessing the power of existing without exchange.

In a general way, every isolable element of the universe always appears as a particle susceptible of entering into the composition in an ensemble

that transcends it. [*In fact, if I envision the universe, it is, one can affirm,
constituted by a great number of* galaxies *(of nebulous spirals). The galaxies
compose the clouds of stars, but does the universe compose the galaxies? (Is it the
organized ensemble of the galaxies?) The question that surpasses understanding
leaves a comical bitterness. It touches on the universe, on its totality . . .*] Being
is always a group of particles whose relative autonomies are maintained.
These two principles—composition transcending the constituent parts, relative autonomy of the constituent parts—order the existence of each "being."

1

From these two principles there follows a third that governs the human
condition. The uncertain opposition of autonomy to transcendence puts
being in a position that slips: at the same time that it encloses itself in
autonomy, for this very reason, each being *ipse* wants to become the whole of
transcendence; in the first place, the whole of the composition from which
it set out, then one day, without limits, the whole of the universe. Its will
to autonomy opposes it at first to the ensemble, but it withers—is reduced
to nothing—to the extent that it refuses to enter into it. It then renounces
autonomy for the ensemble, but provisionally: the will to autonomy only
relaxes for a time and quickly, in a single movement in which equilibrium
is created, the being devotes itself at once to the ensemble and the ensemble
to itself.

This being *ipse*, itself composed of parts and, as such, as result, unpredictable chance, enters into the universe as will to autonomy. It is composed but seeks to dominate. Spurred by anguish, it surrenders to the desire
to submit the world to its autonomy. *Ipse*, the infinitesimal particle, this
unpredictable and purely improbable chance, is condemned to want to be
other: everything and necessary. The movement that it undergoes—that
introduces it into higher and higher compositions—animated by the desire
to be at the summit—bit by bit engages it in an agonizing ascension; this
will to be the *universe* is however only a derisory challenge directed at the
unknowable immensity. The immensity eludes consciousness, it eludes itself
infinitely before an individual who seeks it by eluding the improbability
that he is and knows only to look for that which can be reduced to the
necessity for its authority (in the authority of knowledge, by the means
through which man attempts to take himself for the whole of the universe,

there is necessity, misery undergone, the derisory, inevitable fate that befalls us, but we attribute this necessity to the universe, which we confuse with our knowledge).

This flight directed toward the summit (which is, dominating the realms themselves, the composition of knowledge) is only one of the paths of the "labyrinth." But this path that we must follow from illusion to illusion, seeking "being," cannot be avoided in any way. Solitude, in which we attempt to seek refuge, is a new illusion. No one escapes the composition of society: in this composition, each pathway leads to the summit, to the desire for absolute knowledge, is a necessity for limitless power.

Only an inevitable fatigue turns us away. We stop before a disheartening difficulty. The paths leading toward the summit are crowded. And not only is the competition for power tense, but it is most often stuck in a swamp of intrigue. Error, uncertainty, the feeling that power is vain, the faculty that we retain for imagining some supreme height above the first summit, contribute to the essential confusion of the labyrinth. In fact, we can only say of the summit that it is situated here or there. (In a certain sense, it is never reached.) An obscure man, whom the desire—or necessity—of attaining it has driven mad, approaches it more closely, in solitude, than the highly placed figures of his times. It often appears that madness, anguish, crime forbid access to it, but nothing is clear: who could say of lies and baseness that they distance one from it? Such a great uncertainty is likely to justify humility: but humility is often only a detour that seemed certain.

This obscurity of conditions is so draconian—and even precisely so dreadful—that we have no excuses for renouncing it. Pretexts abound. It suffices, in this case, to rely on one or several intermediary individuals: I renounce the summit, another reaches it; I can delegate my power, a renunciation that offers itself a feeling of innocence. Yet it is through it that the worst happens. It is evidence of fatigue, of the feeling of impotence: in seeking the summit, we find anguish. But in fleeing anguish, we fall into the emptiest poverty. We feel "insufficiency" in it: this is the shame of having been thrown toward the void, which leads to the delegation of one's power (and shame is hidden). It follows that the most superficial of men, and the most tired, feel the weight of their indifference and fatigue: indifference and fatigue leave the largest place for deceit, even provoke deceit. We only escape the aberrant nostalgia for the summit by rendering it deceptive.

2

In what way does the individual human being access the universal?

At the end of irrevocable night, life throws the child into the play of beings; he is then the satellite of two adults: he receives the illusion of sufficiency from them (the child regards his parents as gods). This character of satellite in no way disappears in what follows: we withdraw our confidence from our parents, we delegate it to other men. What the child found in the apparently solid existence of his relatives, man seeks in every place where life comes together and condenses. The individual being, lost in the multitude, delegates to those who occupy its center, the concern for assuming the totality of "being." He is content to "take part" in total existence, which maintains, even in simple cases, a diffuse character.

This natural gravitation of beings has as a consequence the existence of relatively stable social groups. In principle, the center of gravitation is in the city; in ancient times, a city, like a corolla enclosing a double pistil, formed around a sovereign and a god. If several cities formed and renounced their role as center in favor of a single one, an empire fell into place around one city among others, where the sovereignty and the gods were concentrated: in this case, the gravitation around a sovereign city impoverished the existence of the peripheral cities, at the heart of which the organs that formed the totality of being have disappeared or wasted away. Bit by bit, the composition of groups (of cities, then empires) gained access to universality (at least tending toward it).

Universality is singular and cannot struggle against its fellows (barbarians are not entirely fellows). Universality suppresses competition. As long as analogous forces are in opposition, one must grow at the expense of others. But once a victorious force remains singular, this way of determining its existence with the help of opposition is lacking. The universal God, if he comes into play, is no longer, like a local god, a guarantor of a city in a struggle against its rivals: he is alone at the summit, even allows himself to be confused with the totality of things and can only arbitrarily maintain "ipseity" in himself. In their history, men thus engage in a strange struggle of *ipse* that must become everything and can only become everything by dying. [*The "gods that die" have taken the form of universals. The God of the Jews was at first "god of armies." According to Hegel, the defeat, the downfall of the Jewish people removed their god from the personal, animal state, of ancient gods, into the impersonal, primitive mode of existence—of light. The*

God of the Jews no longer upheld the existence of the combat: in the death of his son, he attained true universality. Born of the cessation of combat, profound universality—laceration—does not survive the resumption of combat. Moreover, universal gods, as much as they can, flee this murderous universality in war. Allah, thrown into military conquest, escapes sacrifice in this way. At the same time, He pulls the God of the Christians from his solitude: He engages Him, in turn, in combat. Islam withers from the moment it renounces conquest: the Church declines in compensation.]

To seek sufficiency is the same error as enclosing being in some kind of point: we can enclose nothing, we only find insufficiency. We try to put ourselves in the presence of God, but God alive within us demands death at once, we only know how to grasp Him by killing. [*Incessant sacrifice being necessary for survival, we have crucified once and for all, and nevertheless, each day, once again, we crucify ourselves. God himself crucifies. "God," said Angela of Foligno, "offered his son, whom he loved, a poverty that he himself never had and never would have, a poverty equal to himself. And yet he has the property of Being. He possesses substance, and it is so much his that this possession is above human speech. And yet God has made him poor, as if the substance had not been his."*[16] *"Possession above human speech . . ." a singular inversion! The "property of substance," the "possession" only truly exists in "speech," mystic experience, vision, situates itself alone beyond speech and can only be evoked by it. The beyond that is vision, experience, is related to "yet God has made him poor," not to the possessing, which is only a discursive category. The possessing is there to amplify the paradox of a vision.*]

What bursts in the confusion of the summit comes to light, moreover, as soon as life begins to go astray. The need for an illusion—the necessity, where the autonomy of human being finds itself, of imposing its value on the universe—introduces from the outset a disordering in all life. What characterizes human life from the outset and what leads up to the completed rupture of the summit is not only the will to sufficiency, but the timid, cunning attraction on the side of insufficiency.

Our existence is an exasperated attempt to complete being (completed being would be *ipse* become everything). But the effort is *undergone* by us: it is what leads us astray and how we are misled in every way! We don't dare affirm in its fullness our desire to exist without limit: it scares us. But we are even more uneasy at feeling a moment of cruel joy in ourselves as soon as the evidence of our misery emerges.

The ascension toward a summit where being attains the universal is a composition of parts in which a central will subordinates peripheral elements to its law. Without lassitude, a stronger will in search of sufficiency throws weaker wills into insufficiency. Insufficiency is not only the revelation of the summit: it bursts at each step, when the composition throws its constituent parts to the periphery. If existence thrown into insufficiency maintains its pretension to sufficiency, it prefigures the situation of the summit, but the one that chance follows, unaware of failure, perceives it from outside: *ipse* seeking to become everything is only tragic at the summit for itself, and when its impotence is externally manifest, it is "laughable" (in this last case it cannot itself suffer, if it became conscious of its impotence, it would abandon its pretense, leaving it to someone stronger, which is impossible only at the summit).

In a composition of human beings, the center alone possesses the initiative and throws the peripheral elements into insignificance. The center alone is the expression of the composite being and takes precedence over its component parts. It possesses over the ensemble a power of attraction that it even exerts, partially, over a neighboring realm (whose center is less strong). The power of attraction empties the component parts of their richest elements. Cities are slowly emptied of life in favor of a capital. (The local accent becomes comical.)

Laughter is born of changes in level, sudden depressions. If I pull the rug out . . . the sufficiency of a serious person is suddenly followed by the revelation of a final insufficiency (one pulls the rug out from under pretentious beings). I am happy, no matter what, by the experience of failure. And I lose my seriousness myself, by laughing. As if it were a relief to escape the concern for my sufficiency. I cannot, it's true, abandon my concern forever. I throw it off only if I can do so without danger. I laugh at a man whose failure does not tarnish my effort at sufficiency, at a peripheral figure who had pretensions and compromised authentic existence (mimicking its outward appearance). The happiest laughter is that which is given birth by a child. For the child must grow up and from the insufficiency that it reveals, at which I laugh, I know that it will be followed by the sufficiency of the adult (there is time for that). A child is an opportunity to look into—without deep uneasiness—an abyss of insufficiency.

But just like a child, the laughter grows up. In its innocent form, it takes place in the same sense as the social composition: it guarantees it, reinforces it (it is thrown toward the periphery of weak forms): laughter constitutes those that it assembles in unanimous convulsions. But laughter does not reach the peripheral region of existence, it does not have as its object only fools and children (those who became empty or who are still empty); through a necessary reversal, it returns from the child to the father, from the periphery to the center, each time that the father or the center betrays in their turn their insufficiency. (In both cases, we laugh moreover at an identical situation: the unjustified pretense of sufficiency.) The necessity of reversal is so important that it had, at one time, its consecration: there is no social composition that does not have its compensation in the contestation of its foundations; the rituals show it: the saturnalias and festivals of madmen reversed the roles. [*And the profundity from which the feeling that determined the rituals blindly descended; the numerous, intimate bonds between the themes of the carnival and the putting to death of kings indicate this well enough.*]

If I now compare the social composition to a pyramid, it appears as a domination of the center, of the summit (this is a rough, even difficult sketch). The summit incessantly throws the base into insignificance and, in this sense, waves of laughter traverse the pyramid, contesting bit by bit the pretension to sufficiency of the beings placed at a lower level. But the first network of these waves issued from the summit flows back and the second network traverses the pyramid from low to high: this time the reflux contests the sufficiency of the beings placed higher up. This contestation, in contrast, up to the final moment, preserves the summit: it cannot, however, fail to reach it. In fact, innumerable being is in a certain sense strangled by a reverberating convulsion: laughter, in particular, strangles no one, but if I envision the spasms of multitudes (whom one never encompasses with a single glance)? As I have said, the reflux cannot fail to reach the summit. And if it reaches it? This is the agony of God in black night.

3

Laughter intuits the truth that the laceration of the summit lays bare: that our will to arrest being is cursed. Laughter slips on the surface the length of slight depressions: laceration opens the abyss. Abyss and depressions are an equal void: the inanity of the being that we are. Being eludes itself in us, we lack it, since we enclose ourselves in *ipse* and it is desire—necessity—to embrace everything. And the act of grasping clearly the comedy of this changes nothing. The means of escape (humility, the death of the ego, belief in the power of reason) are only so many paths by which we become more stuck.

Man cannot, by any means, escape insufficiency, nor renounce ambition. His will to flee is the fear that he has of being man: its only effect is hypocrisy—the fact that man is what he is without daring to be so [*in this sense, human existence is only embryonic within us, we are not quite men*]. No harmony is imaginable and man, inevitably, must wish to be everything, to remain *ipse*. He is comical in his own eyes if he is conscious of this: he must therefore *want* to be comical, for he is comical insofar as he is man (it is no longer a question of characters, emissaries of comedy)—without a way out. [*This assumes an agonizing dissociation from oneself, a disharmony, a definitive discord—undergone with vigor—without vain efforts to alleviate them.*]

In the first place—he can't avoid it—man must fight before responding to his will to be alone and to be everything himself. As long as he fights, he is still neither comical nor tragic and everything remains suspended in him: he subordinates everything to the action by which he must translate his will (he must therefore be moral, imperative). But a way out can be opened.

The object of the fight is a composition, more and more vast, and, in this sense, it is difficult to fully access the universal. But with success, the fight comes closer to it (in eminent groups, human life tends to take on universal value). If the fight is lessened a little—or if a life, in some way, escapes from it—man gains access to his final solitude: at this moment the will to be everything pulls him to pieces.

He is then no longer struggling with an ensemble equal to what he represents but with nothingness. In this extreme inner turmoil, he can be compared to the bull in a bullfight. The bull, in the bullfight, is at times heavily absorbed in animal nonchalance—abandoned to the secret weakness of death—at times, seized with rage, rushes toward the void that a phantom matador opens before him without respite. But once this void has been affronted, the bull weds nudity—TO THE EXTENT THAT HE IS A MONSTER—lightly assuming this sin. Man is no longer like the beast, a plaything of nothingness, but nothingness is itself his plaything—he ruins himself in it, but lights the darkness with this *laughter*, which he reaches only *intoxicated* by the very void that kills him.

February 1936

[I am irritated if I think of the period of "activity" that I spent—during the final years of peace—in forcing myself to reach my fellows. I had to pay that price. Ecstasy itself is empty envisioned as a private exercise, important only for a single individual.

Even preaching to the converted, there is, in its predication, an element of distress. Profound communication requires silence. In the end, action, which the predication signifies, is limited to this: closing one's doors so as to stop discourse (noise, the mechanisms of the outside).

At the same time the door must remain open and closed. What I wanted: the profound communication of beings to the exclusion of the bonds necessary for projects, which discourse forms. I became, eventually, touchy, each day intimately more wounded. If I took refuge in solitude, it was constraint. It doesn't matter to me, now, that everything should be dead—or seem to be.

The war put an end to my "activity" and my life became all the less separated from the object of its search. A screen normally separates one from this object. In the end, I was able, I had the strength to do it: I made the screen fall. Nothing restful remained, which rendered the efforts illusory. It became possible, once, to link oneself to the inexorable, crystalline fragility of things—without concern for responding to minds full of empty questions. Desert, not undoubtedly without mirages, suddenly dissipated . . .

Few circumstances were more favorable to ironic drunkenness. Spring rarely made me better understand the happiness of the sun. I dug my garden, not without ardor, gaily calculating the opposite chances (they appeared numerous . . . but only became precise in May.[17] I remember having sown seeds on the 20th—I provoked fate but without believing in it). Extreme anguish and melancholy, the profound disabused serenity gave life many diverse meanings (hardly reconcilable). The conditions lent themselves poorly to expression; my thought, however, freed itself from its chains, reached maturity. I allowed myself to become intoxicated by a feeling of conquest and the shattered world extended itself before me like an open realm. Today these few pages seem indecisive to me—impure, lyrical flight encumbers them—but under the influence of the first vision, I believed that they revealed profound truth.

For almost two years, I had been able to advance in inner experience. In this sense, at the very least, the states described by the mystics had ceased to be closed to me. This experience was independent, it's true, from the presuppositions to which the mystics imagined themselves to be bound. One day its

results converged with those that I drew from long reflections on eroticism and
laughter—as with those which followed a bookish study and the uneasy experi-
ence of the sacred. I broached the problems of method only later and for all that
I remained at first in vagaries—from the point of view at least of the science
of knowledge, of philosophy. When, after more than a year, I got there—I speak
of it in another book—I reached excessive, nauseating clearness—then, I had
nothing to do, could not conceive of a project, I was abandoned to the nausea
that I have described under the name of "torture."]

"Communication"

. . . [18]From one simple particle to another, there is no difference in
nature, nor is there a difference between this one and that one. There is
some of this that is produced here and there, each time in the form of unity,
but this unity does not persevere in itself. Waves, swells, simple particles
are perhaps only multiple movements of a homogeneous element; they only
possess fleeting unity and do not shatter the homogeneity of the whole.

Groups composed of numerous simple particles alone possess this
heterogeneous character that differentiates me from you and isolates our
differences in the rest of the universe. What one calls a "being" is never
simple, and if it has a single enduring unity, it only possesses it imperfectly:
it is undermined by its profound inner division, it remains poorly closed
and, at certain points, open to attack from the outside.[19]

It is true that this isolated "being," foreign to what is not it, is the
form in which existence and truth first appeared to you. You must relate
the meaning of each object to this irreducible difference—which you are.
Yet the unity that you are flees itself and escapes: this unity would only
be a dreamless sleep if chance disposed of it in accordance with your most
anxious will.

What you are comes from the activity that links the countless elements
that compose you to the intense communication of these elements among
themselves. These are contagions of energy, movement, heat, or transferences
of elements, which constitute internally the life of your organic being. Life
is never situated in one particular point: it passes rapidly from one point to
another (or from multiple points to other points), like a current or a kind
of electrical stream. Thus, where you would like to grasp your nontemporal

substance, you only encounter a slippage, only the poorly coordinated play of your perishable elements.

Further on, your life is not limited to this ungraspable inner streaming; it also streams outside and opens itself incessantly to what flows or surges toward it. The enduring vortex that composes you throws itself toward similar vortices with which it forms a vast figure, animated by a measured agitation. Now to live signifies for you not only the flux and the fleeting play of light that unifies itself in you, but the passages of warmth and light from one being to another, from you to your fellow being or from your fellow to you (even in the moment when you read me, the contagion of my fever reaches you): words, books, monuments, symbols, laughter are only so many paths of this contagion, of these passages. Individual beings matter little and enclose unavowable points of view, if one considers what is animated, passing from one to the other in love, in tragic scenes, in movements of fervor. Thus we are nothing, neither you nor I, beside the burning words that could pass from me to you, printed on a page: for I would only have lived to write them, and, if it is true that they are addressed to you, you will live from having had the strength to hear them. (In the same way, what do the two lovers, Tristan and Isolde, signify, considered without their love, in a solitude that leaves them some vulgar occupation? The two pale beings, deprived of the marvelous: nothing counts but the love that tears them apart together.)

I am and you are, in the vast flux of things, only a stopping point favorable to a resurgence. Do not delay in becoming precisely aware of this agonizing position: if it happens that you can attach yourself to goals enclosed within those limits in which no one is at stake but you, your life would be that of the great majority, it would be "deprived of the marvelous." A brief moment of pause: the complex, the gentle, the violent movement of worlds will make of your death a splashing foam. The glories, the marvels of your life come from this resurgence of the wave that was tied in you in the immense noise of the cataract of the sky.

The fragile walls of your isolation, where multiple stops were composed, the obstacles of awareness, will have served only to reflect for a moment the flash of this universe at the heart of which you will never cease to be lost.

If there were only these moving universes, which would never encounter any eddies capturing the too rapid currents of an indistinct consciousness, when it binds we don't know what brilliant, infinitely vague interior, to the most blind movements of nature, without obstacles, these movements would be less vertiginous. The stabilized order of isolated appearances is necessary for the anguished consciousness of the torrential floods that carry it away. But if it takes itself for what it appears to be, if it encloses itself in a fearful attachment, it is no longer the occasion of a laughable error; one more withered existence marks a dead point, an absurd little drop, forgotten for a short time, in the middle of the celestial bacchanalia.

From one end to the other of this human life that is our lot, consciousness of the lack of stability, even of the profound lack of all real stability, liberates the enchantment of laughter. As if suddenly this life passed from a sad and empty solidity to the happy contagion of warmth and light, to the free tumult that water and air communicate to one another: the flashes and reboundings of laughter follow the first opening, to the permeability of a breaking smile. If a group of people laughs at a sentence betraying an absurdity or an absent-minded gesture, a current of intense communication passes through them. Every isolated existence emerges from itself by means of an image betraying the error of fixed isolation. It emerges from itself in a kind of easy flash; at the same time it opens itself to the contagion of a wave that rebounds, for those who laugh together become like waves in the sea, as long as the laughter lasts there is no longer a partition between them, they are no more separated than two waves, but their unity is also undefined, as precarious as that of the agitation of the waters.

Shared laughter assumes the absence of a true anguish, and yet it has no other source than anguish. What engenders it justifies your fear. You cannot imagine that dropped, you don't know from where, into this unknown immensity, abandoned to enigmatic solitude, condemned in the end to sink in suffering, you should not be seized with anguish. But from the isolation in which you grow old to the heart of the universe dedicated to your loss, you are free to derive this vertiginous consciousness of what takes place, consciousness, vertigo, that you only reach bound by this anguish. You could not become the mirror of a lacerating reality if you did not have to be *shattered* . . .[20]

To the extent that you oppose an obstacle to the overflowing forces, you are destined for pain, reduced to disquiet. But you are still free to perceive the meaning of this anguish in you: from the way in which this obstacle that you are must negate itself and wish itself destroyed, from the fact that it is part of the forces that shatter it. This is only possible on this condition: that your laceration not prevent your reflection from taking place, which demands that a *slippage* be produced (that the laceration should only be reflected, and leave the mirror intact for a time). Shared laughter, assuming anguish aside, when it draws reflux from it at the same time, is undoubtedly the cavalier form of this trickery: it is not the one who laughs whom laughter strikes, but one of his *fellows*—though this is still without an excess of cruelty.

The forces that work to destroy us find in us such happy—and sometimes violent—complicities that we cannot simply turn ourselves away from them as interest would lead us to do. We are driven to do the "work of fire."[21] Rarely are men in a state to kill themselves, and not in despair but like a Hindu, throwing themselves royally under a festival cart. But without going to the point of delivering ourselves, we can deliver, from ourselves, a part: we sacrifice goods that belong to us or that are bound to us by so many bonds, from which we distinguish ourselves so poorly: our fellow being. Assuredly, this word, *sacrifice*, signifies this: that men, from the fact of their will, place certain goods in a dangerous region, where destructive forces reign. Thus we *sacrifice* the one we laugh at, abandoning him without any anguish whatsoever, to some degradation that seems slight to us (laughter undoubtedly lacks the gravity of sacrifice).[22]

We can only discover *in others* how to dispose of the light exuberance of things. Hardly have we grasped the vanity of our opposition than we are carried away by the movement; it suffices that we cease to oppose ourselves, we communicate with the unlimited world of those who laugh. But we communicate without anguish, full of joy, imagining not giving ourselves over to the movement that will, however, have us at its disposal, some day, with a definitive rigor.

Without any doubt, someone who laughs is himself laughable and, in a profound sense, more so than his victim, but it matters little that a slight error—a slip—spills joy from the kingdom of laughter. What throws men out of their empty isolation and mingles them with unlimited movements— by which they communicate among themselves, rushing with a great noise one toward the other like waves—could only be death if the horror of this *self* that has folded back on itself was pushed to logical consequences. The consciousness of an external reality—tumultuous and lacerating—which is born in the recesses of self-consciousness—demands that man perceive the vanity of these recesses—to "know" them in a presentiment, already destroyed—*but it also demands that they endure.* The foam that is at the crest of the wave demands this incessant slippage: consciousness of death (and the liberation that it brings to the immensity of beings) would not be formed if one did not approach death, but it ceases to be as soon as death has done its work. And this is why the agony, as if immutable, of all that is, which is human existence in the heart of the skies—assumes the multitude of spectators for those who survive a little (the surviving multitude amplifies the agony, reflects it in the infinite facets of multiple consciousnesses, where the immutable slowness coexists with the rapidity of a bacchanalia, in which lightning and the fall of the dead are contemplated): sacrifice requires not only victims but those who sacrifice; laughter demands not only the laughable persons that we are, but it demands the inconsequential crowd of those who laugh . . .[23]

[*I wrote (from April to May) even more of this, but without adding anything that matters to me. I exhausted myself in vain to* develop.

When I expressed the principle of slipping—*like a law presiding at* communication—*I believed I had reached bottom (I was astonished, having given this text to be read, that no one saw, as I do, the signed trace of the criminal, the* belated, *and yet decisive explanation of the crime . . . It must be said, none of it was).*

Today I don't think I misled myself. I finally offered an account of the comedy—*which is the* tragedy—*and, reciprocally. I affirmed at the same time: existence is* communication—*that every representation of life, of being, and generally of "something" must be reconsidered in this light.*
The crimes—and consequently the enigmas—which I recounted were clearly defined. They were laughter and sacrifice (in what followed, which I didn't think was worth saving, I took up sacrifice, the comedy that demands that one individual die in place of all the others and I prepared myself to show that the path of communication *(the profound bond between peoples) is in anguish (anguish, sacrifice unite men of all times).*

The recourse to scientific facts (fashion perhaps—the present, perishable—in matters of knowledge) appears to me of secondary importance, given the foundation, the ecstatic experience from which I set out.[24]]

Part Four

Post-Scriptum to the Torture (or the New Mystical Theology)

Life will dissolve itself in death, rivers into the sea, the known into the unknown. Knowledge is access to the unknown. Nonsense is the outcome of every possible sense.

It is an exhausting folly that, there where, visibly, all means are lacking, one nevertheless claims to know, in place of knowing one's ignorance, of recognizing the unknown, but what is more sad is the infirmity of those who, if they no longer have the means, admit that they don't know, but stupidly confine themselves in what they know. In any case, that a man should not live with the incessant thought of the unknown makes one doubt his intelligence all the more, as that same man is eager, but blindly, to find in things the part that compels him to love, or shakes him with an inextinguishable laughter, that of the unknown. But it is the same with light: eyes have only reflections of it.

Soon the night seemed to him gloomier and more terrible than any night, as if it had in fact issued from a wound of thought that had ceased to think, of thought taken ironically as object by something other than thought. It was night itself. Images that constituted its darkness inundated him. He saw nothing, and, far from being distressed, he made this absence of vision the culmination of his sight. Useless for seeing, his eye took on extraordinary proportions, developed beyond measure and, stretched out on the horizon, let the night penetrate its center in order to receive the day from it. And so, through this void, it was sight and the object of sight that mingled together. Not only did this eye that saw nothing apprehend something, it apprehended the cause of its vision. It saw as object that which prevented it from seeing. Its own glance entered into it as an image, just when this glance seemed the death of all image.

—Maurice Blanchot, *Thomas the Obscure*[1]

Philosophy never appeared more fragile, more precious, more passionate than at that moment when a yawn caused the existence of God to vanish in Bergson's mouth.

—Ibidem[2]

Outside of the notes in this volume, I only know of *Thomas the Obscure*, where the questions of the new theology (which has only the unknown as an object) are pressing, though there they remain hidden. In a way that is entirely independent from his book, orally, yet in a way that he in no respect lacked the feeling of discretion that demands that close, to him, I thirst for silence, I have heard the author pose the foundation of all "spiritual" life, which can only:

> —have its principle and its end in the absence of salvation, in the renunciation of all hope,
> —affirm of inner experience that it is the authority (but all authority expiates itself),
> —be contestation of itself and nonknowledge.

1

God

God savors himself, says Eckhart. It's possible, but what he savors is, it seems to me, his hatred for himself, to which none, here on earth, can be compared (I could say: this hatred is time, but that bothers me. Why should I say time? I feel this hatred when I cry; I analyze nothing). If God lacked this hatred for a single instant, the world would become logical, intelligible, idiots would explain it (if God did not hate himself, he would be what depressed idiots believe: dejected, imbecilic, logical). What, at bottom, deprives man of every possibility of speaking of God, is that, in human thought, God necessarily conforms to man, insofar as man is tired, famished for sleep, and peace. In the act of saying ". . . all things . . . recognize him as their cause, their principle, and their end . . ." there is this: no longer being able TO BE, a man demands grace, he falls exhausted into degradation, as, not being able to go on, he goes to bed.

God finds rest in nothing and is satisfied with nothing. Every existence is threatened, is already in the nothingness of His insatiability. And God can no more appease himself than He can *Know* (knowledge is rest). He does not know how thirsty He is. And as He *knows nothing*, He knows nothing of Himself. If He revealed Himself to Himself, it would be necessary for Him to recognize Himself as God, but He cannot agree to this even for a moment. He only has knowledge of His nothingness, this is why He is atheist, profoundly: He would cease to be God suddenly (there would no longer be anything in place of His dreadful absence than an imbecilic, stupefied presence, if He saw himself as such).

> *Ghost in tears*
> *o dead God*
> *hollow eye*
> *damp moustache*
> *single tooth*
> *o dead God*
> *o dead God*
> *Me*
> *I hounded you*
> *with hatred*
> *unfathomable*
> *and I would die of hatred*
> *as a cloud*
> *is undone.*

To the soaring of thoughts unchained—eager for distant possibilities—it was vain to oppose a desire for rest. Nothing stops, if not for a time. Peter wanted, on Mount Tabor, to set up tents, in order to jealously protect the divine light. However, thirsting for radiant peace, his steps already led him to Golgotha (to the dark wind, to the exhaustion of *lama sabachthani*).[3]

In the abyss of possibilities, being thrown always further, hurled toward a point where the possible is the impossible itself, ecstatic, breathless, *experience* thus opens a little more each time the horizon of God (the wound), extends a little more the limits of the heart, the limits of being, it destroys the depths of the heart, the depths of being by unveiling them.

Saint Angela of Foligno said: "Once my soul was elevated, and I saw the light, the beauty, and the fullness that is in God in a way that I had never seen before in so great a manner. I did not see love there. I then lost the love that was mine and was made non-love. Afterward, I saw him in darkness, and in a darkness precisely because the good that he is, is far too great to be conceived or understood. Indeed, anything conceivable or understandable does not attain this good or even come near it."[4] A little further on: "When God is seen in darkness it does not bring a smile to the lips, or devotion, fervor, or ardent love; neither does the body or the soul tremble or move as at other times; the soul sees nothing and everything (*nihil videt et omnia videt*); the body sleeps and speech is cut off. And all the signs of friendship, so numerous and indescribable, all the words that God spoke to me, all those that you ever wrote—I now understand that these were so much less than that which I see with such great darkness, that in no way do I place my hope in them, nor is there any of my hope in them."[5]

It is difficult to say to what extent belief is an obstacle to experience, to what extent the intensity of experience overturns this obstacle. The dying saint had a strange cry: "O unknown nothingness!"[6] (*o nihil incognitum!*), which she repeated several times. I don't know if I am wrong to see in it an escape from fever beyond divine limits. The narrative of her death associates it with the knowledge that we have of our own nothingness . . . But the sick woman, completing her thought, gave the only profound explanation for this cry: "Truly a soul cannot have a better awareness in this world than to perceive its own nothingness and to stay in its own cell. There is greater deception in spiritual advantages than in temporal ones—that is, to know how to speak about God, to do great penances, to understand the Scriptures, and to have one's heart almost constantly preoccupied with spiritual matters."[7] She expressed herself in this way, then repeated her cry twice: "O unknown nothingness!" I am inclined to believe that the vanity of what is not the "unknown" opening itself up before ecstasy appeared to this dying woman, who could only translate what she experienced through cries. The notes taken at her bedside attenuate, perhaps, the words (I doubt it).

At times, the burning experience makes little of the limits received from outside. Speaking of a state of intense joy, Angela de Foligno says she is angelic and that she loves even devils.[8]

At first the saint had the life of a woman surrounded by frivolous luxury. She was married, had several sons, and was not unaware of burning desires of the flesh. In 1285, at the age of thirty-seven, she changed her life, devoting herself little by little to miserable poverty. "While looking at the cross," she said of her conversion, "I was given an even greater perception of the way the Son of God had died for our sins with the greatest suffering. I felt that I myself had crucified Christ . . . Nonetheless, this perception of the meaning of the cross set me so afire that, standing near the cross, I stripped myself of all my clothing and offered my whole self to him.

Although very fearful, I promised him then to maintain perpetual chastity."⁹ She goes on, in the same narrative: "It came to pass, God so willing, that at that time my mother, who had been a great obstacle to me, died. In like manner my husband died, as did all my sons in a short space of time. Because I had already entered the aforesaid way, and had prayed to God for their death, I felt a great consolation when it happened."¹⁰ And further on: "My heart was so on fire with the love of God that I never got tired of genuflections or other penitential practices. Afterward, this fire of the love of God in my heart became so intense that if I heard anyone speak about God I would scream. Even if someone stood over me with an axe ready to kill me, this would not have stopped my screaming."¹¹

2

Descartes

In a letter from May 1637, Descartes writes on the subject of the fourth part of the *Discourse*—where he affirms the certainty of God based on the *Cogito*: "If you spend a sufficient time on this meditation, you acquire by degrees a very clear, dare I say intuitive, notion of intellectual nature in general. This is the idea that, if considered without limitation, represents God, and if limited, is the idea of an angel or a human soul."¹² Now this movement of thought is simpler and much more necessary to man than that from which Descartes has drawn, in the *Discourse*, divine certitude (which is reduced to Saint Anselme's argument: perfect being cannot fail to have existence as an attribute).¹³ And this vital movement is essentially what dies in me.

Descartes's intuition founds discursive knowledge. And undoubtedly established discursive knowledge, the "universal science," which was Descartes's *project*, and which occupies such a place today, can ignore the intuition that was discovered at the outset (it passes over it, wanting, if it can, to avoid being more than it is). But what does this knowledge, about which we are so vain, mean when its foundation has been detached? Descartes had offered as a goal for philosophy: "a knowledge clear and assured of what is useful for life."¹⁴ But in his work this goal could not be separated from the foundation. The question thereby introduced touches upon the *value* of reasoned knowledge. If it is foreign to the initial intuition, it is the sign and the evidence of the man who acts. But from the point of view of the intelligibility of being? It no longer has any meaning.

It is easy for each of us to perceive that this science, of which Descartes is so proud, even complete with the answers to all the questions that it can regularly formulate, would leave us in the end in nonknowledge; that the existence of the world cannot, in any way, cease to be unintelligible. No explanation of the sciences (nor more generally of discursive knowledge) would be able to answer for it. No doubt the aptitudes that were given to us to understand this or that from all sides, to bring numerous solutions to varied problems, leave us the impression of having developed in ourselves the faculty of understanding. But this spirit of contestation, which was the tormenting genius of Descartes, if we animate it ourselves in our turn, no longer stops at secondary objects: it is henceforth less a question of the well or poorly founded nature of accepted propositions than of deciding if the best understood propositions, once established, could satisfy the infinite need for knowledge implied in Descartes's initial intuition. In other words, the spirit of contestation now comes to formulate the final affirmation: "*I know only one thing: that a man will never know anything.*"[15]

If I have a "very clear knowledge" of God (of this "intellectual nature considered without limitation"[16]), knowledge would immediately seem to me to know, but only at that price. This clear knowledge of the existence of an infinite knowledge, even if I had only a part of it at my disposal, would certainly give me the assurance that I lack. However I perceive that this assurance was, in Descartes, knowledge necessary for *project* (the former title of the *Discourse* was *Plan for a Universal Science* . . . formula in which the system and the actions of the author are summed up).[17] Without activity linked to *project*, Descartes would not have been able to maintain a deep assurance, which is lost as soon as one is no longer in the spell of the *project*. To the extent that the *project* is realized, I clearly distinguish objects diverse from one another, but once acquired, the results are not longer interesting. And no longer being distracted by anything, I cannot rely on God for the concern of infinite knowing.

Descartes imagined man having a knowledge of God prior to his knowledge of himself (of the infinite before the finite). Yet, he was himself so occupied that he could not represent divine existence to himself—for him the most immediately knowable—in his state of complete idleness. In the state of idleness, this kind of discursive intelligence that is linked in us to activity (as Claude Bernard said, with a rare aptness, to the "pleasure of not knowing"—which obliges one to seek[18]) is no longer anything but the useless trowel once the palace has been completed. As poorly placed as

I am for this, I would like to emphasize that in God, *true knowledge can only have God himself as an object.* This object, whatever access to it that Descartes imagined, remains unintelligible to us.

But it does not follow from the fact that divine nature knows itself in its profound intimacy but escapes man's understanding that it escapes that of God as well.

What seems clear, at the point I have reached, is that here men introduce a confusion by means of which thought slips soundlessly from the discursive level to the nondiscursive level. God undoubtedly can know himself but without following the mode of discursive thought that is ours. "Intellectual nature without limitation" here finds its final limitation. Beginning with man, I can represent to myself—anthropologically—the limitless extension of my power of understanding, but I cannot pass from there to the knowledge that God must have of himself (must, for the good reason that he is perfect). It thus appears that God, before knowing himself is no longer "intellectual nature," in the sense in which we understand it. Even "without limitation," the understanding cannot surpass at least the (discursive) mode without which it would not be what it is.

One can speak of the knowledge that God has of himself only by negations—suffocating negations—images of tongues cut out. In this way one abuses oneself, one passes from one level to another: suffocation, silence arise from experience and not from discourse.

I do not know if God exists or does not exist, but assuming that he does, I attribute exhaustive knowledge of himself to him and assuming that I link to this knowledge the feelings of satisfaction and approbation that are added in us to the faculty of apprehending, a new feeling of essential dissatisfaction takes hold of me.

If it is necessary for us at some moment in our misery to postulate God, it is to succumb by a rather vain flight that submits the unknowable to the necessity of being known. It is to give precedence to the idea of perfection (to which misery is attached) over every representable difficulty and, what's more, over all that is, such that, inevitably, every profound thing slips from an impossible state, in which experience perceives it, to abilities drawing their depth from what they must in the end suppress.

In us, God is initially the movement of a spirit that consists—after having passed from finite knowledge to infinite knowledge—in passing as if through an extension of limits to a different, not discursive, mode of knowledge in such a way that the illusion is born from a satisfaction realized beyond us of the thirst to know existing within us.

3

Hegel

To know means: to relate to the known, to grasp that an unknown thing is the same as another known thing. This assumes either a solid ground upon which everything rests (Descartes) or the circularity of knowledge (Hegel). In the first case, if the ground slips away . . . In the second, even if assured of having a well-closed circle, one perceives the unsatisfying character of knowledge. The endless chain of known things is for knowledge only the completion of itself. Satisfaction rests on the fact that a project of knowledge, which existed, has come to its end, is accomplished, that nothing remains to be discovered (at least nothing important). But this circular thought is dialectical. It entails the final contradiction (affecting the whole circle): *circular, absolute knowledge is definitive nonknowledge.* Assuming that I were to effectively attain it, I know that I would know nothing more than I know now.

If I "mimic" absolute knowledge, I am at once by necessity God myself (in the system, there can be no knowledge, even in God, which goes beyond absolute knowledge). The thought of this self—of *ipse*—could only make itself absolute by becoming everything. *The Phenomenology of Spirit* comprises two essential movements completing a circle: it is the completion by degrees of self-consciousness (of human *ipse*) and the becoming everything (becoming God) of this *ipse* completing knowledge (and thereby destroying particularity within it, completing therefore the negation of itself, becoming absolute knowledge). But in this way, as by contagion and mimicry, I accomplish within myself Hegel's circular movement, I define, beyond the limits attained, no longer an unknown but an unknowable: unknowable not on account of the insufficiency of reason but by its nature (and even, for Hegel, one could only be concerned for this beyond by fault of possessing absolute knowledge . . .). Assuming then that I were God, that I were to be in the world with Hegel's assurance (suppressing shadows and doubt), knowing everything, even why completed knowledge required that man, the innumerable particularities of *selves* and history produce themselves, precisely at this moment the question is formulated that causes human existence, divine existence to enter . . . the furthest into the obscurity without return; why must there be *what I know?* Why is it a necessity? In this question is hidden—it does not initially appear—an extreme laceration, so profound that only the silence of ecstasy responds to it.

This question is distinct from Heidegger's question (why is there being and not nothing?) in that it is only posed after every conceivable response, aberrant or not, to the successive questions formulated by understanding: thus it strikes at the heart of knowledge.

Lack of pride evident in the stubbornness of wanting to know discursively to the very end. It seems however that Hegel lacked pride (was a servant) only apparently.* Undoubtedly he had a tone of one who irritatingly makes empty promises, but in a portrait of him as an old man, I imagine seeing exhaustion, horror of being at the depth of things—of being God. Hegel, at the moment the system closed, believed himself going mad for two years: perhaps he was afraid of having accepted evil—that the system justifies it and renders it necessary; or perhaps linking the certainty of having attained absolute knowledge to the completion of history—to the passage of existence to the state of empty monotony—he saw himself, in a profound way, becoming dead; perhaps even these diverse moments of sadness were composed in him in the more profound horror of being God. It seems to me however that Hegel, shrinking back from the path

---

*No one more than he understood in depth the possibilities of intelligence (no doctrine is comparable to his; it is the summit of positive intelligence). Kierkegaard made a superficial critique of it in that: (1) he had imperfect knowledge of it; (2) he only opposed the system to the world of positive revelation, not to that of human nonknowledge. Nietzsche knew hardly more of Hegel than a standard popularization. *The Genealogy of Morals* is the singular proof of the ignorance in which the dialectic of the master and the slave—of which the lucidity was dazzlingly—remained and remains (it is the decisive moment in the history of self-consciousness and, it must be said, to the extent that we have to distinguish each thing that touches us from other things—no one knows anything of *himself* if he has not grasped this movement that determines and limits the successive possibilities of man). The passage on the master and the slave from the *Phenomenology of Spirit* (Chapter IV, Part A) has been translated and commented upon by Alexandre Kojève in the issue of *Mesures* from 15 January 1939 under the title *Autonomy and Dependence of Self-Consciousness: Mastery and Slavery.* (Reproduced in Kojève, *Introduction to the Reading of Hegel* [1947] trans. James Nichols (Ithaca: Cornell University Press, 1969) pp. 3–30.)

of ecstasy (from the only direct resolution of anguish), *had* to take refuge in an occasionally effective (when he wrote or spoke) but essentially vain attempt at equilibrium and harmony with the existing, active, official world.

My existence, like any other, of course, moves from unknown to known (relating the unknown to the known). No difficulty; I believe I am able, as much as anyone I know, to surrender to the operations of knowledge. This is necessary for me—as much as it is for others. My existence is composed of steps forward, of movements that it directs to points that are suitable. Knowledge is in me, I understand this for each affirmation in this book, linked to these steps, to these movements (these last are themselves linked to my fears, my desires, my joys). Knowledge is in no way distinct from my self: *I am it*; it is the existence that I am. But this existence is not reducible to it: this reduction would demand that the known be the goal of existence and not existence the goal of the known.

There is a blind spot in understanding: which recalls the structure of the eye. In understanding, as in the eye, one can only reveal it with difficulty. But whereas the blind spot in the eye is without consequence, the nature of understanding demands that the blind spot within it have more meaning than understanding itself. To the extent that understanding is auxiliary to action, the spot within it is also as negligible as it is in the eye. But to the extent that one envisions in understanding man himself—I mean an exploration of the possibility of being—the spot absorbs attention: the spot is no longer lost in knowledge but knowledge is lost in it. Existence in this way closes the circle, but it couldn't do this without including the night from which it only escapes in order to return there again. As it moved from the unknown to the known, it is necessary to invert itself at the summit and return to the unknown.

Action introduces the known (the manufactured); then understanding, which is linked to it, relates, one after another, the nonmanufactured elements, the unknown, to the known. But desire, poetry, laughter unceasingly cause life to slip in the opposite way, going from the known to the unknown. Existence, in the end, discovers the blind spot of understanding and right away absorbs it completely. It could go otherwise only if the possibility of rest offered itself at some point. But nothing like that happens: what alone remains is the circular agitation—which does not exhaust itself in ecstasy and begins again from it.

Final possibility: that nonknowledge still be knowledge. I would explore the night! But no, the night explores me . . . Death quenches the thirst for nonknowledge. But absence is not rest. Absence and death are in me without reply and absorb me cruelly, without fail.

Even within the (incessant) completed circle, nonknowledge is end and knowledge means. To the extent that it takes itself for an end, it sinks into the blind spot. But poetry, laughter, ecstasy are not means for other things. In the "system," poetry, laughter, ecstasy are nothing, Hegel hastily rids himself of them: he knows no other end than knowledge. His immense fatigue is linked in my eyes to horror of the blind spot.

The completion of the circle was for Hegel the completion of man. Completed man was, for him, necessarily "work": he could be that man, himself, Hegel, being "knowledge." Knowledge "works," which poetry, laughter, and ecstasy do not. But poetry, laughter, ecstasy are not completed man, do not give "satisfaction." Short of dying of them, one leaves them like a thief (or as one leaves a woman after making love), dazed, stupidly thrown back into the absence of death: in distinct knowledge, activity, work.

4

Ectasy

NARRATIVE OF A PARTIALLY FAILED EXPERIENCE

At the moment of nightfall, when silence invades an increasingly pure sky, I found myself alone, sitting on a narrow white veranda, not seeing anything of where I was but the roof of a house, the foliage of a tree and the sky. Before getting up to go to bed, I felt the extent to which the sweetness of things had penetrated me. I had just had the desire for a violent movement of the spirit and, in this sense, I perceived that the felicitous state into which I had fallen did not differ entirely from "mystical" states. At the very least, as I had passed quickly from inattention to surprise, I felt this state with more intensity than one normally does and as if an other and not me had experienced it. I could not deny that, with the exception of attention, which was lacking only at first, this banal felicity was an authentic inner experience, obviously distinct from project, from discourse. Without giving these words more than an evocative value, I thought that the "sweetness of the sky" communicated itself to me and I could feel precisely the state within that responded to it. I felt it to be present inside my head like a vaporous streaming, subtly graspable, but participating in the sweetness of the outside, putting me in possession of it, making me take pleasure in it.

I remembered having vividly known a felicity of the same kind in a car while it was raining and while the hedges and trees, barely covered with a tenuous foliage, emerged from the spring mist and came slowly toward me. I entered into possession of each damp tree and I only left it sadly for another. At that moment, I thought that this dreamy pleasure would not cease to be mine, that I would live henceforth endowed with the power to enjoy things melancholically and to breathe in their delights. Today I must admit that these states of communication were only rarely accessible to me.

I was far from knowing what I see clearly today, that anguish is linked to them. I could not understand at the moment that a trip that I had much anticipated had only brought me uneasiness, that everything had been hostile to me, beings and things, but above all men, whose lives in remote villages, empty to the point of diminishing the one who perceived them, I was obligated to see at the same time as a self-assured and malevolent reality. It is from having escaped for a moment, by means of a precarious solitude, from so much poverty, that I perceived the tenderness of the damp trees, the lacerating strangeness of their passing: I recall that, in the back of the car, I had abandoned myself, I was absent, happily gay, I was gentle, I gently absorbed things.

I recall having made a comparison of my enjoyment with that described in the first volumes of *In Search of Lost Time*. But I then had only an incomplete, superficial idea of Marcel Proust (*Time Regained* had not yet appeared[19]) and young, I dreamed only of naive possibilities of triumph.

At the moment of leaving the veranda to go to my room, I began to contest within myself the unique value that I then attributed to ecstasy before the empty unknown. Was I to have contempt for the state into which I had just entered without thinking of it? But why? What gave me the right to classify, to place this ecstasy above slightly different possibilities, less strange but more human and, it seemed to me, as profound?

But whereas ecstasy before the void is always fleeting, furtive, and only has little concern to "persevere in being," the felicity in which I was demanded only to last. I should have, by this fact, been warned: on the contrary I took pleasure in it and, in the tranquility of my room, I exerted myself running through the possible depth of it. The streaming of which

I have spoken immediately became more intense: I melted into a more solemn felicity in which I captured a diffuse sweetness by enveloping it. It suffices to arouse in oneself an intense state to be liberated from the agitating importunity of discourse: attention passes then from "projects" to the being which one is, which, little by little, is put in movement, emerges from the shadows; it passes from effects on the outside, possible or real (from project or reflected or realized action) to this inner presence that we cannot apprehend without a leap of our entire being, detesting the servility of discourse.

This plenitude of inner movement emerging from the attention normally paid to the objects of discourse is necessary to arrest the latter. This is why the mastery of this movement, what the Hindus strive to obtain in *yoga*, increases the little chance that we have of escaping from prison. But this plenitude is itself only a chance. It is true that in it, I lose myself, gain access to the "unknown" of being, but *my* attention being necessary to the plenitude, this self attentive to the presence of this "unknown" only loses itself in part, it also distinguishes itself from it: its lasting presence still demands a contestation of the known appearances of the subject that I remain and of the object that it still is. For *I* last: everything escapes if I have not been able to annihilate myself; what I have glimpsed is brought back to the level of objects known to me.

If I only gain access to the simple intensity of the inner movement, it goes without saying that discourse is only rejected for a time, that it remains at bottom the master. I can drop off into a quickly accessible felicity. At the most: I am not abandoned in the same way to the arbitrary power of action, the rhythm of projects that is discourse slows down; the value of action remains contested in me to the benefit of a different possible whose direction I see. But the mind attentive to inner movement only gains access to the unknowable depth of things: by turning to an entire forgetting of self; not being satisfied by anything, always going further toward the impossible. I knew this, however, I lingered that day over the movement that a chance felicity had given birth in me: it was prolonged pleasure, an agreeable possession of a slightly insipid sweetness. I by no means forgot myself in this way, I attempted to capture the fixed object, to envelop its sweetness in my own sweetness. At the end of a very short period of time, I refused the reduction of experience to the poverty that I am. Even the interest of my "poverty" demanded of me that I emerge from it. Revolt often has humble beginnings, but once begun it doesn't stop: at first I wanted to return from a contemplation that brought the object back to me (as usually happens when we enjoy a landscape) to the vision of this object in which I lose

myself at other times, which I call the unknown and which is only distinct
from nothingness by nothing that discourse can enunciate.

FIRST DIGRESSION ON ECSTASY BEFORE AN OBJECT: THE POINT

If I describe the "experience" that I had that day, it is because it had
a partially failed character: the bitterness, the humiliating bewilderments
that I found in it, the breathless efforts to which I was reduced "to get
out" illuminate better the region in which experience takes place than less
labored movements, reaching their goal without error.

However, I will put off until later this narrative (which, for other
reasons, exhausts me, as much as the failed experience exhausted me). I
would like, if it's possible, to leave nothing in the shadows.

If dozing beatitude is linked, as one might expect, to the faculty the
mind offers itself in order to provoke inner movements, it is time for us to
emerge from it, even if we must make ourselves prey to disorder. Experience
would only be a lure if it were not revolt, in the first place, against the
mind's attachment to action (to project, to discourse—against the verbal
servitude of the reasonable being, of the servant), in the second place against
the assurances, the obedience that experience itself introduces.

The "I" incarnates in me currish docility, not to the extent that it is
ipse, absurd, unknowable, but an equivocation between the particularity of
this *ipse* and the universality of reason. The "I" is in fact the expression of
the universal; it loses the wildness of the *ipse* to offer the universal a domesticated appearance; because of this equivocal and submissive position, we
represent the universal to ourselves in the image of the one who expresses
it, in opposition to wildness, as a domesticated being. The "I" is neither the
irrationality of the *ipse* nor that of the whole, and this shows the foolishness
that the absence of wildness (common intelligence) is.

In Christian experience, rebellious anger opposed to the "I" is still
equivocal. But the terms of the equivocation are not the same as in the
reasonable attitude. It is often the wild *ipse* (the proud master) who is
humiliated, but sometimes it is the servile "I." And in the humiliation of
the servile "I," the universal (God) is restored to pride: hence the difference
between a (negative) mystic theology and a positive one (but in the end the
mystic is subordinated, the Christian attitude is servile: in common piety,
God himself is a completed servant).

Ipse and the whole both slip away from the grasp of discursive intelligence (which enslaves); the middle terms alone can be assimilated. But in
its irrationality, the proud *ipse*, without being able to humiliate itself, can,

throwing the middle terms into the shadows, in a single and abrupt renunciation of itself (as *ipse*), attain the irrationality of the whole (in this case
knowledge is still mediation—between me and the world—but negative: it
is the rejection of knowledge, night, the annihilation of every middle term,
that constitutes this negative meditation). But the whole, in this case, is
only called the whole provisionally; the *ipse* losing itself in it goes toward
it as toward an opposite (a contrary), but in this it goes no less from
the unknown to the unknown, and, undoubtedly, there is still knowledge,
strictly speaking, insofar as the *ipse* can distinguish itself from the whole,
but in the *ipse*'s renunciation of itself, there is fusion: in fusion, neither *ipse*
nor the whole subsists; it is the annihilation of everything that is not the
final "unknown," the abyss in which one has sunk.

Thus understood, the full communication that is experience leading
to the "extremity" is accessible to the extent that existence successively strips
itself of its middle terms: of what follows from discourse, then, if the mind
enters into a non-discursive interiority, of all that returns to discourse from
the fact that one can have a distinct understanding—in other words, that
an equivocal "I" can make an object of "servile possession."

In these conditions this still appears: the dialogue from person to
person, from soul to God, is a voluntary and provisional mystification (of
oneself). Existence ordinarily communicates itself, it leaves its ipseity to meet
its fellows. There is communication, from one being to another (erotic) or
from one to several others (sacred, comical). But *ipse* encountering, in a final
step, in place of one of its kind, its opposite, tries nevertheless to recover
the terms of situations in which it was accustomed to communicating, to
losing itself. Its frailty demands that it be available for a fellow being and
that it not be able to make, from the first step, the leap into the impossible
(for *ipse* and the whole are opposites, while the "I" and God are similar).

For one who is a stranger to experience the above is obscure—but
it is not destined for him (I write for one who, entering into my book,
would fall into it as into a hole, never to come out). And from two things
one: either the "I" speaks in me (and most will read what I write as if "I,"
in common terms, have written it) or the *ipse* does. Having to communicate with others who resemble it, *ipse* has recourse to degrading sentences.
It would sink into the insignificance of the (equivocal) "I," if it did not
attempt to communicate. In this way, poetic existence in me addresses itself
to poetic existence in others, and it is a paradox, undoubtedly, if I expect
from my fellows, drunk with poetry, that which I wouldn't expect knowing

them to be lucid. Now I cannot myself be *ipse* without having hurled this cry at them. Only by this cry do I have the power to annihilate in myself the "I" as they will annihilate it in themselves if they hear me.

When the mind rejects the pleasant monotony of inner movements, it can itself be thrown back into disequilibrium. From then on it has meaning only in irrational audacity, can only seize upon fleeting, derisory visions, or even: provoke them.

A comical necessity obliges us to dramatize. Experience would remain inaccessible if we did not know how to dramatize—by forcing ourselves to do so. (What is strange is that bringing to thought, as to experience, a rigor that hadn't been possible previously, I express myself with an unequaled disorder. And the disorder alone is possible while rigor—this character: "one cannot escape, man must pass through this"—is at the price of an effort equal to my disorder, which one will grasp. And yet, I only find, in my rigorous construction, and adapting itself to it, a disorderly expression, not intended so, but so.)

From one hour to the next, I am sickened at the idea that I am writing, that I must pursue. I never have security, certainty. I hold continuity in horror. I persevere in disorder, faithful to passions that I truly know nothing about, that disorder me in every way.

In the felicity of inner movements, the subject alone is modified: this felicity, in this sense, has no object. The movements flow into an external existence: they lose themselves there, they "communicate," it seems, with the outside, without the outside taking a determined form and being perceived as such.

Will I reach the end for once? . . . I exhaust myself: at moments, everything slips away. An effort to which so many contrary efforts are opposed, as if I hated in it a desire to cry out—such that the cry . . . which nevertheless I would utter, was lost in dread. But nothing delirious, nothing forced. I have little chance of making myself understood. The disorder wherein I am is the measure of man, forever thirsting for moral ruin.

I return to ecstasy before the object.
The mind awakening to inner life is, however, in search of an object. It rejects the object proposed by action for an object of a different nature, but cannot occur without an object: its existence cannot close in on itself.

(The inner movements are in no way object nor are they subject in that they are the subject that loses itself, but the subject can in the end bring them back to himself and as such they are equivocal; in the end, the necessity of an object, which is to say: the necessity of getting out of oneself, becomes urgent.)

I will make this obscure remark: the object in experience is at first the projection of a dramatic loss of self. It is the image of the subject. The subject attempts at first to go toward its fellow being. But once it has entered into inner experience, it is in search of an object like itself, reduced to interiority. What's more, the subject whose experience is in itself and from the beginning dramatic (is loss of self) needs to objectify this dramatic character. The situation of the object that the mind seeks needs to be objectively dramatized. Starting from the felicity of movements, it is possible to fix a vertiginous point that is supposed to inwardly contain that which is torn from the world, the incessant slippage of everything toward nothingness: time, if you wish.

But this is only a question of a fellow being. The point, before me, reduced to the most deprived simplicity, is a person. At each moment of the experience, this point can radiate its arms, cry out, set itself on fire.

The objective projection of oneself—that takes in this way the form of a point—cannot, however, be so perfect that the character of the fellow being—that belongs to it—can be maintained without lying. The point is not the whole, nor is it *ipse* (when Christ is the point, man in him is already no longer *ipse*, he can still be distinguished, however, from the whole: it is an "I," but fleeing at the same time in two directions).

This remains of the point, even effaced, that it has given optical form to experience. From the moment it poses the point, *the mind is an eye* (it becomes it in experience as it had become it in action).

In the felicity of inner movements, existence is in equilibrium. The equilibrium is lost in the breathless search, long vain, for the object. The object is the arbitrary projection of oneself. But the self necessarily poses before itself this point, its profound fellow being, given the fact that it can only get out of itself in love. Once it has gotten out of itself it gains access to non-love.

It is nevertheless without artifice that existence, in disequilibrium and anguish, gains access to the "point" that sets it free. In advance, this point is before me like a possible and experience can't do without it. In the projection of the point, the inner movements have the role of the magnifying glass concentrating the light in a very small incendiary focus. It is only in such a concentration—beyond itself—that existence is at leisure to perceive, in the form of an inner flash of light, "what it is," the movement of painful communication that it is, that goes no less from within to without than from without to within. And undoubtedly, this concerns an arbitrary projection, but what appears in this way is the profound objectivity of existence, from the moment this is no longer a corpuscle enclosed in itself, but a wave of life losing itself.

The vaporous flow of inner movements is in this case the magnifying glass at the same time as the light. But in the flow, there was nothing yet crying out, whereas starting with the projected "point," existence collapses in a cry. If I had more than uncertain knowledge of this, I would be led to believe that the experience of Buddhists does not cross the threshold, knows nothing of the cry, limits itself to the effusion of movements.

One only attains the point by dramatizing. To dramatize is what the devout people who follow the *Exercises* of Saint Ignatius do (but not them alone).[20] If one were to imagine the place, the characters of the drama and the drama itself: the torture to which Christ is led. The disciple of Saint Ignatius offers himself a theatrical representation. He is in a peaceful room: he is asked to have the feelings he would have on Calvary. He is told that despite the peacefulness of his room, he *should* have these feelings. One desires that he should get out of himself, deliberately dramatizing this human life, of which one knows in advance that it is likely to be a half-anxious, half-dozing futility. But not yet having had a properly inner life, before having shattered discourse within him, he is asked to project the point about which I have spoken, similar to him—but even more similar to that which he wants to be—in the person of Jesus agonizing. The projection of the point, in Christianity, is attempted before the mind has its inner movements at its disposal, before it has become free of discourse. It is only the rough projection, which one attempts, starting from it, to attain non-discursive experience.

In any case, we can only project the object-point by drama. I had recourse to upsetting images. In particular, I would stare at the photographic image—or sometimes my memory of it—of a Chinese man who must have been tortured during my lifetime.* Of this torture, I had had in the past a

---

*Dumas, who in the *Traité de Psychologie* has reproduced two snapshots (of the five that were taken showing the torture from the beginning and that I had for a long time at home), attributes the torture to a relatively distant time. They date from the time of the Boxer rebellion.

series of successive representations. In the end, the patient, his chest flayed, twisted, arms and legs cut at the elbows and knees. Hair standing on his head, hideous, haggard, striped with blood, beautiful as a wasp.

I write "beautiful" . . . something escapes me, flees from me, fear robs me of myself and, as if I had wanted to stare at the sun, my eyes slip.

I had at the same time recourse to a simple mode of dramatization. I did not set out like a Christian from a single discourse, but also from a state of diffuse communication, from a felicity of inner movements. These movements that I grasped in their stream or river-like flowing, I could set out from them in order to condense them in a point where the accumulated intensity caused a simple escape of water to pass into a precipitation evocative of a waterfall, of a flash of light or lightning. This precipitation could occur precisely when I projected before me the river of existence flowing from me. The fact that existence, in this way, condensed itself into a flash, dramatized itself, stemmed from the disgust that the languor of the flow, which I could enjoy at my leisure, quickly inspired in me.

In languor, felicity, communication is diffuse: nothing is communicated from one term to another, but from oneself to an empty, indefinite expanse, where everything is drowned. In these conditions, existence naturally thirsts for more troubled communications. Whether it is a question of love holding hearts breathless or of impudent lasciviousness, whether it is a question of divine love, everywhere around us I found desire extended toward a fellow being: eroticism is around us so violent, it intoxicates hearts with such force—to finish it, its abyss is so deep in us—that there is no celestial space that does not take its form and fever from it. Who among us does not dream of forcing the gates of the mystical realm, who does not imagine himself to be "dying from not dying," consuming himself, ruining himself with love?[21] If it is possible for others, for Orientals whose imagination is not burning with the names Teresa, Heloise, Isolde, to abandon themselves to the infinite void with no other desire, we cannot conceive of the extreme collapse other than in love. At this price alone, it seems to me, I gain access to the extremity of the possible and if not, something is still missing from the trajectory along which I can only burn everything—to the point of the exhaustion of human strength.

The young and seductive Chinese man of whom I have spoken, left to the work of the executioner, I loved him with a love in which the sadistic instinct had no part: he communicated his pain to me or rather the excess of his pain, and it was precisely this that I was seeking, not to enjoy it, but to ruin in me that which is opposed to ruin.

Before excessive cruelty, be it from men, or from fate, it is natural to rebel, to cry out (the heart fails us): "That can no longer be!" and to weep, to blame some whipping post. It is more difficult to say to oneself: that in me that weeps and curses is my thirst to sleep in peace, my fury at being disturbed. The excesses are signs, suddenly given support, of what the world sovereignly is. It is to this type of signs that the author of the *Exercises* had recourse, wanting to "disturb" his disciples. This didn't prevent him and his own from cursing the world: I can only love him, right to the dregs and without hope.

Now I cite, from memory, an incident that appeared in the *Journal* some fifteen years ago (I cite it from memory, but I add nothing): in a small city or perhaps village in France, a poor worker returned home at the end of the week bringing his pay in bills. A little boy of some years saw the bills, played with them, and threw them in the fire. Noticing this too late, the father sees red, seizes an axe, and in the fit of rage cuts off the child's two hands. The mother was bathing her little girl in the next room. She enters, drawn by the cries, and falls dead. The little girl drowned in the bath. Become suddenly mad, the father fled, wandering in the countryside.*

Although it is hardly apparent, I meant nothing less in the following sentences, written three years ago:

"I fix a point before me and I represent this point to myself as the geometrical locus of all existence and of all unity, of all separation and all anguish, of all unsatisfied desire and every possible death.

"I adhere to this point, and a profound love of what is there burns me until I refuse to be alive for any reason other than for what is there,

---

*I must compare this passage, published in the 1st edition (1943), with the following incident, published in *Ce Soir* (September 30, 1947): "Prague, September 29. A shocking drama has just unfolded in the home of the butcher of Chomutov. The shopkeeper was counting his day's receipts . . . when he had to leave for a moment. His son, aged five years, in order to amuse himself, set fire to the banknotes. The butcher's wife, occupied with bathing her other son, aged one year, could not intervene, but his cries alerted the father who . . . seized his cleaver and cut the child's wrists. At the sight of this, the mother collapsed, killed by an embolism, and the baby that she was washing drowned in the bath. The butcher took flight." Apparently, a simple repetition of a perfect theme, without interest from my point of view. I must however mention the fact.

for this point that, being both the life and death of the loved one, has the burst of a cataract.

"And at the same time it is necessary to strip away all external representations from what is there, until it is nothing but a pure interiority, a purely interior fall into a void: this point endlessly absorbing this fall into what is nothingness within it, which is to say 'past' and in the same movement, endlessly prostituting its apparition, fleeting but fulgurating, to love."[22]

At the same time I wrote in favor of a strangely calmed anguish:

"If I imagine myself in a vision and in a halo that transfigures that vision, the ecstatic face of a dying individual, that which radiates from that face illuminates with its necessity the cloud of the sky, whose gray glow then becomes more penetrating than that of the sun itself. In this representation, death appears to be of the same nature as the illuminating light, to the extent that the light is lost from its source: it appears that no less a loss than death is required for the flash of life to traverse and transfigure dull existence, since it is only its free uprooting that *becomes in me* the power of life and time. Thus I cease to be more than a mirror of death, in the same way that the universe is the mirror of light."[23]

These passages from "Friendship" describe ecstasy before the "point."

"I had to stop writing. I was, as I often am, seated in front of an open window. Just as I sat down, I fell into a kind of ecstasy. This time, I no longer doubted, as I painfully had the previous day, that such a state was no more intense than erotic pleasure. I see nothing: *that* is neither visible nor invisible. *That* makes not dying sad and heavy. If in anguish I describe all that I have loved I would assume the furtive realities to which my love was linked were so many clouds behind which *what was there* was hidden. The images of ravishment betray. *What is there* is equal to the fear, the fear makes it come. There must be an equally violent crash so that *this can be there.*

". . . This time, suddenly, recalling *what is there*, I must have started sobbing. I raised my empty head, through the power of love, of being *ravished* . . ."[24]

SECOND DIGRESSION ON ECSTASY IN THE VOID[25]

Impatience, contestation, change the bursts of illumination, soft or fulgurating, into a more and more bitter night.

At the end of the first of these transcribed texts, I added:

"In vain, love wants to grasp what will cease to be.

"The impossibility of satisfaction in love is a *guide* toward the *accomplishing leap* at the same time that in advance, it is the entombment of every possible illusion."[26]

What I call contestation has not only the appearance of an intellectual approach (of which I speak about Hegel, Descartes—or in the principles of the introduction). Still, often this appearance is lacking (in Angela of Foligno, so it seems). The "contestation" is still a movement essential to love—which nothing can satisfy. What is presumptuous in the little sentence, often cited, from Saint Augustine, is not the first affirmation: "Our hearts find no peace," but the second: "until they rest in You."[27] For there is such disquiet in the depths of the heart of man, that it is not in the power of any God—or any woman—to calm it. This woman or God only calms it, each time, for a period of time: the disquiet would quickly return were it not for fatigue. God undoubtedly, in the immense concealment of vague domains, can for a long time postpone the new calming of a disquiet that has begun again. But the calming will die sooner than the disquiet.

I said (in the second part): "Nonknowledge communicates ecstasy." A gratuitous and deceptive affirmation. It is founded on experience—if one lives it . . . If not, it is suspended.

It is easy to say that one cannot speak of ecstasy. There is in it an element that one cannot reduce, that remains "ineffable," but in this ecstasy does not differ from other forms: I can have, can communicate precise knowledge of ecstasy as much—or more—than of laughter, of physical love—*or of things*; the difficulty, however, is that being less commonly experienced than laughter or things, what I can say about ecstasy cannot be familiar, easily recognizable.

Nonknowledge communicates ecstasy—but only if the possibility (the movement) of ecstasy already belonged, to some degree, to someone who disrobes himself of knowledge. (The restriction is that much more admissible since, from the beginning, I have wanted the extremity of the possible, in that there is no human possible to which I haven't been bound, in these conditions, to have recourse.) The movement of nonknowledge prior to ecstasy is ecstasy before an object (whether this should be the pure point—as the renunciation of all dogmatic faiths would have it, or some upsetting image). If this ecstasy before the object is initially given (as a possible) and if I suppress, after the fact, the object—as "contestation" inevitably does—if for this reason I enter into anguish—into horror, into the night of nonknowledge—ecstasy is near and, when it arises, ruins me further than anything imaginable. If I had known nothing of ecstasy before the object, I would not have attained ecstasy in the night. But *initiated* as I was in the object—and my initiation had represented the furthest penetration of the possible—I could only, in the night, find a deeper ecstasy. From then on the night, nonknowledge, will each time be the path of ecstasy along which I will lose myself.

Earlier, I said of the position of the point that starting from it, the mind is an eye. From then on experience has an optical framework, in that one distinguishes within it a perceived object from a perceiving subject, the way a spectacle is different from a mirror. Moreover, in this case, the apparatus of vision (the physical apparatus) occupies the greatest place. It is a spectator, it is eyes that seek the point, or at least, in this operation, the spectator's existence condenses itself in the eyes. This character does not cease if night falls. What then finds itself in a profound obscurity is a fierce desire to see when, before this desire, everything slips away.

But the desire for existence thus dissipated in the night bears on an object of ecstasy. The desired spectacle, the object, in expectation of which passion exceeds itself, is the reason why "I could die of not dying." This object effaces itself and the night is there: anguish binds me, it withers me, but this night substitutes itself for the object and now alone responds to my expectation? Suddenly I know it, discover it without a cry, it is not an object: it is THAT which I was awaiting! If I had not sought the object, I would never have found it. It was necessary that the contemplated object make me this mirror distorted by a flash, that I had become, for the night to at last offer itself to my thirst. If I had not gone toward IT as eyes go to the object they love, if the anticipation of a passion had not sought it, IT would only be the absence of light. Whereas my exorbitant gaze finds IT, ruins itself in it, and not only does the object loved to the point of crying out leave no regrets, but I almost forget—fail to understand and debase—this object without which however my gaze wouldn't have "become exorbitant," discovered the night.

Contemplating night, I see nothing, love nothing. I remain immobile, frozen, absorbed in IT. I can imagine a landscape of terror, sublime, the earth open as a volcano, the sky filled with fire, or any other vision capable of "ravishing" the mind; as beautiful and upsetting as it may be, the night surpasses this limited possible and yet IT is nothing, it is nothing tangible, not even in the end darkness. In IT everything is effaced, but, exorbitant, I traverse an empty depth and the empty depth traverses me. In IT, I communicate with the "unknown" opposed to the *ipse* that I am; I become *ipse*, unknown to myself, two terms merge into the same laceration, hardly differing from a void—distinguished from it by nothing that I can grasp— nevertheless differing from it more than the world of a thousand colors.

RESUMPTION AND END OF THE NARRATIVE

What I desired:

   . . . Venus wholly fastened upon her prey.[28]

But further on:

   *. . . already the venom having reached my heart
   Into this dying heart casts an unknown chill . . .*[29]
   . . . .
   And death, stealing light from my eyes . . .[30]

"At first," I said, "I wanted to return from a contemplation that brought the object back to me (as usually happens when we enjoy a landscape) to the vision of this object in which I lose myself at another time, which I call the 'unknown' and which is only distinct from nothingness by nothing that discourse can enunciate."[31] In this sentence at which the interrupted narrative stops, I named night as an object, but it hardly matters. Meanwhile, I have shown the way that leads generally from the common state, in which we know the world, to the "unknown." But the day of the half-failed experience that I relate, in my effort to regain access to this void, I exhausted myself in vain. Nothing happened at the end of a long time but this: I perceived the possession of a streaming of existence within me and before me, as if it took place enclosed by two crossed branches (like the tentacles of my avarice). In the end, as if the branches met even more, the flow that I directed escaped beyond itself, in the prolongation of the St. Andrew's cross that it formed. At this moment, this flow was lost in a lively and free current, this current fled before me suddenly freed from an avaricious hold and I remained raised up, in suspense, breathless. This escape was empty of intellectual contents and today I imagine only that it responded to the position of the "point," but the slipping of myself toward the "point," the precipitated confusion were more animated here; and more than before the "point," I remained breathless by what was ungraspable about it. Here I open this parenthesis to complete if I can what I had said previously: as long as this slippage was not graspable, it was captivating; it was so to the ultimate degree of tension. So much so that I now saw in it what is always in the "point," at least what always begins in it: a furtive, distraught flight toward night, but at this moment that hardly lasted, the movement of flight was so rapid that the possession of the "point," which normally limited it, was from the start surpassed, such that, without transition, I had gone from a jealous embrace to complete dispossession. And this word dispossession is so true that I shortly found myself emptied, trying to grasp once again in vain the ungraspable that had definitively escaped; then I felt idiotic.

I found myself in a state comparable to that of a man enraged by a woman he loves and who, suddenly, sees chance deprive him of any outlet: be it the arrival of a visitor. The visitor: inevitable stupefaction, as difficult to dismiss but all the less admissible at that moment in which desire for the ungraspable was at stake. I could have remained there, been discouraged, but even this solution failed: like the enraged man, I was excited and could not relax. Rightly telling myself that it was vain to seek that which had escaped from me, I abandoned the question to the intense flowing of inner movements that I had so lightly aroused. And tired enough to fall asleep, I resigned myself to submit to the law that I believed to be that of those movements: I thought that a voluptuous possession alone was the measure of their resources.

These streams within us are of a disarming plasticity. To imagine suffices, and the dreamed-of form vaguely takes shape. It is thus that years ago, when this streaming remained diffuse within me, without object, in the darkness of my room, I felt myself become a tree and even a tree struck by lightning;[32] My arms lifted little by little and their movement became knotted like that of strong branches broken almost at the level of the trunk. Elsewhere these follies derive their possibility from the indifference one has for them. If I had had this project: to become a tree, it would have failed. I had become a tree as one dreams, without other consequence, but I was awake, I took pleasure in no longer being myself, being different, in slipping. If I have these inner streams at my disposal today, they cannot change me, but become an object distinct from myself. When tired, I told myself that only a voluptuous possession was open to me, I obscurely evoked a presence that the sweetness, the nudity, the night of breasts would have formed: at once this sweetness, this nudity, this warm night became mingled, made of the milky flow emanating from me. For a long time my tenderness drank from this pure incarnation of sin. Then it grew tired. The figure that followed that of femininity was "divine," composed of an internally violent majesty, leaving me the memory of a somber sky where the empty plenitude of the wind rages. This new figure remained graspable: I embraced this vast void and its noise, I experienced its presence only transfixed with fear: but it belonged entirely to me being my thing. And able to enjoy it only tenderly, in the end, I rebelled.

The drama went on, I couldn't disengage myself from it; my disquiet was so great. I was thirsty for other things and suffered from my stubbornness. It so happened that physical fatigue stopped me and as I had been sick for several weeks and, due to a medical condition, had the use of only one lung, on doctor's orders, I had to stretch out from time to time, forcing myself to forget, at the very least to regain my breath.

Despair, impatience, horror of myself—even while I was sometimes trying to recover the bewildering path of ecstasy, sometimes to have done with it, to resolutely go to bed, to sleep—eventually delivered me. Suddenly, I stood up and I was completely taken. As I had earlier become a tree, but the tree was still myself—and what I became differed no less than one of the "objects" that I had just possessed—I became a flame. But I say "flame" only by comparison. When I had become the tree, I had in mind, clearly and distinctly, an idea of a woody plant. Whereas the new change responded to nothing that one could have evoked in advance. The upper part of my body—above the solar plexus—had disappeared, or at least no longer gave rise to isolatable sensations. Only my legs, which remained standing, connected what I had become to the floor, kept a link to what I had been: the rest was inflamed, gushing, *exceeding*, even free of its own convulsion. A character of dance and of decomposing agility (as if made of a thousand distracted futilities and of life's thousand mad laughs) situated this flame "outside of me." And as in a dance everything mingles together, there was nothing that didn't go there to be consumed. I was thrown into this hearth: nothing remained of me but this hearth. In its entirety, the hearth itself was thrown out of me.

The next day, I wrote of this flame: "It is not aware of itself, it is absorbed in its own unknown; in this unknown, it loses itself, annihilates itself. Without this thirst for nonknowledge, it would cease right away. The flame is God, but ruined in the negation of itself."

It is possible that these first sentences account more for the flame, for the silent absorption, for the slipping elsewhere. What I was able to say later remains exact, but muddled by exactitude. And if now, the narrative finished, I come back to myself, I feel sad as happens when, burning, we discover in ourselves that which is not yet consumed and will not be able to be, not being commensurate to the fire. I still have little concern for myself, for the impossible spider, not yet crushed, that I am, so poorly dissimulated in its network of webs. Despite this the spider, lurking in the depths, is horror having become a being, to the point that being the night, it nevertheless radiates like a sun . . .

To the feeling of an indelible shame is added that of having little strength. I can imagine myself remediating the obscurity of my book through a conversation. I can even say to myself that this remedy is the only one, that if truths come down into the complexity of human lives, nothing can insure that they will be given clearly at one time; clarity will be great in one who persists in saying them. But I must remember that a dialogue is wretched, better than a book at reducing its objects to the poverty of discourse. How would I not feel exhausted, knowing of the desired clarity that I call for while awaiting the obscurity for which I thirst, for which man however is dying of thirst—even though his eyes flee from it—as they flee the brightness of the sun?

5

Fortune

"Oh, wretchedness of all givers! Oh, darkening of my sun! Oh, craving to crave! Oh, ravenous hunger in satiation!"

—Zarathustra, The Night Song[33]

What one doesn't normally see while speaking: that discourse, even negating its own value, assumes not only he who engages in it but he who listens to it . . . I find nothing in myself, nothing more than myself, no property of my fellow being. And this movement of my thought, that flees me, not only can I not avoid it, but there is no moment so secret that it doesn't animate me. Thus I speak, everything in me gives itself to others.

But knowing that, no longer forgetting it, undergoing the necessity of giving myself decomposes me. I can know that I am a point, a wave lost in other waves, laugh at myself even, at the comedy of "originality" that I remain; at the same time I can only say to myself: I am alone, bitter . . .

And to conclude: solitude of light, of desert . . .

Mirage of penetrable existences wherein nothing troubling would rise up without being caught in the undertow of a flash, just as spilled blood, death, wouldn't slip without venom, froth, except at the end of a slower ecstasy.

But instead of grasping this unleashing of oneself, a being stops in himself the torrent that gives him to life, and devotes himself, in the hope of avoiding ruin, to fear of excessive glories, to the possession of things. And the things possess him when he believes he possesses them.

O desert of "things" that speak! Hideousness of existence: the fear of being changes a man into a bartender.

Servitude, inextricable decline: the slave liberates himself from the master through work (the essential movement of the *Phenomenology of Mind*), but the product of his work becomes his master.

What dies is the possibility of the festival, the free communication of beings, the Golden Age (the possibility of the same intoxication, the same dizziness, the same sensual pleasure).

What the reflux abandons: disabled, arrogant marionettes, repelling one another, hating one another, challenging one another. They claim to love one another, falling into zealous hypocrisy, hence the nostalgia for tempests, for tidal waves.

By means of misery, life, from contestation to contestation, devoted to ever increased demands—all the more distant from the Golden Age (from the absence of challenge). Once ugliness has been perceived, beauty rarefying love . . .

Beauty demanding wealth, but wealth challenged in turn, glorious man surviving the completed ruin of himself, on the condition of a senseless lost of rest. Like a bolt of lightning, chance—light in the debris—alone escaping from the avaricious comedy.

To conclude, solitude (where I am)—at the limit of a sob strangled by self-hatred. The desire to communicate growing in proportion to the contestation of easy, ridiculous communications.

Existence taken to the extreme, in conditions of madness, forgotten, despised, hunted. Yet, in these mad conditions, torn from isolation, shattering like a mad laughter, given to impossible saturnalias.

Most difficult: renouncing "average" man for extremity, we contest a fallen humanity, removed from the Golden Age, greed, and falsehood. At the same time we contest that which is not the "desert" where the extremity occurs, "desert" where the saturnalias of the solitary are unleashed! . . . There the being is point or wave; but it is, it seems, the only point, the only wave; the solitary is in no way separated from the "other" but the other is not there.

And was the other there?

Would the desert be any less empty? The orgy less "desolate"?

Thus I speak, everything in me gives itself to others! . . .

6

Nietzsche

ON A SACRIFICE IN WHICH EVERYTHING IS VICTIM

While I was writing, anxiety arose. Once begun, the narrative remained, before my eyes, blackened by strikeouts, eager for ink. But having conceived of it sufficed for me. Having to finish it and expecting anything from it disconcerted me.

Remembering Lautréamont's *Poésies*, I thought of inverting the terms of the *Pater*.[34] As a *continued story*, I imagined this dialogue:

I sleep. Though silent, God speaks to me, insinuating, as in love, in a low voice:

—O my father, you, on earth, the evil that is in you delivers me. I am the temptation of which you are the fall. Insult me as I insult those who love me. Give me each day the bread of bitterness. My will is absent in the heavens as it is on earth. Impotence binds me. My name is insipid.

Hesitating, troubled, I respond:
—So be it.

"One is most dishonest to one's god: he is not allowed to sin."
(*Beyond Good and Evil*, § 65a[35])

I rely on God to deny himself, to loathe himself, to throw what he dares, what he is, into absence, into death. When I am God, I negate him to the depths of negation. If I am only myself, I know nothing of God. To the extent that clear consciousness subsists in me, I name him without knowing him: I do not know God. I attempt to know him: immediately I become nonknowledge, become God, unknown, unknowable ignorance.

"There is a great ladder of religious cruelty, with many rungs; but three of these are the most important. Once one sacrificed human beings to one's god, perhaps precisely those whom one loved most: the sacrifices of the first-born in all prehistoric religions belong here, as well as the sacrifice of the Emperor Tiberius in the Mithraic grotto of the isle of Capri, that most gruesome of all Roman anachronisms. Then, during the moral epoch of mankind, one sacrificed to one's god one's strongest instincts, one's 'nature'; this festive joy lights up the cruel eyes of the ascetic, the 'anti-natural' enthusiast. Finally—what remained to be sacrificed? At long last, did one not have to sacrifice for once whatever is comforting, holy, healing; all hope, all faith in hidden harmony, in future blisses and justices? Didn't one have to sacrifice God himself and, from cruelty against oneself, worship the stone, stupidity, gravity, fate, the nothing? To sacrifice God for the nothing—this paradoxical mystery of the final cruelty was reserved for the generation that is now coming up: all of us already know something of this."
(*Beyond Good and Evil*, § 55[36])

I believe that one sacrifices the goods that one abuses (to use is only a fundamental abuse).

Man is greedy, obligated to be so, but he condemns greed, which is only endured necessity—elevates the gift, of self or possessions, that alone makes glorious. Making his food of plants and animals, he recognizes in them, however, the sacred nature, similar to his own, such that one cannot destroy them and consume them without offense. Before each element that man absorbs (to his profit) was felt the obligation of admitting the abuse that he made of it. A certain number of men among others had the responsibility to recognize a plant, an animal having become a victim. These men had sacred relations to the plant or animal, not eating them, they *gave* them to men in the other group to eat. If they ate them, it was with a revealing parsimony: they had recognized in advance the illegitimate character, serious and tragic, of consumption. Is it not a tragedy itself that man can only live on the condition of destruction, killing, absorbing?

And not only of plants and animals but of other men.

Nothing can hold the march of humanity back. There would only be satiety (if not for each man—the majority of individuals must abandon the quest for their part—at least for the whole) if man became everything.

On this path, it was a step, but only a step, that a man enslave other men, make a thing of his fellow beings, possessed, absorbed, as are animals and plants. But the fact that man became the thing of man had this repercussion: that the master for whom the slave became the thing—the sovereign—withdrew from communion, shattered the communication of men among themselves. The sovereign's infraction of the common rule began the isolation of man, his separation in pieces that could be reunited only rarely at first, then never.

The master's possession of prisoners that could be eaten or of unarmed slaves put man himself, like nature subject to appropriation (no longer unduly but as much as the animal or the plant), among the objects that it was necessary to sacrifice from time to time. It so happened moreover that men suffered from the absence of communication resulting from existence separated from a king. They had to put to death not the slave but the king to assure the return to communion of the whole people. Among men, it must have therefore seemed that one couldn't choose one more worthy of the knife than a king. But in regard to military leaders, sacrifice ceased to be possible (a war commander was too strong). Carnival kings (disguised prisoners, pampered before death) were substituted for them.

The saturnalias during which one sacrificed false kings permitted the temporary return to the Golden Age. One inversed the roles: for once the master served the slave and such a man embodying the power of the master—from whence came the separation of men among themselves—was then put to death, assuring the fusion of everyone in a single dance (and even in a single anguish, then in a single rush of pleasure).

But the appropriation by man of every appropriable resource was not only limited to living organisms. I am not speaking so much of the recent and merciless exploitation of natural resources (of an industry whose problems—imbalance—I am often surprised, are hardly perceived at the same time as the prosperity that it brings about), but of the mind of man to whose profit the entire appropriation takes place—different in this way from the stomach, which digests food, and never digests itself—has at last changed itself into a thing (an appropriated object). The mind of man has become its own slave and, through the labor of autodigestion that the operation assumes, has consumed, subjugated, destroyed itself. Cog within the available cogs, the mind of man makes of itself abuse whose effects escape him—to the extent that this effect is only in the end, nothing subsists in the mind of man that is not a useful thing. Right up to God, there is nothing that is not reduced to servitude. A gnawing away, as rodents do, eventually cuts God up, assigns him positions; then, since everything is mobile, reworked without respite, deprives God of them, reveals their absence or uselessness.

If one says that "God is dead," some think of Jesus, whose immolation brought back the Golden Age (the kingdom of heaven) like that of the kings (but Jesus alone died, God who abandoned him was nevertheless awaiting him, sat him on his right); others think of the abuse that I just evoked, that permits no value to subsist—the mind reduced, in accordance to Descartes's formula, to the "clear and distinct consciousness of what is useful for life."[37] But that "God should be dead," victim of a sacrifice, only has meaning if profound and differs as much from the evasion of a God in the notion of a clear and servile world as does a human sacrifice, sanctifying the victim, from a slavery that makes the victim an instrument of work.

Each day a little more I have understood that notions drawn from scholarly books—as are totemism, sacrifice—engage in an intellectual servitude: I can less and less evoke a historical fact without being disarmed by the abuse that consists in speaking of appropriated and digested things. Not that I am struck by the degree of error: it is inevitable. But I am that much less afraid of erring since I accept it. I am humble and don't awaken a long dead past without uneasiness. Whatever knowledge the living have of it, they do not possess the past as they think they do: if they think they hold it, it escapes them. I give myself excuses: building my theory, I didn't forget that it leads to a movement that is elusive; I can only situate in this way the sacrifice that is incumbent upon us.

Because of the increasing servility of intellectual forms within us, it has come down to us to complete a sacrifice more profound than that of the men who preceded us. We no longer have to compensate with offerings for the abuse that man has made of vegetable, animal, and human species. The reduction of men themselves to servitude now receives (moreover for a long time now) consequences in the political realm (this is good, instead of drawing religious consequences from it to abolish the abuse). But the supreme abuse that man belatedly made of his reason demands a final sacrifice: reason, intelligibility, the ground itself upon which he stands, man must reject them, in him God must die, this is the depth of terror, the extremity where he succumbs. *Man can find himself only on the condition of escaping, without respite, from the avarice that grips him.*

DIGRESSION ON POETRY AND MARCEL PROUST

If I feel the weight of which I have spoken, it is usually blindly—this is not unusual. I want to free myself, already poetry . . . But is poetry equal to a completed absorption?

It is true that the effect, even were it of a sacrifice of a king, is only ever poetic: a man is put to death; no slave is liberated. One even aggravates the state of things by adding a murder to the acts of servitude. This was quite quickly the common feeling, far from alleviating horror, human sacrifice created it: other solutions were required; Christianity brought them. Consummated once and for all on the cross, sacrifice was the blackest of all crimes: if it is renewed, it is in an image. Then Christianity initiated the real negation of servitude: it put God—consensual servitude—in place of the master—enforced servitude.

But to conclude, we cannot imagine any real amendment of abuses that can only be inevitable (they are inevitable from the beginning, we cannot conceive of the development of man if there had not been slavery—thereafter, but when in the long run it ceased to be what it was at first—inevitable—one mitigated it, and it was more the aging of an institution than a voluntary change). The meaning of the sacrifice is to maintain as tolerable—living—a life that the necessary greed ceaselessly returns to death. We cannot suppress greed (attempting to do so increases hypocrisy). But if sacrifice is not the suppression of evil, it differs nonetheless from poetry in that it is not normally limited to the realm of words. If man must reach the extremity, his reason collapse, *God die,* words, their sickest games, cannot suffice.

Of poetry, I will now say that it is, I believe, the sacrifice in which words are victims. Words—we use them, we make of them the instruments of useful acts. We wouldn't be human if language within us had to be entirely servile. Nor can we do with the efficacious relationships that words introduce between men and things. But we tear words from these relationships in a delirium.

When words like *horse* or *butter* enter into a poem, they do so detached from interested concerns. For as many times as the words *butter* and *horse* are put to practical ends, the use that poetry makes of them liberates human life from these ends. When the farm girl says *butter* or the stable boy says *horse*, they know butter, horse. The knowledge that they have of them even in a sense exhausts the idea of knowing, for they can make butter or lead a horse at will. Making, raising, using, perfect and even found knowledge (the essential links of knowledge are relations of practical efficacy; to know an object is, according to Janet, to know how to go about making it). But, on the contrary, *poetry leads from the known to the unknown*. It can do what neither the boy nor the girl can do, introduce a butter horse. In this way it places one before the unknowable. No doubt I have barely enunciated the words when the familiar images of horses and butter present themselves, but they are solicited only in order to die. In this poetry is sacrifice, the most accessible sacrifice. For if the use or abuse of words, to which the operations of work oblige us, takes place on the ideal, unreal level of language, the same is true of the sacrifice of words that is poetry.

If I say honestly, naively, of the unknown that surrounds me, from which I come, to which I go, that it is truly such, that, of its night, I neither know nor can know anything—assuming of this unknown that it is concerned or annoyed with the feeling that one has for it, I imagine that no one is in harmony with the concern it demands more than I am. I imagine this not because I need to tell myself, "I've done everything, now I can rest," but because one cannot submit to a greater demand. I can in no way imagine the unknown concerned with me (I said assuming: even if it is true, it is absurd, but after all: I know nothing), it is to my mind impious to think of it. In the same way, in the presence of the unknown, it is impious to be moral (shameful, like a fisherman, to bait the unknown). Morality is the constraint that a man, inserted into the known order, imposes upon himself (what he knows, these are the consequences of his acts), the unknown breaks the constraint, abandons to disastrous consequences.

In the end undoubtedly to better ruin knowledge, I have carried it further than another, and in a similar way the demand to which the hatred of morality carries me is only a hypertrophy of morality. (If one must renounce salvation, in whatever form one gives it: would morality only have been interested?) But would I be where I am if I knew nothing of the turns of the most impoverished maze? (And in everyday life, loyalty, purity of heart, in a word, the true moral laws, are only truly broken by small men.)

The level of morality is the level of the *project*. The opposite of project is sacrifice. Sacrifice falls into the forms of the project, but only in appearance (or to the extent of its decadence). A ritual is the divination of a hidden necessity (forever remaining obscure). And where only the result counts in the project, in the sacrifice, the act concentrates value in itself. Nothing in sacrifice is put off until later; sacrifice has the power to contest everything in the instant that it takes place, to summon everything, to render everything present. The crucial instant is that of death, yet as soon as the action begins, everything is contested, everything is present.

Sacrifice is immoral, poetry is immoral.*

This still: in the desire for an inaccessible unknown, which at all costs we must situate beyond reach, I arrive at this feverish contestation of poetry—where, I believe, I will contest myself with others. But of poetry, I have at first put forward only a narrow form—the simple holocaust of words. I will now give it a more vast and vague horizon, that of the modern *Thousand and One Nights*, which are the books of Marcel Proust.

I have only a breathless interest in the philosophies of time—offering apparent answers in the form of an analysis of time. I find it more naive to say: to the extent that things known in an illusory way are nevertheless the defenseless victims of time, they are give over to the obscurity of the unknown. Not only does time alter them, annihilate them (if necessary, knowledge could follow them a bit in these alterations), but the evil that is time, that dominates them from on high, shatters them, negates them, is the unknowable itself, which, in each successive instant, opens itself in them, as it opens itself in us, who would experience it if we didn't force ourselves to flee it in false pretenses to knowledge. And to the extent that Proust's work is an effort to link time, to know time—in other words that it is not, according to the author's desire, poetry—I feel far from it.

But Proust writes of love that it is "time made tangible to the heart"[38] and the love that he lives, however, is only a torture, an enticement in which what he loves endlessly eludes his grasp.

---

*It is so barely paradoxical that the sacrifice of mass is in its essence the greatest of all crimes. The Hindus, the ancient Greeks knew the profound immorality of sacrifice.

Of Albertine, who was perhaps Albert, Proust went so far as to say that she was "like a mighty goddess of Time";[39] what he wanted to say was, it seems to me, that she will remain for him, no matter what he does, inaccessible, unknown, that she was going to escape him. At all costs, however, he wanted to enclose her, to possess her, "to know her," and it is too little to say that he wanted to: the desire was so strong, exceeding, that it became the token of loss. Satisfied, the desire would die: if she ceased to be the unknown, Proust would cease wanting to know, he would cease to love. Love returned with the suspicion of a lie, by which Albertine eluded any knowledge, any will to possession. And Proust imagined grasping the definitive distress of love—when it is not that of love, but only that of possession—by writing: "The image which I sought, upon which I relied, for which I would have been prepared to die, was no longer that of Albertine leading an unknown life, it was that of an Albertine as known to me as it was possible for her to be (and it was for this reason that my love could not be lasting unless it remained unhappy, for by definition it did not satisfy the need for mystery), an Albertine who did not reflect a distant world, but desire nothing else—there were moments when this did indeed appear to be the case—than to be with me, to be exactly like me, an Albertine who was the image precisely of what was mine and not of the unknown."[40] But the exhausting effort was revealed to be vain: ". . . this beauty which, when I thought of the successive years in which I had known Albertine, whether on the beach in Balbec or in Paris, I found that I had but recently discovered in her, and which consisted in the fact that she existed on so many planes and embodied so many days that had passed, this beauty became almost heartrending. Then beneath that rose-pink face I felt that there yawned like a gulf the inexhaustible expanse of the evenings when I had not known Albertine. I could, if I chose, take Albertine on my knee, hold her head in my hands, I could caress her, run my hands slowly over her, but, just as if I had been handling a stone that encloses the salt of immemorial oceans or the light of a star, I felt that I was touching no more than the sealed envelop of a person who inwardly reached to infinity. How I suffered from that position to which we are reduced by the obliviousness of nature that, when instituting the division of bodies, never thought of making possible the interpenetration of souls! And I realized that Albertine was not even for me (for if her body was in the power of mine, her thoughts eluded the grasp of my thoughts) the marvelous captive with whom I had thought to enrich my home, while concealing her presence there completely, even from the friends who came to see me and never suspected that she was at the end of the corridor, in the room next to my own, as did that person whom nobody knew that he kept the Princess of China sealed in a bottle; urging me with cruel and fruitless insistence in quest of the past, she resembled, if anything, a mighty goddess of Time."[41] Is the young girl in this game not what the man's greed, from time immemorial, wanted to grasp, jealousy, the narrow path that in the end can only lead to the unknown.

Other paths lead to the same point; the unknown that life reveals definitively, what the world is, at every instant is embodied in some new object. There is in each of them a share of the unknown that has the power to seduce. But the unknown (seduction) slips away if I want to possess, if I attempt to know an object: while Proust never tired of wanting to use, to abuse objects that life proposes. Such that he hardly knew anything of love but impossible jealousy and not the communication in which the feeling of the self softens, when we offer ourselves in an excess of desire. If the truth that a woman proposes to one who loves her is the unknown (the inaccessible), her lover can neither know her nor reach her, but she can shatter him: if he is shattered what does he become, if not that which lay dormant in him, the unknown, the inaccessible? But from such a game neither the lover nor the beloved could ever grasp anything, nor immobilize it, nor make it last. That which communicates (is penetrated in each of them by the other) is the blind share, which neither knows nor knows of itself. And no doubt there are no lovers whom one doesn't find busy, intent on killing love, attempting to limit it, to appropriate it, to give it barriers. But rarely does the obsession to possess, to know, decompose to the degree that Proust described in *The Captive*, rarely is it linked to so much disintegrating lucidity.

The lucidity that tore him apart before his beloved must, however, have been absent in him when, with just as great an anguish, he believed he could apprehend, forever capture fleeting "impressions": does he not say he has grasped the ungraspable?
"So often," he said, "in the course of my life, reality had disappointed me because at the instant when my senses perceived it my imagination, which was the only organ that I possessed for the enjoyment of beauty, could not apply itself to it, in virtue of that ineluctable law that ordains that we can only imagine what is absent. And now, suddenly, the effect of this harsh law had been neutralized, temporarily annulled, by a marvelous expedient of nature that had caused a sensation—the noise made both by the spoon and by the hammer, for instance—to be mirrored at one and the same time in the past, so that my imagination was permitted to savour

it, and in the present, where the actual shock to my senses of that noise, the touch of the linen napkin, or whatever it might be, had added to the dreams of the imagination the concept of 'existence' that they usually lack, and through this subterfuge had made it possible for my being to secure, to isolate, to immobilize—for a moment brief as a flash of lightning—what normally it never apprehends: a fragment of time in the pure state."[42]

I imagine that Marcel Proust's pronounced eagerness for pleasure was linked to the fact that he could only take pleasure from an object by being assured of its possession. But these moments of intense communication that we have with that which surrounds us—whether it is a matter of a row of trees, of a sunlit room—are in themselves ungraspable. We only take pleasure to the extent that we *communicate*, that we are lost, inattentive. If we cease to be lost, if our attention is concentrated, we cease for all that to *communicate*. We seek to understand, to capture the pleasure: it escapes us.

The difficulty (which I have attempted to show in the introduction) consists principally in that by wanting to grasp, nothing remains in our hands but the bare object, without the impression that accompanied it. The intense release of life that had occurred, as in love, moving toward the object, losing itself in it, escapes us, because in order to apprehend it, our attention is turned naturally toward the object, not toward ourselves. Being most often discursive, its progress is reducible to the linking of words, and the discourse, the words that permit us to reach the objects easily, attain poorly the inner states, which remain strangely unknown to us. We have consciousness of these states but in a fleeting way, and to want to stop ourselves there, to make them enter the field of vision, is in the first movement to want to know them, and we only became aware of them to the extent that we let go of our discursive mania to know! Even motivated by good will, we can do nothing about it; wanting to pay attention to the inner, attention nevertheless slips towards the object. We only emerge from this starting from states proceeding from objects that are in themselves barely graspable (silence, breath). To bring Proust's attention back to the inner, memory—certainly involuntary, not expressly elicited memory—played a role recalling that of breath, in the suspended attention that a monk from India conjures within himself.

If the impression is not current and comes out of memory—or, if you like, the imagination—it is the same communication, the same loss of self, the same inner state as the first time. But we can grasp this state, stop for a moment, since it has itself become "object" in memory. We can know it—at least recognize it—consequently possess it, without changing it.

It seems to me that this felicity of reminiscences, opposing itself to the ungraspable void of first impressions, derives from the author's character. Proust imagined himself discovering a kind of way out: but the way out that mattered to him had, I believe, no meaning for anyone else. In any case it derives from this: that *recognition*, which is not discursive—and destroys nothing—give Proust's will to possession a sufficient appeasement, analogous to that of *knowledge*, which, itself, is discursive and destroys.

This opposition between knowledge and recognition is moreover that of intelligence and memory. And if intelligence is open to the future, even when the object of its analysis is past, if intelligence is nothing more than the faculty of project, and thereby the negation of time, memory, consisting in the union of past and present, is time itself within us. What I must nevertheless indicate is that Proust lazily only half understood the opposition, for barely does he say that the "marvelous expedient" of memory has permitted his being to "secure, to isolate, to immobilize—for a moment brief as a flash of lightning—what normally it never apprehends: a fragment of time in the pure state,"[43] then he adds: "The being which had been reborn in me when with a sudden shudder of happiness I had heard the noise that was common to the spoon touching the plate and the hammer striking the wheel, or had felt, beneath my feet, the unevenness that was common to the paving-stones of Guermantes courtyard and to those of the baptistery of St. Mark's, this being is nourished only by the essences of things, in these alone does it find its sustenance and delight. In the observation of the present, where the senses cannot feed it with this food, it languishes, as it does in the consideration of the past made arid by the intellect or in the anticipation of a future that the will constructs with fragments of the present and the past, fragments whose reality it still further reduces by preserving of them only what is suitable for the utilitarian, narrowly human purpose for which it intends them. But let a noise or a scent, once heard or once smelt, be heard or smelt again in the present and at the same time in the past, real without being actual, ideal without being abstract, and immediately the permanent and habitually concealed essence of things is liberated and our true self, which seemed—and perhaps for long years seemed—to be dead but was not altogether dead, is awakened and reanimated as it receives the celestial nourishment that is brought to it. A minute freed from the order of time has re-created in us, to feel it, the man freed from the order of time. And one can understand that this man should have confidence in his joy, even if the simple taste of a madeleine does not seem logically to contain within it the reasons for this joy, one can understand that the word 'death' should have no meaning for him; situated outside time, why should he fear the future?"[44] Thus "time in the pure state" is, on the following page, "freed from the order of time." Such is the illusion of memory that the unfathomable unknown of time—that, profoundly, it acknowledges—is confused in itself with its opposite, knowledge, through which we sometimes have the illusion of escaping from time, of gaining access to the eternal. Memory is usually linked to the faculty for project, to intelligence, which never functions without it, but the memory evoked by the sound, the contact, was pure memory, free of all project. This pure memory, in which are our "true self," *ipse* different from the "I" of project, is inscribed, liberates no "permanent and habitually concealed essence of things," if not communication, the state into which we are thrown when, uprooted from the known, we no longer grasp in things anything but the unknown usually elusive in them.

The known—ideal, freed from time—belongs so little to the moments of felicity that on the subject of a line from the Vinteuil *Septet* (situated near another about which he says: "This phrase was what might have seemed most eloquently to characterize—as contrasting so sharply with all the rest of my life, with the visible world—those impressions that at remote intervals I experienced in my life as starting points, foundation stones for the construction of a true life: the impression I had felt at the sight of the steeples of Martinville, or a line of trees near Balbec . . ."[45]). He says this: "I saw [one] reappear five times or six without being able to distinguish its features, but so caressing, so different . . . from anything that any woman had ever made me desire, that this phrase—this invisible creature whose language I did not know but whom I understood so well—which offered me in so sweet a voice a happiness that it would really have been worth the struggle to obtain, is perhaps the only Unknown Woman that it has ever been my good fortune to meet."[46] A woman's desirable qualities—he says this in twenty ways, were in Proust's eyes, her share of the unknown (if the thing had been possible, to take pleasure in her would have been to extract from her "something like the square root of her unknown"[47]). But knowledge always killed desire, destroying the unknown (which "a mere introduction was generally enough to dispel"[48]). In the realm of "impressions," at least knowledge could reduce nothing, dissolve nothing. And the unknown formed their attractions as it does those of desirable beings. A phrase from the septet, a ray of summer sunlight, steal from the will to know a secret that no reminiscence will ever make penetrable.

But in the "impression" brought back to memory, as in the poetic image, remains an equivocation deriving from the possibility of grasping what, in essence, is elusive. In the inner turmoil that follows from opposing the will to take and the will to lose—the desire to appropriate and the contrary desire to communicate—poetry is on the same level as the states of "consolation," the visions, the words of the mystics. The "consolations" translate an inaccessible (impossible) element into strictly familiar forms. In the "consolations," the devout soul, taking pleasure in the divine, possesses it. Whether she emits cries or faints, she is not speechless, does not attain the depths, the dark void. The most inner images of poetry—and which cause the greatest loss—the "impressions" about which Proust was able to say, "such that I remained in ecstasy on the uneven paving stones . . ."[49] or "if the actual site had not immediately conquered me, I would have lost consciousness . . ."[50] or "they force . . . our will . . . to teeter on the edge of an uncertainty similar to that which one experiences before an ineffable vision, at the moment of falling asleep . . ."[51]—the poetic images or "impressions" reserve, even while they overflow, a feeling of ownership, the persistence of an "I" relating everything to itself.

The share of the inaccessible in the "impressions"—the sort of insatiable hunger that precedes them—emerges better from these pages of *Within a Budding Grove* than from the commentaries of *Time Regained*: "Suddenly I was overwhelmed with that profound happiness that I had not often felt since Combray, a happiness analogous to that which had been given me by—among other things—the steeples of Martinville. But this time it remained incomplete. I had just seen, standing a little way back from the hog's-back road along which we were traveling, three trees that probably marked the entry to a covered driveway and formed a pattern that I was not seeing for the first time. I could not succeed in reconstructing the place from which they had been as it were detached, but I felt that it had been familiar to me once; so that, my mind having wavered between some distant year and the present moment, Balbec and its surroundings began to dissolve and I wondered whether the whole of this drive were not a make-believe, Balbec a place to which I had never gone except in imagination. Mme de Villeparisis a character in a story and the three old trees the reality that one recaptures on raising one's eyes from the book that one has been reading and that describes an environment into which one has come to believe that one has been bodily transported.

"I looked at the three trees; I could see them plainly, but my mind felt that they were concealing something that it could not grasp, as when an object is placed out of our reach, so that our fingers, stretched out at arm's length, can only touch for a moment its outer surface, without managing to take hold of anything. Then we rest for a little while before thrusting out our arm with renewed momentum, I should have to be alone. What would I not have given to be able to draw aside as I used to do on those walks along the Guermantes way, when I detached myself from my parents! I felt indeed that I ought to do so. I recognized that kind of pleasure that requires, it is true, a certain effort on the part of the mind, but in comparison with which the attractions of the indolence that incline us to renounce that pleasure seem very slight. That pleasure, the object of which I could only dimly feel, which I must create for myself, I experienced only on rare occasions, but on each of these it seemed to me that the things that had happened in the meantime were of little importance, and that in attaching myself to the reality of that pleasure alone could I at length begin to lead a true life. I put my hand for a moment across my eyes, so as to be able to shut them without Mme de Villeparisis's noticing. I sat there thinking of nothing, then with my thoughts collected, compressed, and strengthened I sprang further forward in the direction of the trees, or rather in that inner direction at the end of which I could see them inside myself. I felt again behind them the same object, known to me and yet vague, which I could not bring nearer. And yet all three of them, as the carriage moved on, I could see coming toward me. Where had I looked at them before? There was no place near Combray where an avenue opened off the road like that. Nor was there room for the site that they recalled to me in the scenery of the place in Germany where I had gone one year with my grandmother to take the waters. Was I to suppose, then, that they come from years already so remote in my life that the landscape that surrounded them had been entirely obliterated from my memory and that, like the pages that, with a sudden thrill, we recognize in a book that we imagined we had never read, they alone survived from the forgotten book of my earliest childhood? Were they not rather to be numbered among those dream landscapes, always the same, at least for me in whom their strange aspect was only the objectification in my sleeping mind of the effort I made while awake either to penetrate the mystery of a place beneath the outward appearance of which I was dimly conscious of there being something more, as had so often happened to me on the Guermantes way, or to try to put mystery back into a place that I had long to know and that, from the day when I had come to know it, had seemed to me to be wholly superficial, like Balbec? Or were they merely the image freshly extracted from a dream of the night before, but already so worn, so faded that it seemed to me to come from somewhere far more distant? Or had I indeed never seen them before, and did they conceal beneath their surface, like certain trees or tufts of grass that I had seen beside the Guermantes way, a meaning as obscure, as hard to grasp, as a distant past, so that, whereas they were inviting me to probe a new thought, I imagined that I had to identify an old memory? Or again, were they concealing no hidden thought, and was it simply visual fatigue that made me see them double in time as one sometimes sees double in space? I could not tell. And meanwhile they were coming toward me; perhaps some mythical apparition, a ring of witches or of Norns who would propose their oracles to me. I chose rather to believe that they were phantoms of the past, dear companions of my childhood, vanished friends who were invoking our common memories. Like ghosts they seemed to be appealing to me to take them with me, to bring them back to life. In their simple and passionate gesticulation I could discern the helpless anguish of a beloved person who has lost the power of speech, and feels that he will never be able to say to us what he wishes to say and we can never guess. Presently, at a crossroads, the carriage left them. It was bearing me away from what alone I believed to be true, what would have made me truly happy; it was like my life.

"I watched the trees gradually recede, waving their despairing arms, seeming to say to me: 'What you fail to learn from us today, you will never know. If you allow us to drop back into the hollow of this road from which we sought to raise ourselves up to you, a whole part of yourself that we were bringing to you will vanish for ever into thin air.' And indeed if, in the course of time, I did discover the kind of pleasure and disquiet that I had just felt once again, and if one evening—too late, but then for all time—I fastened myself to it, of those trees themselves I was never to know what they had been trying to give me nor where else I had seen them. And when, road having forked and the carriage with it, I turned my back on them and ceased to see them, while Mme de Villeparisis asked me what I was dreaming about, I was as wretched as if I had just lost a friend, had died myself, had broken faith with the dead or repudiated a god."[52]

Isn't the absence of satisfaction more profound than the feeling of triumph at the end of the work?

But Proust, without the feeling of triumph, would have lacked a reason to write . . . What he said at length in *Time Regained*: the act of writing regarded as an infinite reverberation of reminiscences, of impressions . . .

But the share of satisfaction, of triumph, is opposed by a contrary share. What the work attempts to translate is nothing less than the moments of felicity, the inexhaustible suffering of love. Otherwise what sense would these affirmations have: "As for happiness, that is really useful to us in one way only, by making unhappiness possible,"[53] or: "It almost seems as though a writer's works, like the water in an artesian well, mount to a height that is in proportion to the depth to which suffering has penetrated his heart."[54] I even believe that the final absence of satisfaction was, more than a momentary satisfaction, the motivation and purpose of the work. In the final volume there is like an equilibrium between life and death— between recovered impressions, "freed from time," and the aging characters who represent, in the Guermantes' salon, a herd of passive victims of this same time. The visible intention was that the triumph of time regained should accordingly emerge. But sometimes a stronger movement exceeds the intention: this movement overflows the whole work, assuring its diffuse unity. The ghosts recovered in the Guermantes' salon, worn and aged after long years, were already like objects eaten from within, that turn into dust the moment you touch them. Even young they only ever appeared ruined, victims of the author's cunning intrigues—all the more intimately corrupting because motivated by sympathy. In this way the very beings to whom we normally attribute the existence that they imagine for themselves—possession of themselves and of a part of others—was no more than poetic, a field where capricious havoc was wreaked. For the strangest things about this movement, which completed the putting to death of Berma by her children, then that of the author by his work, is that it contains the secret of poetry. Poetry is only a havoc that restores. It gives time, which eats away, that which a dull vanity tears away from it, it dissipates the false pretenses of an ordered world.

I did not mean to say that *In Search of Lost Time* was an expression of poetry purer and more beautiful than any other. One even finds elements of poetry decomposed in it. In it the desire to know is ceaselessly mixed with the contrary desire, to extract from each thing the share of the unknown that it contains. But poetry is not reducible to the simple "holocaust of words." In the same way it would be childish to conclude that we escape from stupor (from foolishness) only passively—if we are ridiculous.

For in this time that defeats us, which can only undo what we want to strengthen, we have recourse to bearing a "heart to be devoured."[55] Orestes or Phaedre—ravaged—is to poetry what the victim is to sacrifice.[56]

The triumph of the reminiscences makes less sense than one imagines. Linked to the unknown, to nonknowledge, it is ecstasy disengaging itself from a great anguish. With the help of a concession made to the need to possess, to know (abused, if you will, by *recognition*), equilibrium is established. Often the unknown gives us anguish, but this is the condition for ecstasy. Anguish is the fear of losing, the expression of the desire for possession. It is a stop before the communication that excites the desire but that causes fear. Given a change in the need to possess, anguish, suddenly, turns into ecstasy.

The appeasement given to the need to possess must still be great enough to sever every possibility of discursive links between us and the unknown object (the foreignness—the unknown—of the object revealed to anticipation must not be resolved by any inquiry). In the case of reminiscences the will to possess, to know, receives a sufficient response. "The dazzling and indistinct vision fluttered near me, as if to say: 'Seize me as I pass if you can, and try to solve the riddle of happiness that I set you.' And almost at once I recognized the vision: it was Venice . . ."[57]

If poetry is the path followed at all times by the desire felt by man to repair his abuse of language, it takes place, as I said, on the same level; or on those, parallel, of expression.

It differs in this from the reminiscences whose play occupies within us the realm of images that assail the mind before it expresses them (without them becoming for all that, expressions). If some element of sacrifice enters into this play, the object is still no more unreal than that of poetry. In fact, the reminiscences are so close to poetry that the author himself links them to their expression, which he could only give them in principle. One will compare the realm of images with that of inner experience but understood in the way that I have articulated, experience questions everything, by which it attains what is least unreal from diverse objects (and yet if it appears so scarcely real, it is because it does not attain it outside of the subject with which it is united). What's more, as poetry itself tends to do, the reminiscences (less bitterly) tend to question everything, but at the same time avoid this tendency—and always for the same reason. Like poetry, the reminiscences do not imply the refusal of possession, they maintain desire on the contrary and consequently can only have a particular object. Even a cursed poet is eager to possess the moving world of images that he expresses and through which he enriches the heritage of man.

The poetic image, if it leads from the known to the unknown, attaches itself however to the known that gives it body, and even though it lacerates it and lacerates life in this laceration, maintains itself in it. Hence it follows that poetry is almost entirely poetry in decline, the enjoyment of images that are, it's true, drawn from the servile realm (poetic as well as noble, formal) but denied the inner ruin that is access to the unknown. Even profoundly ruined images are in the realm of possession. It is unfortunate to no longer possess anything but ruin, but this is not to no longer possess anything, it is to retain with one hand what the other gives.

Even simple minds felt obscurely that Rimbaud pushed back the possible of poetry by abandoning it, by completing its sacrifice, without equivocation, without reserve. That he only reached a tiring absurdity (his African existence) is what was of secondary importance in their eyes (in that they were not wrong, a sacrifice must be paid for, that's all). But these minds could not follow Rimbaud: they could only admire him, Rimbaud having by his flight, at the same time pushed back the possible for himself, suppressed this possible for others. From the fact that they admired Rimbaud only through love of poetry, some continued to enjoy poetry or to write, but with a bad conscience; others enclosed themselves in a chaos of inconsequentiality wherein they took pleasure and, letting themselves go, did not hesitate before any distinct affirmation. And as often happens, "the one and the other" together—in numerous cases, each time in a different form—in one single person composed a definite type of existence. Bad conscience could suddenly be translated into a humble attitude, childish even, but on another level than that of art, the social level. In the world of literature—or of painting—on the condition of observing certain rules of impropriety, one returns to habits in which abuse (exploitation) was difficult to distinguish from the reserve of the best people. I don't mean to say anything hostile but only that nothing, or almost nothing, remains of Rimbaud's unspoken contestation.

The sense of a beyond is far from escaping those who designate poetry as a "land of treasures."[58] In the *Second Surrealist Manifesto*, Breton wrote: "It is clear that Surrealism is not interested in giving very serious consideration to anything that happens outside of itself, under the guise of art, or even anti-art, of philosophy or anti-philosophy—in short, of anything not aimed at the annihilation of the being into a diamond, all blind and interior, which is no more the soul of ice than that of fire."[59] The "annihilation" had from the first words a "beautiful" allure, and there was no point in speaking of it, without contesting the means brought to this end.

If I wanted to speak at length about Marcel Proust, it is because he had a perhaps limited inner experience (how engaging, nevertheless, with so much frivolity, so much happy nonchalance mixed in), but free from dogmatic obstacles. I will add friendship, for his way of forgetting, of suffering, a feeling of sovereign complicity. And again this: the poetic movement of his work, whatever its weakness, takes the road by which poetry touches the "extremity" (which one will see further on).

Among diverse sacrifices, poetry is the only one whose fire we can maintain, renew. But its misery is even more tangible than that of other sacrifices (if we envision the part left to *personal* possession, to ambition). What is essential is that on its own, the desire for poetry renders our misery intolerable: certain of the inability of the sacrifice of objects to truly liberate us, we often experience the necessity of going further, up to the sacrifice of the subject. This cannot have consequences, but if he succumbs, the subject lifts the weight of avidity; his life escapes avarice. The one who sacrifices, the poet, having unceasingly to bring ruin into the ungraspable world of words, quickly tires of enriching a literary treasure. He is condemned to it: if he lost the taste for treasure, he would cease to be a poet. But he cannot fail to see the abuse, the exploitation made of personal genius (of glory). With a parcel of genius available to him, a man comes to believe that it is "his," like a farmer does a parcel of land.[60] But just as our more timid ancestors felt before the harvest, the herds—which they had to exploit in order to live—that there was in those harvests, those herds an element (that each recognized in a man or in a child), that one cannot "use" without qualm, so others, at first were reluctant to "use" poetic genius. And when that reluctance is felt, everything darkens, the evil must be vomited out, it must be "expiated."

If one could, what one would want, without any doubt, would be to suppress the evil. But the desire to suppress only had as an effect (genius remains obstinately personal) the expression of desire. Witness these phrases, whose intimate resonance takes place of an external efficacy that they don't have: "All men," Blake said, "are alike in the Poetic Genius."[61] And Lautréamont: "Poetry must be made by all. Not by one."[62] I would like one to try, honestly, as one can, to give these intentions some consequences: is poetry any less the act of those who are visited by genius?

The poetic genius is not a verbal gift (the verbal gift is necessary, since it is a question of words, but it often leads astray): it is the divination of ruins secretly anticipated, so that so many set things become undone, lose themselves, communicate. Nothing is rarer. This instinct that divines and acts certainly even demands, of one who is in possession of it, silence, solitude: and the more it inspires, all the more cruelly it isolates. But as it is instinct of required acts of destruction, if the exploitation that the most impoverished make of their genius demands to be "expiated," an obscure feeling suddenly guides the most inspired toward death. Another, unknowingly, not being able to die, short of destroying himself entirely, destroys at least poetry within him.[63]

(What one doesn't grasp: that, literature being nothing if it is not poetry, poetry being the opposite of its name, literary language—the expression of hidden desires, of obscure life—is the perversion of language a little more even than eroticism is the perversion of sexual functions. Hence the "terror" raging in the end "in letters," like the search for vices, new excitements, at the end of a debauched person's life.)

The idea—which deceives some, permitting them to deceive others—of a unanimous regained existence that would animate the inner seduction of poetry, surprises me so much that:

No one more than Hegel gave more importance to the separation of men among themselves. He was the only one to give this fatal laceration its place—every place—in the realm of philosophical speculation. But it is not romantic poetry, it is "obligatory military service" that seemed to him to guarantee the return to this common life, without which there was, according to him, no knowledge possible (he saw in it the sign of the times, the proof that history was completing itself).

I have often seen Hegel cited—as if by chance—often by those haunted by the fate of a poetic "Golden Age," but one neglects this fact, that Hegel's thoughts are in solidarity, to the point that one cannot grasp their meaning, if not in the necessity of the movement that is their coherence.

And this cruel image of a "Golden Age"—dissimulated beneath the appearance of an "Iron Age"—I have several reasons at least to propose it for the meditation of changeable minds. Why continue to fool ourselves? Driven by a blind instinct, the poet feels that he is slowly distancing himself from others. The more he enters into the secrets *that are those of others as much as his own* and the more he separates himself, the more he is alone. His solitude in the depth of himself begins the world again, but it does not begin it again only for himself alone. The poet, carried too far, triumphs over his anguish, but not that of others. He cannot be turned away from the destiny that absorbs him, far from which he would perish. He must always go a little farther on, this is his only country. No one can cure him of not being the crowd.

To be known![64] How could he not be aware that he is himself the *unknown*, under the mask of one man among others.

The death of the author by his work: "Happiness alone is salutary to the body, but unhappiness develops the forces of the mind. But unhappiness, even if it did not on every occasion reveal to us some new law, would nevertheless be indispensible, since through its means alone we are brought back time after time to a perception of truth and forced to take things seriously, tearing up each new crop of the weeds of habit and skepticism and levity and indifference. Yet it is true that truth, which is not compatible with happiness or with physical health, is not always compatible even with life. Unhappiness ends by killing. At every new torment that is too hard to bear we feel yet another vein protrude, to unroll its sinuous and deadly length along our temples or beneath our eyes. And thus gradually are formed those terrible ravaged faces, of the old Rembrandt, the old Beethoven, at whom the whole world mocked. And the pockets under the eyes and the wrinkled forehead would not matter much were there not also the suffering of the heart. But since strength of one kind can change into strength of another kind, since heat that is stored up can become light and the electricity in a flash of lightning can cause a photograph to be taken, since the dull pain in our heart can hoist above itself like a banner the visible permanence of an image that is done to us for the sake of the spiritual knowledge that grief brings; let us submit to the disintegration of our body, since each new fragment that breaks away from it returns in a luminous and significant form to add itself to our work, to complete it at the price of sufferings of which others more richly endowed have no need, to make our work at least more solid as our life crumbles away beneath the corrosive action of our emotions."[65] The gods to whom we sacrifice are themselves sacrificed, tears wept to the point of dying. This *In Search of Lost Time* that the author would not have written, if, shattered by pain, he had not ceded to these pains, saying: "Let us allow our bodies to disintegrate . . ." What is this if not the river, flowing in advance toward the estuary, which is the sentence itself: "Let us . . ."? And the sea that opens the estuary is death. So much so that the work was not only what led the author to the tomb but the way in which he died; it was written on his deathbed . . . The author himself wanted us to imagine him dying a little more with each line. And it is himself that he depicts while speaking of those, the invited: "who were not at the party because they were too weak or too ill to be there, those whom their secretary, seeking to give the illusion of their survival, had excused by one of those telegrams that from time to time were handed to the Princess."[66] One must only substitute a manuscript for the Rosary of "those invalids, moribund for years, who no longer leave their beds, no longer move, and even in the midst of the frivolous attentions of visitors, drawn to them by the curiosity of the tourist or the pious hopes of a pilgrim, with their eyes closed and their rosaries clutched in hands that feebly push back the sheet that is already a mortuary shroud, are like monumental figures, carved by illness until the skeleton is barely covered by a flesh that is white and rigid as marble, lying stretched upon a tomb."[67]

ON A SACRIFICE IN WHICH EVERYTHING IS VICTIM
(CONTINUATION AND CONCLUSION)

"Have you not heard of that madman who lit a lantern in the bright morning hours, ran to the marketplace, and cried incessantly: 'I seek God! I seek God!'—As many of those who did not believe in God were standing around just then, he provoked much laughter. Has he got lost? asked one. Did he lose his way like a child? asked another. [. . .] Thus they yelled and laughed.

"The madman jumped into their midst and pierced them with his eyes: 'Whither is God?' he cried; 'I will tell you. We have killed him—you and I! All of us are his murderers. But how did we do this? How could we drink up the sea? Who gave us the sponge to wipe away the entire horizon? What were we doing when we unchained this earth from its sun? Whither is it moving now? Whither are we moving? Away from all suns? Are we not plunging continually? Backward, sideward, forward, in all directions? Is there still any up or down? Are we not straying as through an infinite nothing? Do we not feel the breath of empty space? Has it not become colder? Is not night continually closing in on us? Do we not need to light lanterns in the morning? Do we hear nothing as yet of the noise of the gravediggers who are burying God? Do we smell nothing as yet of the divine decomposition?

"Gods, too, decompose. God is dead. God remains dead. And we have killed him. How shall we comfort ourselves, the murderers of all murderers? What was holiest and mightiest of all that the world has yet owned has bled to death under our knives: who will wipe this blood off us? What water is there for us to clean ourselves? What festivals of atonement, what sacred games shall we have to invent? Is not the greatness of this deed too great for us? Must we ourselves not become gods simply to appear worthy of it?

"THERE HAS NEVER BEEN A GREATER DEED; AND WHOEVER IS BORN AFTER US—FOR THE SAKE OF THIS DEED HE WILL BELONG TO A HIGHER HISTORY THAN ALL HISTORY HITHERTO."
(The Gay Science[68])

This sacrifice *that we consummate*[69] is distinguished from others in this way: the one who sacrifices is himself touched by the blow that he strikes, he succumbs and is lost with his victim. Once again: the atheist is satisfied with a world complete without God, this practitioner of sacrifice is, on the contrary, in anguish before an unfinished, unfinishable world, forever unintelligible, which destroys him, tears him apart (and this world destroys itself, tears itself apart).

Another thing that stops me: this world that destroys itself, tears itself apart . . . does not usually do this with a crash, but in a movement that escapes one who speaks. The difference between this world and the orator derives from the absence of will. The world is profoundly mad, without design. At first the madman is histrionic. It happens that one of us inclines toward madness, feels ourselves become everything. Like a peasant who, stumbling over a little raised piece of earth infers the presence of the mole, in no way thinking of the little blind being but of the means of destroying it, so, from a few signs, the friends of the unhappy being infer his "megalomania," asking themselves to which doctor they will entrust the sick man. I prefer to stick to the "little blind being," who plays the major role in the drama, that of the agent of sacrifice. It's madness, the megalomania of the man who throws himself on the throat of God. And what God himself does with an absent simplicity (in which only the madman grasps that he has the time to weep), this madman does with cries of impotence. And these cries, this unleashed madness in the end, what are they if not the blood of a sacrifice in which, as in the old tragedies, the whole stage, when the curtain falls, is strewn with the dead?

It is when I collapse that I leap. At this moment: everything up to the plausibility of the world dissipates. It was necessary, in the end, to see everything with lifeless eyes, to become God, otherwise we would not know what it is to sink, to no longer know anything. For a long time Nietzsche held himself on the incline. When it was time for him to yield, when he understood that the preparations for the sacrifice were finished, he could only say gaily: I am, myself, Dionysus, etc.[70]

Curiosity arises here: Did Nietzsche have a fleeting understanding of "sacrifice"? A sanctimonious understanding? An understanding of sacrifice as such? Or another still?

Everything takes place in divine confusion! Only blind will, "innocence," save us from "projects," errors, where the eye, eager for discernment,
drives us.

Having the vision that one knows of the eternal return, the intensity
of Nietzsche's feelings made him at once laugh and tremble.[71] He wept too
much: these were tears of jubilation. Walking the woods, along the lake
of Silvaplana, he had stopped "at a powerful pyramidal rock not far from
Surlei."[72] I imagine myself arriving at the shore of the lake and, imagining
it, I weep. Not that I have found in the idea of the eternal return anything
that can move me in my turn. What is most evident about a discovery that
was to make the ground give way under our feet—in Nietzsche's eyes a
kind of man transfigured alone would know how to overcome the horror of
it—is that it leaves the best will indifferent. Only the object of his vision,
what caused him to laugh and tremble, was not the return (and not even
time), but what the return laid bare, the impossible depth of things. And
this depth, should one reach it by one path or another, is always the same
since it is night and since, perceiving it, nothing remains but to swoon (to
become agitated to the point of fever, to lose oneself in ecstasy, to weep).

I remain indifferent attempting to apprehend the intellectual contents
of the vision, and through that content how Nietzsche was torn apart, in
place of perceiving a representation of the time that questioned life right
up to its lack of sense, that he ended up through this vision by losing his
bearings and saw in this way what one only sees in a swoon (what he had
seen the first time the day that he understood that God was dead, that he
had killed God himself). I can inscribe time at will in a circular hypothesis,
but nothing has changed: each hypothesis on the subject of time is exhausting, acts as a means of access to the unknown. What is least surprising is
that, in a movement toward ecstasy, I have the illusion of knowing and
possessing, as does a work of science (I wrap the unknown in some kind
of known, as I can).

Laughter in tears. The putting to death of God is a sacrifice that,
making me tremble, lets me laugh nevertheless, for in it, I succumb no
less than the victim (whereas the sacrifice of Man saved). In fact, what succumbs with God, with me, is the bad conscience that those who sacrificed
had in turning away from sacrifice[73] (the confusion of the soul in flight,
but stubborn, assured of eternal salvation, crying out that it is not worthy
of this, obviously).

This sacrifice of reason is apparently imaginary; it has neither a bloody conclusion nor anything analogous. It differs nonetheless from poetry in that it is total, does not reserve any pleasure, if not by arbitrarily slipping, which one cannot maintain, or by abandoned laughter. If it by chance leaves a survivor, it has forgotten itself, like a wildflower after a harvest.

This strange sacrifice assuming a final state of megalomania—we feel ourselves become God—nevertheless has ordinary consequences in one case: should the pleasure be avoided through slipping and should the megalomania be entirely consumed, we remain condemned to making ourselves "recognized," to want to be a God for the crowd; a condition favorable to madness, but to nothing else. In any case, the final consequence is solitude; madness can only make it greater, through its lack of awareness.

If someone is satisfied by poetry, has no nostalgia to go further, he is free to imagine that one day everyone will know of his royalty and, having recognized themselves in him, commingled themselves with him (a little naiveté abandons one without return to this easy charm: to taste the possession of the future). But he can, if he wishes, go further. The world, the shadow of God, which the poet himself is, can suddenly seem to him to be marked by ruin. So much so that the unknown, the impossible that they are in the end, become visible. But then he will feel so alone that solitude will be like another death to him.[74]

If one goes right to the end, one must efface oneself, suffer solitude, suffering harshly from it, renouncing being *recognized*: be therein as though absent, insane, suffer without will and without hope, be elsewhere. One must bury thought alive (because of what it has in its depths). I publish this knowing it in advance to be misunderstood, before it is. Its agitation must end, so that is can remain hidden, or almost, an old woman in a corner, without honor. I and she with me can only sink to this point in nonsense. Thought ruins and its destruction is incommunicable to the crowd, it addresses itself to the least weak.

What is hidden in laughter must remain hidden.[75] If our knowledge goes further and if we know what is hidden there, the unknown that destroys knowledge, this new knowledge that blinds us, must be left in the shadows (where we are), such that others remain blind naively.

The extreme movement of thought must offer itself for what it is: foreign to action. Action has its laws, to which practical thought responds.

Extended to the beyond in search of a distant possible, autonomous thought can only reserve the realm of action.[76] If action is "abuse," nonutilitarian thought sacrifice, the "abuse" must take place, has every right. Inserted in a cycle of practical goals, a sacrifice has as a goal, far from condemning abuse, making abuse possible (the greedy use of the harvest is possible once the prodigality of the first fruits has ended). But as autonomous thought refuses to judge the realm of action, in exchange, practical thought cannot oppose the rules which are valid for it in the prolongation of life into the distant limits of the possible.

Consequence of solitude. "Around every profound spirit a mask is growing continually, owing to the constantly false, namely *shallow*, interpretation of every word, every step, every sign of life he gives."

(*Beyond Good and Evil* § 40[77])

Remark on tonic side of solitude. ". . . They take suffering itself for something that must be *abolished*. We opposite men, having opened our eyes and conscience to the question where and how the plant 'man' has so far grown most vigorously to a height—we think that this has happened every time under the opposite conditions, that to this end the dangerousness of his situation must first grow to the point of enormity, his power of invention and simulation (his 'spirit') had to develop under prolonged pressure and constraint into refinement and audacity, his life-will had to be enhanced into an unconditional power-will. We think that hardness, forcefulness, slavery, danger in the alley and the heart, life in hiding, stoicism, the art of experiment and devilry of every kind, that everything evil, terrible, tyrannical in man, everything in him that is kin to beasts of prey and serpents serves the enhancement of the species 'man' as much as its opposite."

(*Beyond Good and Evil* § 44[78])

Is there a solitude more suffocating, more soundless, further beneath the earth? In the dark unknown, breath fails. The lees of possible agonies are sacrifice.

If I have known how to create the silence of others within myself, *I am*, myself, Dionysus, *I am* the crucified. But if I forget my solitude . . .

Extreme flash: I am blind, extreme night: I remain so. From one to the other, always there, the objects that I see, a slipper, a bed.

Final and pure joke of fever. In the cloudy silence of the heart and the melancholy of a gray day, in this expansive desert of oblivion that only presents to my fatigue a sick bed, soon a deathbed, this hand that I in a sign of a distress have let drop by my side, hanging with the sheets, a ray of sunlight that slips toward me gently asks me to take it up again, to raise it before my eyes. And as if there were awakened in me, dazed, mad, emerging suddenly from a long fog in which they believed themselves dead, lives like a crowd, jostling one another at the miraculous moment of a festival, my hand holds a flower and carries it to my lips.[79]

Part Five

Manibus Date Lilia Plenis[1]

Gloria in Excelsis Mihi[2]

At the height of the heavens
the angels, I hear their voices, glorify me.
I am, under the sun, an errant ant,
small and black, a rolling stone
reaches me,
crushes me,
dead,
in the sky
the sun rages
it blinds,
I cry out:
"it will not dare"
it dares.

Who am I
not "me" no no
but the desert the night the immensity
that I am
what are
desert immensity night beast
quick nothingness without return
and without having known anything
Death
answer
sponge streaming with solar
dreams
sink into me
that I no longer know anything
but these tears.

Star
I am the star
o death
thunderous star
mad bell of my death

Poems
not courageous
but gentleness
ear of delight
a lamb's voice howls
beyond goes beyond
torch   extinguished.

God

With eager hands
I die you die
where is he
where am I
without laughter
I am dead
dead and dead
in the ink night
arrow shot
at   him.

Method of Meditation

If man does not sovereignly *close his eyes, he will end by no longer seeing what it worth being looked at.*

—René Char[1]

Foreword

My ambition—in the following pages—is the most remote ever known.

However worthy of interest a political task might be—or anything else equal to bold ideas—(when on this topic, I think, I evaluate or judge, imbued with a feeling of my limits: the humility of a comical character, indifference to oneself, a happy negation of what is not a rapid movement liberates me from hesitation): I perceive nothing that a man proposes to himself that is not reduced by some failing, a subordinate operation (which differs in some point from that which delays me, which would be a *sovereign operation*).

I imagine I would weaken the affirmation of my intention explaining myself further. I would voluntarily limit this foreword to these first words, but I think the moment has come to dissipate, if possible, the misunderstandings created by the disorder of my books—which touch the subjects broached further on.[2]

I

I Situate My Efforts As A Continuation Of But Alongside Surrealist

A daring, provocative demand manifested itself under the name Surrealism. It was confused, it's true, often loosing the prey for the shadow. The present confusion, the general settling (what today formulates the least demand?) sometimes appears preferable to me. I nevertheless think that, the Surrealism ambition persisting, I cannot say exactly what I just said. And, in any case, I am surprised by what is now discovered: with a few rare exceptions, I see around me neither intellectual conscience nor temerity nor desire nor force. Still, I can only speak with exasperation.*

---

*I cannot avoid expressing my thought in a philosophical mode. But I am not addressing philosophers. Besides, what I have to say is hardly difficult to grasp. Even leaving aside the obscure passages, because of the intensity of the feelings, would entail fewer misunderstandings than reading a professor.

II

My Method Is At The Antipodes Of "Yoga"

In principle, a method of meditation would have to respond to the teachings of *yoga* (Hindu exercises in concentration).

It would be pleasant if some manual existed, stripping the *yogi's* practices of the moral and metaphysical beliefs. The methods, what's more, could be simplified.

Calm deep breathing, prolonged but as in sleep, in the manner of an incantatory dance, the slow ironic concentration of thoughts toward the void, the able conjuring of the mind on meditational themes, where the sky, the earth, the subject successively collapse, could be the object of teaching. A bare description of this discipline would help lead to the "ecstasy of the *yogis.*"

The interest at stake is appreciable, in that there is no shorter means of escaping the "sphere of activity" (or, if you like, the real world).

But this is precisely why it is the best *means*, on the subject of *yoga*, the question is posed narrowly: if *recourse to means* defines the sphere of activity, how can this be ruined, when from the first one speaks of *means?* *Yoga* is nothing if not this ruin.

III

My Reflections Are Founded On A "Privileged" Experience; Nevertheless, "To Go The Furthest Possible" Only Has Meaning Once The Primacy Of The "Continuum" Has Been Recognized

By *continuum*, I understand a continuous milieu that is the human ensemble, opposing itself to a rudimentary representation of indivisible and decidedly separated *individuals.**

Among the criticisms made of *Inner Experience*, one that gives "torture" an exclusively individual meaning reveals the limit, in relation to

---

*The separation of beings, the abyss separating *you* from *me*, habitually has the first sense. In our sphere of life, however, the difference between one and another is only a deepening of precarious possibilities. If it is true that in one case, at a given time, the passage from *you* to *me* had a continuous character, the apparent discontinuity of beings is no longer a fundamental quality.

This is the case of twins from the same egg. Mark Twain used to say that if one of the twins drowned we'd never know which one.[3] The egg, which I was, the *continuum*, of the *individuals* who make the criticism. There is a point in the *continuum* wherein the experience of "torture" is inevitable, not only cannot be denied, but this point, situated at the extremity, defines human being (the *continuum*).

IV

I Separate Myself In No Way From Man In General And Take Upon Myself The Totality Of What Is

To me, the exclusion commonly made of the worst (folly, vice, indolence . . .) seems to translate servility. The *servile* intelligence is in the service of folly, but folly is *sovereign*: I can change nothing with it.

V

The Essential Is Inavowable

What is not servile is inavowable: a reason for laughing, for . . . : it's the same with ecstasy. What is not useful must be hidden (beneath a mask). Addressing himself to the crowd, a dying criminal was the first to formulate this *commandment*: "Never confess."

VI

The Apparent Relaxation Of Rigor Can Only Express A Greater Rigor, To Which It Must Respond In The First Place

This principle must still be inverted.

The apparent rigor affirmed here and there is only the effect of a profound relaxation, of the abandonment of something essential that is in any case, the SOVEREIGNTY OF BEING.

---

could divide itself in two individuals different one from the other in that the one saying "me" would have in this way radically excluded the other, but I don't know *how* each of them differed from this me who is neither one nor the other. In fact, this difference that we deepen like a wound is only a lost *continuum*.

Part One

Contestation

The idea of silence (the inaccessible) is disarming!

I cannot speak of an absence of meaning without giving it a meaning that it does not have.

The silence was broken, since I said . . .

Always some *lama sabachthani* ends the story, and cries out our inability to keep ourselves silent: I must give meaning to that which lacks meaning: in the end, being is given to us as impossible!

This immense folly, arrogant childishness, the crude futility of laughter, and the entirety of an ignorance frozen in servile rages returns me from every side to the same response: *impossible!* The being that is there, man, is the *impossible* incarnated in every sense. He is the inadmissible and only admits, only tolerates what he is that renders his essence more profound: inadmissible, intolerable! Lost in a maze of aberrations, of deafness, of horrors, eager for tortures (eyes, fingernails torn out) ruined without end in the satisfied contemplation of an absence.[4]

That one dares to hope for a way out, amending this, cursing that, denouncing, condemning, decapitating or excommunicating, depriving (it seems) of value (of meaning) what others . . . engages a new platitude, a new ferocity, a new hypocritical bewilderment.

But how (I am addressing all men) could I renounce your folly? When I know that, without it, I would not exist! What would I be—what the rocks or wind are—if I was not an accomplice to your errors?

I am a cry of joy!
There is no error, no horror that does not raise my flames.

Think the way a girl lifts her dress.
At the extremity of its movement, thought is shameless, obscenity even.

Under no circumstances is an excessive conflagration contrary to the murderer, the usurer, the teacher. It forsakes neither the lost girl nor the "man of the world."
It completes the movement of foolishness, of insipid jest, of cowardice.

MEDITATION I

I demand an audience with an important person.
With a kick in the behind, the minister leaves me in a huff.
I enter into an ecstasy in the waiting room: the kick enraptures me, binds me, penetrates me; it opens itself in me like a rose.

*

MEDITATION II

I find a glistening worm between two graves.
I put it, in the night, in my hand.
The worm looks at me from there, penetrates me to the point of shame.
And we lose ourselves, one another, in its gleam: we commingle, one another, with the light.
The wonderstruck worm laughs at me and at the dead and I marvel equally, laughing at being divined by the worm and by the dead.

*

MEDITATION III

The sun comes into my room.
It has a thin neck of flowers. Its head resembles the skull of a bird.
It grasps my coat button.
Strangely I take hold of a button on my pants.
And we look at one another like children:

> *"I take you*
> *you take me*
> *by the beard.*
> *First . . ."*

*

Every problem is in a certain sense one of the *use of time*.
It implies the preliminary question:

—What do I have to do (what should I do or what is in my interest to do or what do I want to do) here (in this world where I have my human and personal nature) and now?

Writing, I wanted to touch the depth of these problems. And having given myself this occupation, *I fell asleep.*

My response expressed the day's fatigue. But it is also the faithful image of my view of the world. This also profoundly expresses the nature of the being in the operation of knowledge: the being cannot be so indifferent that an inclination counters the desire to know.

Philosophy, if it is being striving to reach its limits, must first resolve an initial problem in the person of the philosopher: is this occupation (this striving to reach one's limits) urgent? For me? For man in general?

The fact that it is not for a great number of people is usually attributed to the *primum vivere* (that is "eating"), on the one hand; on the other hand, to some insufficiency on the part of those who effectively have the time for philosophy (lack of intelligence, weak character).

If philosophy is only one science among others, only with a different domain, the urgency is to consider it as a *subordinate* task, where the calculation of inconveniences and of advantages is related to judgments foreign to the problem at stake. But if it is knowledge with no other end than itself, the calculations related to other ends deprive the operation of its exceptional character (emasculating it, aligning it with minor activities, voluntarily restricted from knowledge). From here the professorial tradition of philosophy and this accumulation of material that in no way resembles the sovereign operation. And not only do these kinds of work not lead to the sovereign operation, they turn away from it (blindly, prevent one from knowing its urgency).

The critique Hegel addressed to Schelling (in the preface to the *Phenomenology*[5]) is no less annoying. The preliminary work of the operation isn't within the capacities of an unprepared intelligence (as Hegel says: likewise it would be senseless, if one were not a cobbler, to make a shoe[6]). These labors, by the mode of application that belongs to them, nevertheless inhibit the sovereign operation (the being going the furthest that it can). Specifically, the sovereign character demands the refusal to submit the operation to preliminary conditions. The operation only takes place if the urgency appears: if it appears, it is no longer time to begin works whose essence is to be subordinated to ends exterior to oneself, which are not ends in themselves.

Scientific work is more than servile; it's crippled. The needs to which it responds are foreign to knowledge. These are:
1. The curiosity of people who do crossword puzzles: a discovery fails to provoke interest, the search for truth the way it is practiced assumes a "pleasure of not knowing" (Claude Bernard): it is the foundation of scientific truths that they only have appreciable value when *new*: we measure the *novelty* of old discoveries after centuries;
2. The needs of a collector (to amass and organize curiosities);
3. Love of work, intense output;
4. The taste for a rigorous honesty;
5. The worries of the academic (career, honor, money).
Often, at its origin, a desire for sovereign knowledge, to go as far as one can go: this desire so quickly born, nullifies itself, by accepting subordinate tasks. The disinterested character—independent of application—and the persistent use of empty words make the change. Science is done by men in whom the desire to know is dead.

For the moment I am not trying to define the *sovereign operation*. It is possible that I have spoken of it without even knowing it. And if necessary I would admit that speaking of it as I did would be childish (indicating an impotence to measure the effort as possible). It nevertheless remains for me, having imagined it, to reveal to myself the lure of operations that subordinate themselves.

Now I must start over:
Servility ordinarily specifies its limits: to contribute to the advancement of the mathematical sciences, or others . . . From limit to limit, one comes to pose, at the summit, some sovereign operation. And I add: the way that leads toward it is not a subordinate operation. It is necessary to choose: one cannot at once subordinate oneself to some ulterior result and "be sovereignly." (Because "to be sovereignly" signifies "not being able to wait.") I cannot however go without subordinate operations, which an authentic sovereignty demands *have been* as complete as possible. At the summit of intelligence is an impasse where the "immediate sovereignty of being" seems decidedly to alienate itself: a region of supreme folly, of sleep.

Beyond a certain point, the feeling of foolishness is inescapable. Intelligence offers me the certainty of being stupid (a calm certainty). The idea of it is breathtaking. It suffices nevertheless to be indifferent: begin a friendship with odious chattering, silences, terrors, whims. Unimagined friendship. Nothing seems more foolish to me than the sovereign contempt for others to which my position condemns me. This feeling in me, losing myself in a void, opens illumination to a lightness "without form and without mode." I would voluntarily define ecstasy: feeling gay but anguished—from my measureless stupidity.[7]

*

I can no longer sustain this poignant emotion, this light as if airy intoxication, linked to excessive tensions.

My feelings already enclose me like a tomb and nevertheless, above me, I imagine a song similar to the modulation of the light, from cloud to cloud, the afternoon, in the unbearable expanse of the skies . . .

How can one endlessly avoid the intimate horror of being? . . . This heart cries out a thousand tender joys, how can I not open it to the void?

My joy infinitely extends an ungraspable game. But, I know, night is coming. Black tapestries fall on all sides.

Long, sad death, the smothered silence of a tomb, under grass alive with worms, supports this feeling of airy lightness, of gaiety lost to the height of the stars.

And nothing . . .

*

I WALK WITH THE HELP OF FEET, I PHILOSOPHIZE WITH THE HELP OF FOOLS. EVEN WITH THE HELP OF PHILOSOPHERS.[8]

I incarnated the ungraspable.

If I lead being to the extremity of reflection and to the misunderstanding that it has of itself, like the infinite starry expanse of the night, I FALL ASLEEP.

And the IMPOSSIBLE is there. (I am IT).

How could I fail to recognize philosophers from every era whose endless cries (impotence) say to me: YOU ARE THE IMPOSSIBLE?

How could I, what's more, fail to adore these voices reverberating in the infinite silent expanses the misunderstanding that men have of themselves and their world?

Sleep of reason! . . . and, as Goya said: THE SLEEP OF REASON BREEDS MONSTERS.
The essential is the aberration. The comical the most grand . . .

What is the worst aberration?
The one we know nothing about, gravely taking it for wisdom?
The one from which, when we see it, we know there is no way out?[9]

*

From extreme knowledge to vulgar understanding—divided most generally—the difference is nonexistent. The understanding of the world, in Hegel, is the first to come (the *first to come*, not Hegel, decides for Hegel the key question: touching on the difference between madness and reason: "absolute knowledge," on this point, confirming the vulgar notion, is founded on it, is one of its forms). Vulgar understanding is in us like another *tissue*! The human being consists not only of visible tissues (bones, musculature, skin); a tissue of understanding, more or less extensive, appreciably the same in each of us, is found equally in adults.

Labors preparatory to philosophy are critical (negative) or growths of tissue.

In a sense, the condition in which *I would see* would be on exiting, emerging, from the "tissue."

And undoubtedly I must immediately say: the condition in which I *would see* would be dying.

At no moment will I have the possibility of *seeing*!

Among the philosophers who are opposed to me, who are only so many ways of weaving the fabric of the tissue, stupidity is the only contribution that agrees with me. Rigorous stupidity (linking them to this series of ruptures, from which we laugh ceaselessly, which undoes the mirage in which activity encloses us) is a window, through which *I would see*, if it was, from the start, the sleep (a death) of intelligence (of the apparatus of vision).

The sphere of known elements wherein our activity inscribes itself is only its product.

A car, a man entering a village: I *see* neither one nor the other, but the tissue woven by an activity of which I began. There where I imagine *seeing* "what is," I *see* the *links subordinating* what is there to the activity. I do not see: I am in a tissue of understanding, reducing to itself, to its servitude, the freedom (the sovereignty and the primary nonsubordination) of what is.

This world of objects that transcend me (in the emptiness within me) encloses me in its sphere of transcendence, encloses me in some way in my exteriority, weaving a thread of *exteriority* within me. In this way, my own activity annihilates me, introduces within me a void *to which I am subordinated.* I nevertheless survive this alteration by binding ties of immanence (returning me to indefinite immanence, which admits superiority nowhere):

1. *Erotic.* I succeed in seeing a woman, I draw her out, strip her from the sphere of objects linked to activity—the *obscoena* are immanence itself, we are generally absorbed, integrated in the sphere of objects, but with the genitals, we still hold onto an undefined immanence (as if with an indestructible, hideous, hidden root); (otherwise the genitals, the erotic links, it's true, are perishable: no matter to whom we bind them, shared activity tends to substitute those objects that subordinate us for them . . .).

2. *Comical.* We are carried in the stream of hilarity: laughter is the effect of a rupture in the chain of transcendent bonds; these comical bonds with our fellows, ceaselessly broken and ceaselessly retied, are most fragile, the least heavy.

3. *Bonds of kinship.* We are connected to our parents at birth, and we bind ourselves thereafter to children.

4. *Sacred bonds.* We unite ourselves with the fundamental immanence of an ensemble of which we are a part; beyond that, as in each immanent relation, to undefined immanence (the limitation of a group defines a hybrid character of the ensemble that the immanent bonds unite); in the manner of finite objects, these ensembles have the possibility of transcendence (the community transcends its members, God the soul of the faithful, thereby introducing new voids within the domain of activity); they substitute themselves for pure activity, they subordinate themselves to the chain of objects, propose themselves as an end, but conceived in the transcendent mode of the objective world of activity, in the long run, no longer differing from this world, they are its sumptuous doubles.

5. *Romantic.* Touching on the love of nature (of wild, hostile nature, foreign to man); the exaltation of the eroticism from the heart, the cult of poetry, of poetic laceration; valuing fiction to the detriment of the *order of things*, of the official and real world.

*

The domination of activity is accomplished more than corrupted by the domination of the State, this "empty block," introducing into the inert consciousness a dominant part of stark elements (transcendent, of another nature, colorless).

In myself, the State opens a dominant and sad void that, truly, gives me a polluted disposition.

Activity dominates us (it is the same with the State), making acceptable—possible—what would be *impossible* without it (if no one worked, if we had neither police nor laws . . .). The domination of activity is that of the *possible*, that of a sad void, a decay in the sphere of objects.

To subordinate ourselves to the POSSIBLE, is to let ourselves banish stars, winds, volcanoes from the sovereign world.

God subordinates himself to the POSSIBLE, diverts chance, abandons the choice to exceed limits. The star exceeds divine intelligence. The tiger has the silent and lost grandeur that God lacks. Man is genuflection . . .

Fear extends the shadow of God over the world like a school uniform over a perverse adolescent girl's nudity.

Whatever fever carries it, the love of God announces: (1) an aspiration to the state of an object (to transcendence, to definitive immutability); (2) the idea of a superiority to such a state. The order of things come from God, not arbitrarily, essentially, is SUBMITTED to the principle of the POSSIBLE: the IMPOSSIBLE is no longer my disadvantage, it is my crime.

One says of the content of the word God that it exceeds the limits of thought—but no! It admits into a point, a definition, limits. The narrow aspect is even more striking: God condemns the shame of a child (if the guardian angel sees him in the wardrobe), he condemns the limitless right to foolishness and discordant infinite laughter: which, being neither God nor matter, neither the identity of God and matter—being unbearable, is nevertheless there, impossible—screaming! Impossible—wanting to die!

*

We alleviate the empty character of the transcendent world through sacrifice. Through the destruction of a vitally important object (but one whose the alteration, resulting from a utilitarian use, was painfully felt), we shatter in one point the limit of the *possible: the impossible* was, in this point, liberated by a crime, stripped bare, unveiled.

Earlier I said: ". . . my own activity annihilates me, introduces within me a void *to which I am subordinated.* I nevertheless survive this alteration by binding ties of immanence: 1. *Erotic* . . . 2. *Comical* . . . 3. *Bonds of kinship* . . . 4. *Sacred bonds* . . . 5. *Romantic* . . ." I have not shown anything except that, in order to form these bonds, it is necessary that "we shatter in one point the limit of the *possible.*" A bond of immanence demands a laceration preliminary to the transcendent realm of the activity: such as stripping bare, childbirth, putting to death . . . (On the level of the comic, a joke reveals the impossible at the heart of the possible. The romantic movement raises laceration, in principle, not without vain ostentation.)

*

At the limit of silence, to speak in the heavy dissolution of thought, to slip lightly into sleep—without sadness, without irony, without surprise—already, softly responds to the demand of the night, brings not absence but the disorder of these processes.

Often enough, leisure has permitted me to order my thought, in obedience to the rules. But today I express this movement: "Sleep invades me . . ." It's more difficult! In other words, I touch on the sovereign operation, where thought does not accept any subordinated object and loses itself in a sovereign object, annihilates in itself the demand of thought.

If my book means: you, the most intelligent man, this new Hegel . . . (or some other), are nonetheless the most stupid, narrow, and nailed to the "possible" by inertia . . . (how can it be concealed that, generally, existence seems underwater to me, subsumed by foolishness—in error—which is its condition; the condition of consciousness, at the limit of the laughter that denounces it . . .): I don't mean that I . . . "You are more intelligent, but I anesthetize my intelligence to relieve myself of yours for a moment."

Reassured: "man aspires to stupidity . . . more than to philosophy (a baby leaves us enraptured)."

*

I am not really concerned about myself: I would love to count on others (the distribution of being in numerous individuals hardly matters).

But I have not known of an interrogation more tiring than mine.

I perceive from all sides, as a fruit of labor, a naive feeling of power linked to the great capacities of man exerting his intelligence!

With a puerile carelessness, we lend *possibility* (possible character) to existence, which everything in the end contradicts: it is the result, the postulate of labor. When I laugh or when I have an orgasm the *impossible* is before me. I am happy but each thing is *impossible*.[10]

The simple truth:
Servile activity is *possible* (on the condition of remaining enslaved, subordinate—to other men, to principles, or even to the necessity of production—human existence has a *possible* before it);
But a sovereign existence is in no way, even for an instant, separated from the *impossible*; I will live *sovereignly* only at the *height of the impossible* and what does this book mean if not:

LEAVE THE POSSIBLE TO THOSE WHO LOVE IT.

Despite everything, my life was also an immense labor: in paying this price, I got to know, sufficient to my taste, a part of what is *possible* for man (which today permits me to say: "*possible*, yes, I bowed my head!"). Nevertheless, what gives me the power to write is having loved, sometimes, *doing nothing* even more.

I see hardly anything in laziness (rather, I have, I think, an excess of vitality). At thirteen (?), however, I asked a fellow student who was the laziest in the class: it was me; but in the whole school, me again. At that time, I made my life difficult, *by failing to write under dictation*. The teacher's first words docilely took form under my pen. I remember my childhood notebook: I quickly limited myself to doodling (I had to seem like I was writing). I was unable to do the homework for the next day because I had not listened to the text: under redoubled punishment, I lived for a long time as the martyr of indifference.

What is an accomplishment if not granted in a privileged experience? Ultimately it is a moment of foolishness.

And the martyr himself, *if he so commands*, is subordinated to his own orders: sleep and laughter, at the summit, mock him, detach themselves, forget. So much anguish in indifference? Who can be believed? Would these words announce the raptures of ecstasy?

. . . some words! Exhaust me without respite: I will nevertheless go to the end of the miserable possibility of words.

There I want to find that which reintroduces—in a point—the sovereign silence that interrupts articulate language.

Part Two

Decisive Position

PRINCIPLES

1. If I wish it, *laughter* is thought, but it is a sovereign moment.

2. To say that in laughing I open the depth of worlds is a gratuitous affirmation.[11] The opened depth of worlds does not have a *meaning*. But it is precisely for this that I can relate other objects of thought to it.

3. In common understanding (which philosophy surpasses, but to which it is linked), every object of thought is related to a solid. This point of departure is such that no other point is conceivable: understanding proceeds from the solid, posed as the known, to which one assimilates, in order to know it, what is not yet known.

4. Every operation relating thought to the position of a solid subordinates it. Not only through its particular end but by the following method: the solid object is an object that one can make and use: *is known as what one can make and use* (or what we assimilate in order to know it, to that which we can make or use).
   Good sense relates the world to the sphere of activity.

5. Returning to an attitude (long affirmed), I will now say:
   —that I haven't received (accepted) a subordinated world that wanted me subordinated;
   —that I saw what a burst of laughter revealed as being the essence of things, to which I acceded freely;
   —that I made no distinction between laughing at a thing and possessing the truth; that I imagined *not seeing* an object at which I did not laugh;*

---

*I agree with few propositions more than this one, from *Zarathustra*, 3rd part: "And we should call every truth false which was not accompanied by at least one laugh" (On Old and New Tablets, § 23).

189

—that it was not only comic themes, but generally the existence of "what is" and myself in particular that made me laugh;

—that my laughter engaged me, thoroughly delighted me, and had no limit;

—that I already had a vague consciousness of the reversal that I effected; I thought that, laughter explained, I would know the meaning of man and the universe: that with laughter, on the contrary left unexplained, knowledge avoided the essential;

—but all of this from authority.

6. Today I add:

—I do not *see* the object that does not make me laugh[12] but only a relationship to the sphere of activity (relation of this object to a solid—to what we can make and use);

—in the same way that common knowledge relates objects to solids, which is to say to the moment of subordinated activity, I can relate them to the sovereign moment, in which I laugh.[13]

7. Relating the objects of thought to sovereign moments assumes a sovereign operation, different from laughter and, generally, from every common effusion. This is the operation in which thought stops the movement that subordinates it and, laughing—or abandoning itself to some other sovereign effusion—identifies itself with the rupture of the bonds that subordinated it.

8. The sovereign operation is arbitrary and even though its effects legitimate it from the perspective of subordinated operations, it is indifferent to judgment from this perspective.

9. Descartes's "I think" is linked, despite everything, to our consciousness of not being subordinated, but:

—this consciousness cannot be the point of departure for objective knowledge;

—beyond the "I think," Descartes alone apprehended, thought in its developed—and *subordinated*—form has no basis in itself but in the manipulation of solids;

—the relationship of objects to unchained thought is a point of arrival; before which a multitude of operations developed without thought ever having any other "object" than subordinated (the idea of freedom designates in principle a power of choice between two or several subordinations).

10. In the sovereign operation, not only is thought sovereign (as it is if we laugh) but its object is sovereign, and recognized as such, independently from its insertion in the useful order: what is, is subordinated to nothing and, revealing itself as such, makes us laugh, etc. . . .[14]

11. The sovereign operation, had it been possible only once, the science relating the objects of thought to sovereign moments* remains possible (it does not present insoluble difficulties).

It nevertheless encounters some obstacles:

—Not only does the sovereign moment not subordinate itself to anything, it is indifferent to the effects that might result; if, after the fact, I want to attempt the reduction of subordinated thought to sovereign thought, I can do it, but what is authentically sovereign has no cure, at any moment it disposes me in another way (this what I said in the first part);

---

*If we had knowledge worthy of the name, which didn't limit itself to fragmentary percep- tions, we could relate each object to any other, indifferently. But the operation has value only if one of the terms of this relation occupies one or the other of two positions in the series of appearances, *solidity* or *sovereignty*. The first in that it withdraws at most an object that others depend upon, assuring its autonomous subsistence. The second in that it denies the possibility of other objects in relation to which the sovereign moment would have a meaning. The solidity still maintains its autonomy by remaining apart, through a principle of conservation. And this conservation of the solid has its meaning in definite ends: it is the condition of activity. In sovereignty, quite the reverse, autonomy proceeds from a refusal of conservation, from a limitless prodigality. The object in a sovereign moment is not a substance *in that it loses itself*. Sovereignty is in no way different from a limitless dissipation of the "wealth" of substance: if we limited this dissipation, there would be a reserve for other moments, which would limit—*abolish*—the sovereignty of the immediate moment. The science relating the object of thought to sovereign moments is in fact only a *general economy*, envisioning the meaning of these objects, one in relation to the others, finally in relation to the loss of meaning. The question of this *general economy* is situated on the level of *political economy*, but the science designed by this name is only a *restricted economy* (restricted to market values). This is a question of the essential problem of the science treating the use of wealth. *General economy* makes evident in the first place that a surplus of energy is produced that, by definition, cannot be used. Excessive energy can only be lost without the slightest goal, consequently without any meaning. It is this use- less, senseless loss that *is* sovereignty. (In that the *sovereign*, like the *solid*, is an inevitable and constant experience.) The science that it envisions, far from being from the domain of dreams, is the only rational, complete *economy*, changing Keynes' "bottle" paradox into a fundamental principle.

I have no intention of adding to this short explanatory more than an allusion to the "work" that it *introduces* (*The Accursed Share*, volume 1, 1949; volumes 2 and 3 forthcoming).[15]

—The voluntary subordination of the operations of thought subordinated to the sovereign moment, even though it does not introduce particular presuppositions (as in theology or philosophy)—but only the position of an arbitrarily chosen moment of being (to which one will be able to relate, or *not to relate*, objects of thought); —No longer allows thought to proceed by chance as science commonly does, advancing only where it can and placidly leaving decisive problems to be resolved. *From the start* I had to operate in a global way, *from the start* leading to propositions chosen for another reason than the possibility of establishing them: an approximation, even an error, was apparently preferable to nothing (I could return to this point through what followed, I couldn't open a void in any case): the description that I had to make could only have bearing on the ensemble of the tableau. This method proceeded from the authenticity of my process, this authenticity imposed itself, and if I can, to speak of it, describe an aspect offering itself from outside, I could not *prove* it through considerations that only the subordinated mind would know to introduce.

12. Some consequences of such a use of thought follow in another way from a possibility of misunderstanding: knowledge relating objects to the sovereign moment risks in the end being confused with this moment itself.

This knowledge that one might call liberated (but that I prefer to call neutral) is *the use of a function detached (liberated) from the servitude that is its principle: the function related the unknown to the known (to the solid), whereas dating it from the moment in which it was detached, it relates the known to the unknown.*[16]

13. What I've just said seems to be opposed to the fact that without an outline, at least, of a neutral knowledge, a sovereign operation cannot be represented. I can, if I so desire, have an attitude, a sovereign behavior, but if I *think—when man cannot be distinguished from his thought—*I take into consideration, in principle, the subordinated character of common operations of thought. The sovereign thought (without which in the end simple sovereign moments insert themselves in the order of things[17]) wants a conscious coincidence of a sovereign moment and an operation of thought. But if some movement, some outline of neutral knowledge, *begins* a sovereign operation, the possible developments of this new mode of knowledge are distinct from it.

The sovereign operation *engages* these developments: they are the residue of a trace left in the memory and of the subsistence of functions, but insofar as it takes place, it is indifferent and *mocks* this residue.*

THE SOVEREIGN OPERATION

14. Essentially, neutral knowledge, within the common domain, reverses the movement of thought. In a sense, it is also a new domain, but in a secondary aspect (this new domain could just as well, without making a difference, allow nothing to appear, amid the others, that might differentiate it from them). The movement that grounds the sovereign operation is also grounded on it: but certainly (any effort, at each hour, appears vain to me, *like works to a Calvinist*), this operation is the end, *it is the path of an experience.*

15. In the first place, this discipline is a *method of meditation*. Its *teaching* is closer to that of the *yogis* than to that of the professors. The least inexact image of a sovereign operation is the ecstasy of the saints.

16. In order to describe it better, I would like to situate it in an ensemble of apparently sovereign behaviors. These are, other than ecstasy:
   —intoxication;
   —erotic effusion;

---

*The parallelism between Heidegger's descriptions and this position is incontestable. This is the case:

—despite the reserve Heidegger inspires in me;

—despite the difference between the paths followed.[18]

Even more however than the text of volume one of *Sein und Zeit* [*Being and Time*] (in appearance at least), his inability to write volume two links me to Heidegger.

On the other hand, I want to indicate these notable differences:

—I set out from laughter and not, as Heidegger does in *Was ist Metaphysik?* [*What is Metaphysics?*], from anxiety: some consequences perhaps result, precisely on the level of sovereignty (anxiety is a sovereign moment, but in flight from itself, negative);

—Heidegger's published oeuvre, so it seems to me, is more a fabrication than a glass of alcohol (it is even only a treatise on fabrication); it is a professorial work, whose subordinated method remains *glued* to its results: what counts, on the other hand, in my eyes, is the moment of *detachment*, what I teach (if it is true that . . .) is an intoxication, this is not a philosophy: I am not a philosopher but a *saint*, perhaps a madman.[19]

—laughter;
—sacrificial effusion;*
—poetic effusion.**

17. This effort at description tends to specify the movement to which it relates, in what follows, the different objects of thought, but in itself it is already obligated to establish the relationships to the sovereign moment of some common objects of thought.

18. The behaviors that I just listed are effusions in that they demand little important muscular movements and consume energy without other effort than a kind of inner illumination (that sometimes precedes anguish—even, in certain cases, is entirely limited to anguish).

19. Previously, I designated the sovereign operation under the names of *inner experience* and the *extremity of the possible*. Now I also designate it under the name of *meditation*. Changing the word signifies the problem of using whatever word it might be (*sovereign operation* is of all the names the most fastidious; *comical operation* in a sense would be less misleading). I like *meditation* better but it has a pious appearance.

20. In laughter, sacrifice, or poetry, even, in part in eroticism, effusion is obtained by a modification, voluntary or not, of the order of objects: poetry arranges changes on the level of images, sacrifice, in general, destroys beings, laughter results from diverse changes.

In intoxication on the contrary, and voluntarily, the subject himself is modified: it is the same in meditation.

21. Intoxication and meditation also have this in common: the vague effusions of each are linked, can at least be linked to other determined effusions. The modification of the object—erotic, comic—in intoxication

---

*Here I understand by *sacrifice* not only ritual but every representation or narrative in which destruction (or the threat of destruction) of a hero or more generally of a being plays an essential role; and by extension, the representations and narratives in which the hero (or the being) is at risk in an erotic mode (thus by *sacrificial effusion* I designate that which the processes of film and the novel strive to obtain (rather poorly) as well).

**This statement is not complete: heroic behavior, anger among others, finally absurdity, are also sovereign moments.[20]

appropriately responds to the modification of the subject. This is limitless in meditation. The origin of the effusion is less, in the two cases, than the activity of the subject: in intoxication, a toxin releases it; in meditation, *the subject contests himself,* hunts himself (capriciously, often even gaily).

22. In meditation, the subject, exceeded,[21] seeks himself.

He refuses himself the right to remain enclosed in the sphere of activity.

He refuses, meanwhile, the external means that are toxins, erotic partners, or alterations of the object (comical, sacrificial, poetic).

The resolute subject seeks himself, offers himself a meeting with an auspicious shadow.

And more completely than with a toxin, he puts himself, not objects, at risk.

23. Meditation is a comedy in which even the meditating person is comical. But also a tragedy in which he is tragic. But the comedic in a comedy or the tragic in a tragedy are limited. Whereas a meditating person is prey to the comedic or the tragic without limit.[22]

24. The closest effusion to meditation is poetry.

Poetry is initially a natural mode of expression of tragedy, of eroticism, of comedy (of heroism even above all). In the order of the words it expresses a great squandering of energy; it is the power that words have to evoke effusion, the immoderate expenditure of their own forces: thus it adds to the determinate effusion (comical, tragic . . .) not only the flows and rhythms of verses but the particular faculty of the disorder of images to annihilate the ensemble of signs that is the sphere of activity.

If one suppresses the *theme,* if one admits at the same time the negligible interest of *rhythm,* a hecatomb of words without gods or reason is for man a major means of affirmation, through an effusion *stripped of meaning;* a sovereignty upon which, apparently, *nothing crosses.*

The moment when poetry renounces *theme* and meaning is, from the perspective of meditation, the rupture that opposes it to the humiliated stammerings of the ascetic. But in becoming a game without rules, and in the impossibility, lacking a theme, of determining violent effects, the exercise of *modern* poetry subordinates itself, in turn, to *possibility.*[23]

25. If poetry weren't accompanied by an affirmation of sovereignty (offering a commentary on its absence of meaning), it would be like laughter and

sacrifice, or like eroticism and intoxication, *inserted* in the sphere of activity. *Inserted* is not exactly *subordinated*: laughter, intoxication, sacrifice, or poetry, eroticism itself, subsisted in an autonomous reserve, *inserted* in the sphere, *like children in a house*. In their limits, they are sovereign minors, unable to contest the *empire* of activity.[24]

26. It is clear, at this point, that the question of power has been posed and poetry cannot avoid it. In the end, poetry is only an *evocation*; poetry only changes the order of the words and *cannot change the world*. The sentiment of poetry is linked to the nostalgia to change more than the order of words, *the established order*. But the idea of a revolution *starting* with poetry leads to that of poetry *in the service* of a revolution.[25] I have no other intention than to put into evidence the drama dissimulated in the words: *limited, poetry cannot affirm full sovereignty, the negation of all limits: it was, from the start, condemned to insertion; escaping its limits, it had to link itself (attempt to link itself) to such a contestation of the facts of the order of things.*

27. Now, what does the contestation—political, in fact—of the established order signify? It demands power and could, theoretically, do this in the name of that which exceeds servile necessity (this used to be the principle of the poetic revolution). They act differently, it's a fact, but one must not contradict them. The *major* positions of political sovereignties (including those of the past, founded on heroism and sacrifice*) were, no less than the *minor* ones, inserted in the sphere of activity. The classical idea of sovereignty is linked to that of commandment.** The sovereignty of the gods, of God, of monarchs, submits itself to all activity: but it was no more altered thereby than a burst of laughter or a child. For *engaging* the order of things became its meaning and it was no longer independent. In these conditions, the sovereignty that would like to remain sovereign quickly abandons *power* to those who want to maintain it authentically with ineluctable necessity.

28. Sovereignty is revolt; it is not the exercise of power. Authentic sovereignty refuses . . .

---

*Sacrifice that, in the form of art, has, in modern societies, the minor position once had the major one.

**But not yet to what we can call *archaic sovereignty*, which seems rather implicated in a kind of impotence.

29. Full sovereignty differs from minor sovereignty in this way: it demands the adherence without reserve of the subject, who must, if possible, be a free man, having, in the sphere of activity, real resources.

30. From the start, the sovereign operation presents a difficulty so great that one must seek it in a slippage.

The slave-subject of Christianity attributed (returned) sovereignty to the god-object, whose purpose intended that one grasp oneself, in effect, as an object of *possession*. The god of the mystics is free (relatively) by definition; the mystic is not (on the contrary, he is voluntarily submissive to moral servitude).

31. A Buddhist is more proud. The Christian submits, in suffering, to the empire of activity, believing he reads therein the divine will, which *wants* his subordination. The Buddhist denies this empire, yet behaves in turn as a slave: he considers himself as fallen, and he must situate the sovereignty that he wants for himself in the other world. He also engages in the contradiction of *work* from the perspective of a sovereign moment.

32. But man only has to do the work, if for no other reason than to assure and repair his forces. Ascetic work is bound to the condemnation of every sovereign moment that is not the moment it pursues! Whatever its power of seduction and whatever successes, *in spite of* its principles, it has known, the mystic tradition, burdened by subordinate presuppositions, is also an equivocal platitude, a foot stuffed in a shoe.

33. We cannot in any way fabricate a sovereign moment from a servile state: sovereignty cannot be acquired. I can in the sovereign operation become conscious of that operation, but the operation *assumes* a sovereign moment, it cannot fabricate one.[26]

34. This sovereignty cannot even be defined as a good. I value it, but would I value it if I did not equally have the certainty that I could laugh at it? On such a summit (it is rather the tip of a needle), I can live on this condition: that at every moment I say: "Sovereign? But why?" I define a neutral knowledge, describing sovereign moments: my sovereignty welcomes this knowledge the way a bird sings and I know no gratitude for my work.

35. I am writing in order to nullify a play of subordinate operations (it is, all told, superfluous).

36. The sovereign operation, *whose authority derives only from itself—expiates that authority at the same time.** If it did not expiate itself, it would have some point of application, it would seek an empire, duration. But authenticity refuses this: it is only powerlessness, the absence of duration, hateful (or gay) destruction of itself, a lack of satisfaction.

37. Still, I want to define it a little more precisely at the limit. Not that one must or could speak . . . , but *it speaks*, gathering at one time the totality of the "meditating person" . . .

What it says is the object of the following chapter . . .

---

*I intentionally recall in this conclusion the terms of a passage borrowed from Maurice Blanchot in *Inner Experience*.

Part Three

Nudity [27]

In the end everything puts me at risk, I remain suspended, stripped bare, in a definitive solitude: beyond the impenetrable simplicity of *what is*; and, the depths of the world open, what I see and what I know no longer have meaning, no longer have limits, and I will stop myself only after I have advanced as far as I can.

Now I can laugh, drink, abandon myself to the pleasure of the senses, deliver myself to the delirium of words; I can sweat in torture and I can die: if I had not entirely dissolved the world in myself, I would remain subordinate to necessity, I could not risk myself more than in joy, torture, or death.

I risk myself if sensuality and pain project me beyond a sphere wherein I have only one meaning: the sum of the responses that I give to the demands of utility; I risk myself when, at the end of the possible, I tend so strongly toward that which will overturn the pleasure the idea of death gives me—and that I laugh taking pleasure in it.

But the smallest activity or the least project brings an end to the game—and I am, lacking play, brought back to the prison of useful objects, loaded with meaning.

*

....
........................this, nevertheless, is the *instant*.......................
....
...........................this, presently, neither my absence nor me, neither death nor light—and my absence and me, death and light—a light laugh rises in me like the sea, it fills the absence immensely. All that is—IS TOO MUCH.

*

. . . this no longer matters, I am writing this book, and *clearly* and *distinctly,** I wanted it to be what it is.

*

In the plenitude of rapture, when nothing counted but the instant *itself, I escaped the common rules. But only to find them again quickly, unchanged; and similarly that, in the burst, ecstasy—or the freedom of the instant—escapes the possible utility, even the being useful, which defines humanity, appears to me linked to the need for material goods, and I poorly imagine giving them superior ends. My method is at the antipodes of elevated ideas, of salvation, of all mysticism.*

---

*Evidently, I was unable to define *in the night* what I call the *sovereign operation*. I have described the play of complex elements, still equivocal movements and the *sovereign moments* are exterior to my efforts. These moments are of a relative banality: a little ardor and abandon suffices (a little cowardliness however turns them around and a moment later we babble). Laughing to tears, sensually coming to cry out, evidently nothing is more common (what is most strange is the servility that after the fact we have spoken of serious matters, *as if nothing were serious*). Ecstasy itself is close: one imagines the provoking enchantment of poetry, the intensity of mad laughter, a dizzying feeling of *absence*, but these elements simplified, reduced to the geometric point, in indistinction. I will again represent the apparition, in the night, at the window of an isolated home, of the beloved but frightful face of a dead woman: suddenly, beneath this blow, night changes to day, the trembling from cold into a mad smile, *as if it were nothing*—because this sharp rapture hardly differs from any state whatsoever (only the painful, boring moments offer an exchange, betraying the richness of their means).

Post-Scriptum
1953

I am uncomfortable with this book,* wherein I wanted to exhaust the possibility of being. It does not really displease me. But I hate its slowness and obscurity. I would like to say the same thing in fewer words. I would like to free its movement, save it from what bogs it down. This would be for all that neither easy nor satisfying.[1]

In the manner of thought that I introduce, affirmation is never what counts. What I say, I believe without doubt, but I know that I carry within me the movement that wants affirmation, further on, to disappear. If a place in the history of thought were granted to me, I think it would be for having discerned the effects, in our human life, of the "disappearance of the discursive real," and for having drawn from the description of these effects a fading light:** this light is perhaps blinding, but it announces the opacity of the *night*; it announces only the night.

Often, it seems to me, today, that I was wrong to play a crepuscular game with a kind of levity, candidly advancing hypotheses, without being in the state to pursue the works that they implied. My previous pride nevertheless pleases me more than it bothers me. Now, I strive clumsily—in a slow search—and nevertheless, I can only doubt, the informality of a game alone responds to this undue situation that necessity leaves to the mind.

This game of the "discursive real" and its disappearance exists *in fact*. It demands the honesty, loyalty, and generosity of the player (there is no generosity without loyalty). But when I exceed the "discursive real," there is no longer a game, and the honesty about which I spoke is that of the law. The law is the foundation of the real, it creates its absolute value, but it would not if it was not the blackmail of a mysticism that it draws from death and pain. Death and pain being the principle of servitude (no slaves without the fear of death and pain) are also the mystical foundations of the law.

Method of Meditation is situated in my eyes as an extension of *Inner Experience*.

**Here I can only clarify a proposition that inevitably, by its nature, can only be expressed in an faltering manner.

205

Only *violent thought* coincides with the disappearance of thought. But it demands a meticulous fury and it yields to violence—its contradiction—only in the end and insofar as, become itself, against itself, violence releases itself from the indolence wherein it endured. But the annihilation of thought—letting only the servile coherence of thought subsist, denounced, spectral, and its multiple failings, gay or tragic—can only turn toward the other the violence that founds it. Violence linked to the movement of thought leaves no way out.

*

I will stop myself on a point that, it seems, has little to do with the movement of *Inner Experience*. I would like to situate my thought in its narrow perspectives, far from the world of facility where one might easily appreciate it.

At the origin of baseness, I perceive the emphatic value given to the human species. Without any doubt, the difference between animal and man is grounded since the human being is opposed to nature. But man poorly surmounts the advantage that he has achieved. Man said of himself: "I am divine, immortal, free . . ." (or he says solemnly "the person"). But this is not all. Each admits naively, without control, principles taken as unassailable: we consider it inhuman to kill, more inhuman still to eat men . . . We ordinarily add that it is no less odious to exploit them. I oppose nothing to these principles; and I even hate those who observe them poorly (besides, as a general rule, they revere them as much as they infringe upon them). But this is mysticism, and it is hypocrisy. The exploitation of man by man, as hateful as it is, is a fact of *humanity*. Even anthropophagy, when it is the convention, coexists with the prohibition of which it is the ritual violation.

Once again, I approve of neither exploitation nor murder (and for cannibals, it goes without saying . . .); and I admit without stopping to think about it that we exploited, slaughtered and ate animals.* But I cannot doubt that these reactions are arbitrary. They are convenient, humanity

---

*Must the zoophilic be cited on this occasion? More seriously, naïve men attribute to animals ways of being and of reacting analogous to those of men. The beliefs of Hindus and Buddhists grant souls to animals... It is a question, if I am not mistaken, of the inconsistencies of the illogicality of childish thought and dreams. These ways of seeing first assume the affirmation according to which it is wrong and atrocious to treat what we are as a thing. In this or that measure, then, an animal fictively receives the prerogatives of the human being, it is assimilated from outside into that which the human being has determined separates itself from the animal.

without them would be still more base than it is. It is nevertheless weak to see more than an effective and traditional attitude in them. Thought that does not limit this arbitrariness to what it is is mystical thought.[2]

What makes mystical humanism a platitude is the misrecognition of the human specificity that it implies. It is proper to man to oppose himself to the beast in a movement of nausea. But the nausea that grounds us in this way does not cease: it is itself the principle of a game animating our life from one end to the other. We are never more human than when impugning one another in horror. The propensity for nausea is stronger if it concerns entire peoples: from then on, it plays itself out blindly! But if it concerns individuals or classes, it has precise objects. The opposition of one man to another in whom he perceives a foul attitude is still the opposition that initially opposes man to beast. It does not have the same clarity: it is henceforth attackable and most often founded on an error. When it is contested, a new mode of opposition, and of disparagement, begins: opposition now has the principle of opposition between these different types of human for its object! If I make a final effort, going to the end of human possibility, I reject in the night those who, with a cowardice that does not acknowledge itself, stop themselves en route.[3]

In this, I distance myself from mysticism more deeply than in fact the mass of my contemporaries. I even feel myself awakening, on the contrary, being on the level of the demand of thought in the state of a hunted beast. In the end, rigor is the point on which I agree with the avowed judgments of men. The tension and the desiccation of the mind, rigor, the desire to force weakness into its final retrenchment . . . I feel something like grace, a kind of rage that opposes me to facility. But often informality is the naked aspect, the obscene aspect of rigor.

These weaknesses and these unintentional ambiguities in my book, these joys and these anguishes that found nothing, never have any being beyond themselves, being only the privilege of the game. The tone often linked to my—too weighty—sentences exposes an unlimited opening that the game, if it is no longer inferior, tolerated, serious, arranges for the idle mind (the sovereign mind, which is never laughable or tragic, but at once infinitely one and the other). Seriousness has only *one meaning*: the game, which is no longer a game, is only serious insofar as "the absence of meaning is also a meaning," but always lost in the night of indifferent nonsense. Seriousness, death, and pain, founding obtuse truth. But the seriousness of death and of pain is the servility of thought.

Notes

The following notes reproduce the editorial notes from Georges Bataille, Oeuvres Complètes, *volume 5 (Paris: Gallimard, 1973), 421–92. I have occasionally amended or expanded, often silently, the notes provided by the Gallimard editors for clarity and continuity and for a contemporary Anglophone readership. Editorial remarks, whether my own or by the Gallimard editors, generally appear in italics. Additional annotation is generally indicated: Trans.*

Inner Experience

Published in 1943 by Editions Gallimard and reissued in 1954 (our text) as the first volume of La Somme athéologique, *augmented by a text that appeared in 1947,* Method of Meditation, *and a post-face,* Post-Scriptum 1953. *(Bataille had projected far more significant revisions for this reissue that we examine in our notes for* Post-Scriptum 1953 *below.)*

Bataille dates the composition of Inner Experience *in an additional unpublished note from 1953 [see Bataille manuscripts at Bibliothèque Nationale de France, Box 9 E, 3]:*

This book was begun in Paris during the winter of 1941 (*Torture*) and finished during the summer of 1942 at Boussy-le-Château. But the texts in roman type in the third part (*Antecedents to the Torture*) are earlier; only the first and the last of them had not been previously published; the second appeared under the title *Sacrifices*, accompanied by etchings by André Masson; the third, prior to 1930, and the forth appeared respectively, under their titles, in *Minotaure* and *Recherches philosophiques*. All of these texts were modified in 1942. Finally, I want to specify that the oldest of these writings, dating undoubtedly from 1926, expresses the feelings that I had no longer felt for some time when it was published. (I had to obviate in this way a factual misunderstanding [*crossed out:* like those that might still be occasioned].)

This note is related to this fragment of a plan for a preface for Madame Edwarda *(see Bataille,* Oeuvres Complètes, *volume 3, notes, p. 491):*

I wrote this little book in September–October 1941, right before *Torture*, which forms the second part of *Inner Experience*. The two texts, to my way of thinking, are closely interdependent and one cannot understand one without the other [. . .]

One does not find a complete manuscript for Inner Experience *in Bataille's papers, but:*

N [Notebook 4, August 1942] = manuscript for pages 4–5

A [Notebook 3] =
  — Draft for the Foreword (6 pages not paginated)
  — Manuscript for pages 9–16 and 23–24 (pages numbered 1–24 and 3 pages not numbered).

B [Envelope 66] =
  — First draft of pages 9–11 (8 pages of a notebook);
  — Rough notes for pages 13–35 (pages numbered 1–52, 1–29, a–n, 101–45, and 5 pages not numbered);
  — Rough notes for pages 149–157 (17 pages not numbered);
  — Notes and scattered fragments (50 pages not numbered).

  (Bataille used ten envelopes for this manuscript, postmarked July 1942, giving his address as the home of Madame Moré [Marcel Moré's mother], in Boussy-Saint-Antoine par Brunoy (Seine et Oise)—one envelope from May 1942 addressed 3 Rue de Lille, [Bataille's companion Denise Rollin's apartment] in Paris.)

C [Box 9, L]= Communication, *pages 96–100 (12 typewritten pages, the last six of which are unpublished; the manuscript of this text is dispersed [Box 13, E, F, and G] in a group of notes for the first version of* The Accursed Share*).*

See also Socratic College *in Georges Bataille,* The Unfinished System of Non-knowledge *[(Minneapolis: University of Minnesota Press, 2001) pp. 5–17] for the text of an unpublished lecture dating from spring 1942 extending Bataille's reflections on "inner experience."*

Here now is the publisher's insert for the 1943 edition of Inner Experience:

Beyond Poetry
(on the band wrapped around the book)

We are perhaps the wound, the sickness of nature.

In this case it would be necessary for us—and also possible, "easy"—to make this wound into a festival, a strength of the sickness. The poetry that loses the most blood would be the strongest. The saddest dawn? Announces the joy of the day.

Poetry would be the sign announcing the greatest inner lacerations. The human musculature would only be entirely at stake; it would only attain its highest degree of strength and the perfect movement of "decision"—that which, whatever happens, being demands—in ecstatic trance.*

Can one not free from its religious antecedents the possibility of mystical experience, which remains open, no matter how it seems, for the nonbeliever? Free it from the asceticism of dogma and from the atmosphere of religions? Free it in a word from mysticism—to the point of linking it to the nudity of ignorance?

Beyond all knowledge is nonknowledge and he who would become absorbed in the thought that beyond his knowledge he knows nothing, even if he had Hegel's inexorable lucidity, would no longer be Hegel but a painful tooth in Hegel's mouth. Would a sick tooth alone fail the great philosopher?

Epigraph

"Night is also a sun."
Friedrich Nietzsche, Thus Spoke Zarathustra *(1883–85) in Nietzsche,* The Portable Nietzsche, *trans. Walter Kaufmann (New York: Viking Penguin, 1954) p. 435. Translation modified.* Trans.

Foreword

1. *Here, in A, this sketch of a preface begins:*
The preface properly speaking should turn on this precise point. I have known [*crossed out:* 20 years ago] a time of effervescence and prophecy, many glimmers surged up attempting to dazzle. Some minds in revolution were drunk, others gritting their teeth, dreaming of cataclysms, and others were speaking, were intoxicated with speaking. As in all things human (but a little more undoubtedly) comedy, affectation, feelings and words beyond feelings, half-false (literary) feelings gave the whole situation a halo of deception. I thought: I don't believe so many of the words that I hear, I poorly understand how . . . But I shared a deep belief. Independently from what I was hearing, I thought that there existed in us an intimate force demanding I don't know what (no one knows) but demanding it with madness, desiring it like a woman in love crying in the dark. And it matters little that, whatever the desiring being means, the tears that flow are like death and I

---

*These first lines, dated January 24, 1943, can be found in Georges Bataille, Guilty (Albany: SUNY Press, 2011) p. 225.

believe—although undoubtedly, I am the only one to believe it—that the death of the sick is the eager anticipation of the joys of those who survive. And when I say joys, I say too little. So many sobs, so many agonies, so many pains demand a response that blinds, something gentle, insane, transfiguring.

It seemed obvious to me that one could not respond to such an anticipation with poems, paintings, exhibitions. And I think that this was obvious to everyone. But an anticipation is never well defined: there were others linked to literature, to fine art, to business, to personal fame. In the confusion, staying with a profound answer to the profound anticipation that they had had—or believed they had—most forgot it. And little by little there were no more glimmers, nor effervescence, nor prophecy. At least I ceased to discern the appearance in the attitude or the words of others. However, the anticipation in me had become no less bitter, no less glaring. I only felt myself become alone, gradually.

When I spoke of confusion, I did not mean to say that it did not exist in my mind. And when I spoke of painting, of poems, I did not think that these objects were worthy of contempt or that there was nothing else that that had entirely exhausted. I will also not pretend to have never thought of such impoverished answers. My anticipation outlasted that of others—but I will seize the occasion to say that without doubt my persistence betrays an insane, often unjustified presumption on my part. It survived in any case, as did my ceaseless pursuit of an answer.

And as always I hurried and though I should have kept myself silent in the sense that nothing was yet [*stripped bare?*] in myself and that I could do no more than catch a glimpse, I spoke on several occasions as if I bore the answer. I affirmed that this answer was the sacred and it is true that I still today believe that I reached it, but today I no longer think that it was a question of a complete answer and then I believe that I could not have made it accessible. Today I say that it is inner experience and I will say what I mean by that in my book. But in the meantime those who were anticipating with me have disappeared, the answer that I gave is given to the desert—in a profound silence. And even more, although I am in no way led to see providence behind acts and their coincidences, I cannot regret to any extent, given what it was, that this answer disappeared so totally. It no longer exists other than in the hidden part of the heart, it no longer has a public existence. This is addressed not to a public eager for new and striking sensations but to those who can only descend to the depths of human possibilities.

This answers to such an extent, in any case, to my feeling that I can ask myself if I should not have had to avoid this preamble. It is in certain respects misplaced to link this about which I am now about to speak to a past of literary agitation. But exactitude in the sense of mediocrity as in the other sense. And although the old preoccupations seem in general to have rotted those who possessed them and cannot surpass them, it can make sense to link them to this "experience" rather than to any other thing.

Perhaps. It seems to me in fact that in this way I put an immediate clarity into a book in which, as one will see, one may ask oneself if the author is not victim of an incorrigible moral sadness and singularly removed from the living world. However, this clarity, after the fact, seems insufficient to me. "Rather than to any other thing," it's quickly said. Perhaps, given the earlier concerns of some. But not for the better. For in myself, without any doubt, this about which I speak is linked to what I imagine to be as far from deliquescence, at the same time from pessimism, from the perverse and unfortunate contempt for health, for human strength often linked to the exercise of poetry. I must say it loudly, since the movement of my book engages confusion. No one is more gay than I, no one more of a friend of man—of his virtues, and of the most juvenile—hostile to his failures, to his judicial chains, to his compassions. How I would like to say of this book the same thing that Nietzsche said of *The Gay Science*: "In almost every sentence profundity and passion go tenderly hand in hand." And I am not wrong to oppose the literary cafés and the Mediterranean sky of Zarathustra, to which all my life has bent. Misfortune to he who curses! I am content, blurting out this cry, to introduce it at the head of a bitter book. And since one could see in it an inexplicable contradiction, to resolve this right away by calling as witness Nietzsche who wrote in *Ecce Homo*: "Another ideal . . ."

(At the end of the preface, vital necessity for man to no longer flee to outside of himself—ex. pictures in order to fix his attention for a moment.

That now I no longer have the possibility, as before, of resolving, or believing I can resolve, through a bold move, a challenge to the world, the difficulties that it presents to me, but only through an attention to each moment.)

2. *Friedrich Nietzsche,* Ecce Homo, *in Nietzsche,* Basic Writings, *trans. Walter Kaufmann (New York: Modern Library, 1992) p. 749. Translation modified.* Trans.

3. *Though Bataille attributes this quotation to* Ecce Homo, *it originally appeared in Nietzsche's* The Gay Science. *It appears in* Ecce Homo *as a quotation from the earlier work. For the original citation, see Friedrich Nietzsche,* The Gay Science *(1887), trans. Walter Kaufmann (New York: Vintage, 1974) § 382. Translation modified. For the citation from* Ecce Homo, *see Nietzsche,* Basic Writings, *trans. Walter Kaufmann (New York: Modern Library, 1992) p. 755.* Trans.

4. *Quoted by Bataille from Friedrich Nietzsche,* La Volonté de Puissance, *t. 2, ed. Friedrich Würzbach, trans. Geneviève Bianquis (Paris: Gallimard, 1938) § 585.* Trans.

5. *In N, this text precedes:*
8-23-42.

In a depression (the bottom of the bowl, scraping bottom):

The sense of man is nonsense. That a being should need (to subsist, even to appear) to conform to particular senses (successive, discordant, saying, man is made for this, for that, always the equivalent of "the carpenter for the plane" only with the general appearance), one day the accounts will come due, someone will contest, nothing will remain. The final demon, chance (nothing has a final meaning—no treasure is hidden from thieves), but that chance should give way! I was lucky: in the end, I wasn't lucky. I had what I loved, *what fulfilled my heart*. What I loved is taken from me. Everything is finished. I can only say, after Job: "The Lord has given, the Lord takes away . . ."

Interrupted. (It is Sunday morning, the sun gilds the foliage of the tall trees before me, a song begins very full, voices of men and women together; it is the *Kyrie eleison*. O miserable echo, hardly soft, of another *superman* that I heard on the shores of Lake Maggiore!* . . . And which remains in me the sign less of my chance than of that of men. And now? A sermon! Of which only the stiff accents reach me, unintelligible.)

"The Lord takes away . . ."

But when chance is the Lord, what is it once it has been withdrawn? Nonsense. I tell myself: would nonsense be my plane? Before chance abandons me, in advance I have often found nonsense like a little fragment of bone breaking off atrociously while one savors a morsel. Today neither morsel nor savor. Nothing but non-sense, truth deserted, creating a desert, glimpsed tearing through the leaves of trees in the pale blue of the sky (which is the absence of man and of all sense). What defeats me most is that I reached a truth today only by chance too great for me, by the excess of strength that it offers. Today when something sickly has spoiled my life, I can only say: it is not a truth for the sickly, the ill-advised cannot bear it. But finally this with a very gentle start: this truth demands my strength, if this is so, I mock my bad luck, I must raise myself to my highest height and, now that chance has left me, *nevertheless* find the strength (and perhaps, at bottom, the only type of strength equal to such a deserted truth, is the strength one finds *nevertheless*). Yesterday, at midnight, at the height of discouragement, I heard in the lobby of the hotel some card players talking, speaking as loudly as possible, their hackles up over diamonds or clubs—and in this absurd Passy garden, the continual quacking of ducks with insomnia; never in me did the vice-grip of idiocy grasp more cruelly the world, I was there, in bed, lights out, my shutters closed, alone and sick. To feel the expanse of the sky and the absence of an answer, evidence that if no one had found an answer, after so much time, it wouldn't be me who would find one, that we were enclosed forever within the idiocy of the ducks, the card players, as in a prison without any imaginable key (and perhaps chance on the inside like a flight, a means of avoiding the dirty walls one bangs against in the darkness: yesterday in my weakness, I banged against them like a giant). Another thing, I said to myself one moment: either there will never be an answer or it has already been given (in the past). And I forced myself, I evoked the answer from the past. Nothing frightened me: not even my cowardice. As at other times, I asked God to enlighten me: he gave I don't know what kind of sickly response . . . There was no longer at that moment anything in my head to surpass the limits of a duck. And this morning I am bursting, absorbed in a frightening, yet simple truth. These lines, written slowly, still like a screen, but . . . it's finished, I want to remain alone with nonsense.

See Antecedents to the Torture, p. 79.

Supposing that there were in the world a sense—as one has always created it, but a sense saying: "this is clear . . ." another saying: "this, that no one before had seen . . ." and endlessly—the sense would be given, man would have to discover it. I accept it, and even want to imagine having reached it, without a doubt. I could not then prevent myself from saying: this world so full of sense, I will see it right to its very depths, *right to the point where it loses* . . . this sense that it indubitably has for me.

To experience (to question—oneself and the world—to perceive in knowledge a lure, an obstacle) is a simple resolution among others. In experience, one must laugh at the foolishness without which one would not have come to form the experience. I wanted to return to [*illegible; cross out:* human] simplicity. If I have followed strange paths, I do not excuse those who amuse themselves endlessly with eccentricities. The human mind is as if decomposed, but to linger over the decomposition, to take pleasure in it, is more and more hostile to my way of thinking. I would have liked to write a book such that one could not draw easy consequences from it. I would not want one to give my book dishonest sequels: I would prefer that one disparage it, or better, that no one care about it.

I have proposed: the friendship of man for himself, the effacement of the self in the evidence of pride, a "desert" in which solitude accesses the "innumerable," and in the exercise of life the most rigor possible.

The key to the integrity of man:
    TO NO LONGER WANT TO BE EVERYTHING,
This is the hatred of salvation.
6. *N:* [. . .] it did not seem so to me [. . .]
7. *This work would be a first version of* The Accursed Share *(see below,* Method of Meditation, *note 20).*
8. *N, continues:* I have now finished this austere, strict book, in which it is as though I have left the earth beyond approachable problems.

Part One

1

1. *In B, attached to drafts for the* Introduction, *these pages numbered 1–8:*
I should have said, all along, what "inner experience" is, and responded to the questions that are asked about it. This was more difficult than one might believe.
To begin with, I fail to define it. I must content myself with empiricism. By "inner experience," I understand what one usually designates under the name "mystical experience," the experience of living states of ecstasy, of rapture, at least of meditated emotion. But I envision less "confessional experience"—to which one in

general refers—than experience in itself, free of ties, however vague, to any confession whatsoever. This is what justifies the abandonment of the word "mystical," to which I could adhere without inviting confusion.

I will not propose a more concise definition. In the end, I will show that inner experience is linked to the necessity, for the mind, of questioning everything—without any conceivable respite or rest. This necessity came to light despite religious presuppositions, but its effects go much further if one sets those presuppositions aside. Useless to insist on the meaning, the implication of this eviction. That philosophical presuppositions should have directed these experiences, as they did in any case, was not necessarily favorable to the development of the experience itself; in any case the intellectual consequences of this were quickly limited. But I must go further. Even consequential suppositions are dangerous and vain. And as "inner experience" exists at the *heart* of the possible, there is no definition that I can give that is not linked to the necessity, of which I have spoken, to question everything without measure.

Nothing further from the possibilities which are mine—or from the intentions of this book—than any mysticism whatsoever, in accordance with poetic imagination. At all times, minds inclined to inner experience indulged in any facilities that they could find: "Such minds," Hegel said, "when they give themselves up to the uncontrolled ferment of the [the divine] substance, imagine that, by drawing a veil over self-consciousness and surrendering understanding they are the beloved of God to whom He gives wisdom in sleep; and hence what they in fact receive, and bring to birth in their sleep, is nothing but dreams . . ." [Hegel, *Phenomenology of Spirit* (1807), trans. A. V. Miller (Oxford: Oxford University Press, 1977) p. 6.] "Experience" does not affect beings who are less intellectually careful in the same way: it is the source of visions. The mind surpasses its limits with such force that the whole world, external in appearance, in fact becomes dependent upon it. What is contemplated in experience is perceived with a surprising intensity and in conditions of general uneasiness. Evidence relevant to the fact itself—the intensity—slips without difficulty from an ungraspable notion to objectivization in a predictable form. The visionary, no doubt, cheats with less difficulty than the philosopher, but it is always an act.

A "mystic" sees what he wants—this depends upon relative abilities. And in the same way he discovers—what he knew. No doubt there are wills, beliefs that are unequally favorable, but as such [*man?*] the experience introduces nothing that has not at first been within one's understanding—*if not the contestation of understanding as the origin of beliefs*.

I represent, one will see, inner experience under the appearance of things best made to be off-putting. But it is not desirable that it be attractive. One must on the contrary offer it as barely accessible. In fact, it is even the inaccessible heart of man.

First of all, one must cease to believe that one can approach it through a science that passes over experience itself. Without denying the interest of scholarly works, how can one not see the extent to which they turn their backs on experience by studying the lives of dead people. The experience that is not living and is no longer even conceivable as a possible is derision. It is a mode of knowledge that one cannot procure for oneself through intermediaries, above all when those people are from another time.

Moreover, I will try to make it understood why the work of scholars, who know nothing of experience, are thereby strangers to the subject that they discuss. This is my means of making known what experience precisely consists of (which a definition does not permit). Science, scientific knowledge, can, it's true, present itself with experience as an object, but in the course of scholarly studies it happens that the conditions of observation change the nature of the observed phenomenon. This is the case, if there is one, of "inner experience." First of all, I have shown experience entering into one who thereby has errors of judgment. And in the same way, if one envisions science with a true faith—if one asserts the kind of judgment that founds the belief in discursive knowledge—this amounts to saying: if experience itself has not put faith and judgment into question—the object to which knowledge lays claim can only apparently coincide with that of a mystical search.

The destruction of the object by the observer is disproportionately tangible, according to the case. It is strange in that of Pierre Janet.* This scholar in no way adheres to bookish knowledge, to which mystical studies are usually limited. He had the luck to care for an "ecstatic" patient in a hospital ward. He designates her in his writings by the familiar name of Madeleine. For six years, he had this creature entirely at his disposal. He had her half undress in order to photograph her in ecstasy (in a pose of crucifixion). There was no desire for blasphemy in this but a concern for meticulous science (Janet observed everything, breathing, heart, excretions). A paternal, ironic, and, all told, infinitely contemptuous benevolence presided over his work. His affectionate kindness won him the blind confidence of the subject.

2. *A, first draft crossed out:*

[. . .] categories of understanding.

The rigor that I bring to my refusal surprises and even risks being [*illegible; crossed out:* remaining a dead letter] in the sense that it is difficult to maintain a position contrary to one's habits. But this rigor [*crossed out:* is no less founded on the intimate necessity for "experience" than on the firmness of a principle] imposes itself upon me without discussion.

If I say decisively [. . .]

See note 10 below.

3. *A:*
[. . .] uneasily hostile to the idea of perfection [*crossed out:* this hostility exists in me as a laceration, links itself to my *blind* gaze, to the state of "nonknowledge" in which the mind sinks in the lost depths of darkness].

[*A first draft, crossed out, reads:*]
I cannot forget that in any case God signifies the salvation of the soul and other relationships of the imperfect to the perfect. What I call the "inconceivable unknown," there is neither the desire nor the means within me to assume it to be perfect. And I can add this: as soon as I have the *vision* of the "unknown," the idea that I have of the perfect is with "that"—in fact—in a state of obvious antagonism and this antagonism is the same thing as the laceration that results from my *blind* state of "nonknowledge" that then sinks me into the most hidden depths of darkness. Without this, everything would result, I think, in something calming.

4. *Pseudo-Dionysius,* Divine Names, *in Pseudo-Dionyius,* The Complete Works, *trans. Colm Luibheid (New York: Paulist Press, 1987) 1: 5 (593c). Bataille borrowed Saint Denys L'Aréopagite, Oeuvres, trans. from Greek by Mgr Darboy (A. Tralin, 1932), from the Bibliothèque Nationale on May 7, 1942, returning it on July 16 of that year. Trans.*

5. *Eckhart von Hochheim (c. 1260–c. 1327), commonly known as Meister Eckhart, a German theologian and mystic of the Dominican Order, conceived of God as a "pure nothingness" (ein bloss niht). Nothingness for Eckhart is best understood as akin to the notion of poverty. In sermon 28, for example, Eckhart writes: "He is a poor man who wants nothing, knows nothing, and has nothing." Eckhart was tried for heresy by the Papal court in Avignon. Trans.*

6. *Pseudo-Dionysius,* Divine Names, *1: 7 (596c), in Pseudo-Dionyius,* The Complete Works, *trans. Colm Luibheid (New York: Paulist Press, 1987). Trans.*

7. *San Juan de la Cruz (1542–1591), known in English as St. John of the Cross, was a Spanish friar, priest, and mystic of the Carmelite Order. Major works by St. John of the Cross include* The Ascent of Mount Carmel, The Dark Night of the Soul, *and* The Spiritual Canticle. *In* The Ascent of Mount Carmel, *for example, he writes: "We apply the term 'spiritual feelings' to whatever is perceived after the manner of the other senses, such as the supernaturally enjoyable experience of a sweet spiritual fragrance, savor, or delight. The intellect derives knowledge or spiritual vision from all of these communications, without the apprehension of any form, image, or figure of the imagination or natural phantasy. For these experiences are communicated immediately to the soul through a supernatural work and through a supernatural means." See St. John of the Cross, Selected Writings, trans. Kieran Kavanaugh (New York: Paulist Press, 1987) p. 136. On December 8, 1941, Bataille borrowed Jean Baruzi's* Saint Jean de la Croix et le problème de l'expérience mystique *(Paris: Alcan, 1924) and* Aphorismes *by Saint Jean de la Croix (Bordeaux: Feret, 1924) from the Bibliothèque Nationale. He returned the first book on May 8, 1942, and the second on March 22, 1943. See Bataille, Oeuvres Complètes, volume 12, p. 617. Trans.*

8. *Teresa Sánchez de Cepeda y Ahumada (1515–1582), commonly known as St. Teresa of Avila, was a Spanish nun and mystic of the Carmelite Order. Her major*

works include her autobiography and The Interior Castle. According to St. Teresa, an intellectual vision is one that is accompanied by neither internal nor external images. It is thereby to be distinguished from common sight and from imaginative vision.

On January 30, 1939, Bataille borrowed Juan Berrueta and Jacques Chevalier's Sainte-Thérèse et la vie mystique *(Paris: Denoël et Steele, 1934) from the Bibliothèque Nationale, returning it on August 16 of that year. He references her thought in the last lecture at the Collège de Sociologie, on July 4, 1939. See Denis Hollier, ed.* Le Collège de Sociologie *(Paris: Gallimard, 1995) p. 812. Three years later, on April 20, 1942, while writing* Inner Experience, *Bataille borrowed Gaston Etchegoyen's* L'Amour Divin: Essai sur les Sources de Sainte Thérèse *(Bordeaux: Feret, 1923) from the Bibliothèque Nationale, returning it on July 16, 1943. See Bataille,* Oeuvres Complètes, *volume 12, pp. 612 and 617.* Trans.

9. *A:*

[. . .] an empire without shares.

April 1942

2

It is no less necessary to oppose "experience" to the progress of science than to pull it out of a dogmatic slumber. The end of "experience" is "experience" itself and not a certain knowledge acquired after the fact without going through it.

"Experience" is often studied with the help of written documents, without perceiving that, without having reached "experience" oneself, one speaks of it in an empty way. "Experience" can no doubt become an object of science, like one psychological fact among others, but the interest of this object is clearly distinct from that of "experience" itself.

Science apprehends objects in order to distinguish them, one from another, and in order to grasp the constant relationships between them. "Experience" flees from knowledge of this order: it distinguishes itself most clearly from discursive thought, which cannot

[All of this crossed out and replaced by:]

10. *A:*

2

8-2-42

This "introduction" was to have six parts, specified in advance. Having only written the first one, I provisionally gave up, going on to the "Post-Scriptum." I have to come to the point where I explain my way of writing. The "introduction" had three pages: I dropped it, I wrote the preface, which was unforeseen. I finished what touches on "dogmatic servitude" with great difficulty. Then I began reading

Janet, imagining it necessary to use its subtlety to go further.* I worked out, without writing it, a development that began with it. But as soon as it existed in my mind, since it had a sufficient precision, I ceased to concern myself with it; I forgot it. In fact, "inner experience" abandons life to incessant disorder.

I continue the "introduction" I began without holding myself to the initial intention. The change, it's true, affects less the outline than the execution; I will simplify everything.

From the outline that I had decided upon I give [. . .]

11. *Bataille evoked an authority that expiates itself in the final issue of* Acéphale *nº 5 (juin 1939) n.p.; see "La Folie de Nietzsche" in Bataille,* Oeuvres Complètes, *volume 1, p. 549. Here, however, he is alluding to meetings organized between December 1941 and March 1943 with two different groups of friends and friends of friends to discuss materials related to* Inner Experience. *One group included Pierre Prévost, Xavier de Lignac, Romain Petitot, Georges Pelorson, Louis Ollivier, and others, many of whom knew one another through their affiliation with the Vichy government–supported cultural group Jeune France. The other perhaps more "literary" group included Michel Leiris, Raymond Queneau, Raoul Ubac, Jean Lescure, and Michel Fardoulis-Lagrange, among others. Maurice Blanchot participated in both groups, though he was undoubtedly more closely affiliated with the first. A lecture prepared for one or both of these groups appears as "Socratic College" in* The Unfinished System of Nonknowledge, *pp. 5–17. For additional biographical information, see my* Georges Bataille *(London: Reaktion Books, 2007) pp. 164–6. Trans.*

12. *In B, these scattered notes:*

Inner experience is a movement in which man questions himself entirely.

Heidegger addresses himself to a community of men who refuse this interrogation. He does it, but as it is addressed to the scientific community, it is in fact as an interrogation, a rather sordid, stunted gnome, too polished to be a monster, embarrassed if not ashamed of being so.

those who are not freed from the fatal habits (intelligence) of school, I should regard as absent (ex. Mr. Janet)

aberration of the nonexistence of a community

[*on the other side:*]

difference between immediate sympathy and the desert where sympathy dies—toward the extremity

In the community: to put on guard the one whose intelligence has been formed at the University. He cannot grasp: He is missing an essential element.

See above reference in note one. Here, Bataille is probably alluding to Janet's De l'angoisse à extase—Études sur les croyances et les sentiments *(Paris: Alcan, 1926–28). He borrowed the book from the Bibliothèque Nationale in May 1942 (as well as in January and February 1935).*

difference between the domesticated state and the wild state—mountain and
plain

*

Show that it is not a matter of addition
knowledge + this or that
and that it is not a new value either

no renewal of method with regard to philosophy: one applies existing intelligence from the moment when the exp. begins
reserve: the method of Holocausts

that communication cannot be authority but only experience

The point of view of judgment from now on must be that of the lack that
resulted from the suppression of authorities.

[*on the other side, crossed out:*]

And in religion the situation is reversed. Whereas previously without being
able to establish [*relations with a?*] God
It is through a non-recourse to God that a less limited path is opened. But
this must be made tangible on another level, that of method.

*

coincidence of a new discourse and of the impotence of discourse
now what is the key to dramatization, it is authority, such that one can say,
if one comes to grasp the drama, that one touches authority—and reciprocally that
if one is lacking authority, if nothing has a particular value, no drama is possible
in the same way if an authority, a value exists, there is necessarily drama
for this is to say: one can only take it totally seriously
further: but authority is always something common, commonly felt, or it is
not. One must seek its authenticity. One can only seek it in common.

*

one could believe
reduction of the possible for example possibility of an inner experience
but from the moment when the little phrase is pronounced, authority itself
is inner experience, man once again has his possible at disposal, and this time even,
all that is possible
next after authority

principle of sacrifice, that is of all religion, is a dramatization tending to take on a general value

this leads to the sacrifice in which everything is victim

but it has two [*sources?*] (Blanchot)

development of intelligence

13. *B*: [. . .] this time without authority, on the contrary against authority, in a movement of divine ease.

14. *B*: [. . .] important (but it is in a less empty form—a little less empty— what I have already said: experience is authority): external means [. . .]

15. *B, crossed out:*

[. . .] my eyes are closed.

The practical difficulty of inner experience [*crossed out*: of the method (dramatization)] derives from the dogged faithfulness of man to discourse.

[*in margin:*]

story of the tempest by the fireside

that I don't write for one who would be unable to wait but for one who, entering into this book, would fall as into a hole.

It is through an "intimate [. . .]

16. *Ignacio de Loyola (1491–1556), a Spanish nobleman, knight, priest, and theologian, who founded the Society of Jesus. See Saint Ignatius of Loyola,* The Spiritual Exercises and Selected Works *(1522–48), ed. George Ganss (New York: Paulist Press, 1991). Bataille referenced Loyola's* Exercises *earlier in "Nietzschean Chronicle" (1937; see* Visions of Excess, *ed. Allan Stoekl [Minneapolis: University of Minnesota Press, 1985] p. 211). He borrowed a French translation of the book,* Exercices spirituels *(Paris: J. de Gigord, 1913), from the Bibliothèque Nationale on March 25, 1939, returning it on June 10, 1940. Trans.*

17. *B:*

[. . .] we let their useless sound fade away.

The effort is worth more than the trouble in that those states perhaps indifferent in themselves lift us literally outside of discourse (get us out of the mire). Indifferent moreover is quickly said. Aesthetic criticism of these states can go as far as one wishes, it is not what is important. But they are that which no sentence can grasp, bits of free existence and the escape of the mind into the unknowable. This, even the escape, is what they are.

But if the spirit of contestation was not in us, we could get caught in the languor of these states, enjoy them as we do those states that are commanded by graspable objects and in the end grasp the states themselves, appropriating them for ourselves. From then on, there is a necessity for constant exchanges, for frenzies following bursts of energy, for an agitation, sometimes burning, feverish, sometimes icy, for an interrogation undertaken endlessly in a new way. It is through these— often comical always breathless—episodes that the mind slowly gets itself out of the sand. These silent "movements" are nothing yet we must release their light and, projecting it outside of ourselves, adore it then extinguish it.

I will initially limit myself to principles whose developments are further on, often in great disorder (and the essential in part four, chapter five). I would only like to again show this: that

no innovation

this is yoga, which is to say essentially the art of mastering inner movements, but represented in the form—by presenting it in my way—of a rough recipe, which removes its pedantic character, on the contrary allowing to emerge

In addition, in yoga, at least such as it is transmitted to Westerners, the mastery of inner movements appears as hygiene and as an aesthetic: whereas I insert it into a movement that continues. I imagine that in India, there is a tendency to drone on about the method, to be the virtuoso, but that the mind being everywhere the same, the practice of yoga develops from the feeling of dissatisfaction, from a nostalgia for going beyond. But what is expressed to us is rather, it must be said, the aspects of coarseness, of platitude, for example, Vivekananda, even if he goes further is no less than this, through his very poor intellectual means . . . And what I have been shown of it as having practically the most meaning did not have any.

This is not a reason to distance oneself from it with too much humor

what I say is insufficient

in any case necessity despite the example of Christianity

for Christianity is the [*forcing*?] or individual faculties

To say formula is to recall poetry . . .

In every method including the mastery of moments [*movements*?] one must give inspiration the greatest role without ignoring formulas.

The essence of the Hindu formula is in some way to listen to breathing

and also one must put words in one's head, at once to serve as food for the need for words and to introduce feelings

silence

Search for all affectivity that one can link to this word that is barely a word since as a word it is already the abolition of sound. One must seek this silence in the sick delectation of the heart as one of those ungraspable lovers born in the most vaporous regions of dream. Nothing more than the shadow of summer heat, the transparency, in a room, of a ray of moonlight. When the scent of a flower is heavy with the secret fragrances of a past of childhood vacations, we linger alone in breathing in the flower [*see page 23*]

18. *In* The Tears of Eros, *Bataille recalls: "In 1938, a friend initiated me into the practice of Yoga"* (The Tears of Eros *[1962], trans. Peter Connor [San Francisco: City Lights Books, 1989] p. 206). Four years later, on July 8, 1942, during the final months of writing* Inner Experience, *Bataille borrowed Paul Oltramare's* L'Histoire des idées théosophiques dans l'Inde *(Paris: Geuthner, 1923) from the Bibliothèque Nationale, returning it on March 22, 1943. Trans.*

19. *B:*

[. . .] the abysses of the heart.

Hindus still have recourse to a means of the same type. They pronounce in a cavernous way, prolonged with a strangely virile but troubled resonance, evocative for us of silence, of the night of cathedrals, the syllable OM. This syllable is sacred for them. In this way they maintain themselves in a kind of religious torpor, full of troubled, even majestic divinity, the prolonging of which, in interiority, is infinite (but personally the "local color" of this procedure, even more than its aspect of "pious artifice" displeased me, if I have attempted to pronounce the syllable it is hardly enough to have grasped the sought-after effects and, moreover, I have never known how to give it the desired resonance).

Hindus do not limit themselves to these simple means; they also have more weighty ones. Certain among them occasionally take drugs (to my taste nothing is more repugnant or more contrary to the spirit, for me necessarily rebounding, torrential in the end, of "inner experience"). Tantric *yoga* uses sexual pleasure, not in order to ruin oneself in it, but to detach oneself from the object, the woman, whom they use, before the end: they avoid the last moment of pleasure. In these practices, it is always a question of an object having powerful prolongations in us but an object which in one way or another we neglect, having in mind only these prolongations, entering into possession of interiority, acquiring the mastery of inner movements, detached from the objects of our life.

Culture in excess of these means, all the more dangerous since they are rich, testifies to a disquieting inclination toward virtuosity. Not being easily offended by licentiousness, I find it vile to "abuse" a woman and pleasure for other ends than themselves, vile certainly to "exploit" experience, to make it into an affected exercise, as in a competition.

[*In the margin*:]

a royalty exercised upon ourselves
royal commandment
expiation = here direction toward experience
putting to death of the king which lays bare if it does not kill
it is not an exceptional path
it puts animal life into human (or divine) rhythm
Expiation is what project seeks to avoid and precisely the project that preserves some and engages others
Link to the end of the book.

I imagine that it is best to oppose the poorest means to this thick, suffocating vegetation. Particularly as they quickly have a powerful effect. Barely have we grasped the path of interiority when we enter into a fabulous region, with pleasant, ungraspable but exhilarating landscapes. For what one attains at the same time as the interior states is the possibility of increasing their intensity. Barely have we succeeded in directing attention toward them when they have fecundated it: what remained unnoticed up till now assumes the fullness, not of a storm—it is a question of slow states—but of an invading flood. What is exalted, in such moments, is sensibility within us. It sufficed that we detach from it the neutral objects that we usually offer it. It becomes such that—the Hindus have remarked—a minute cracking (the Hindus say, the drop of a pin) has an incredible resonance, as if they immediately touched, delicately but intensely, our heart.

But I know little, almost nothing, about India [*see page 24*]

20. *B, scattered notes:*

I imagine that it is the same, [*crossed out:* awakening of sensibility] in this case, as in vision. We keep our pupil almost closed against the intense light and in the darkness we dilate it. But this time it is no longer a particular organ that is at stake, it is the heart of the sensuous being. This is because in us, in a general way, we have turned the objects into night. And it is this that makes the journey to the end of being possible. For

normally hoarded, thereby detached

result responding to the introduced facts

but in the same way, we only relatively have

misleading possibilities

with intense moments one can recompose from objects

but starting from that . . .

21. *The* Advaita Vedenta *is a traditional school of Hindu religious philosophy with a coherent approach to interpreting the* Upanishads, *the* Bhagavad Gita, *and the* Brahma Sutras, *among other books. In the terms of this tradition, adherents seek liberation through knowledge of the identity of Atman, or pure consciousness of the true Self, and Brahman, the highest Reality. For Nietzsche's remarks on the Vedenta, see for example,* On the Genealogy of Morals (1887), trans. Walter Kaufman (New York: Random House, 1967) III, § 17. Trans.

22. *B:*

[. . .] no longer being reborn. [*crossed out:* What strikes me in this topic: assuming that I myself were at first a peasant of Louis XIV (or some other absurd simple man, or a girl, it matters little). In any case, what I am now would have been unimportant to the simple man. In the same way I am indifferent to what would be . . . And what does the identity of a self without the necessity of concern mean. I would very much like to concern myself, actually, with what will happen to me tomorrow, next year, and further on . . . I cannot escape from this necessity. But to extend it beyond a threshold, like death! That I should have to burn in hell forever, I couldn't care less about this if *I* were any other human being, unknown to me, arriving]

What I find striking on this topic: assuming X is dead [. . .]

23. *This is the last line of Psalm 39. Bataille is quoting the Vulgate version that prints Psalms 9 and 10 as one Psalm, reducing the numbers of all the following Psalms by one.* Trans.

24. *B:*

[. . .] appear to be of the same nature (strictly speaking, it's true, it is not so arbitrary, it is touching to concern oneself [*absurdly?*] with K: K contains in itself, at bottom, the multitude of being but in an incongruous form).

To imagine oneself [. . .]

25. *Friedrich Nietzsche*, La Volonté de puissance, *t. 2. (1938), ed. Friedrich Würzbach, trans. Geneviève Bianquis (Paris: Gallimard, 1995) § 612.* Trans.

26. *B, on the other side*:

It is possible that I want to be everything, to enclose everything: in this case I would enclose in order to stream out, to flow out, to lose myself, my concern to be everything would be my total absence of concern.

27. *Saint John of the Cross*, The Ascent of Mount Carmel, *book 1, chapter 13, section 11. See John of the Cross, Selected Writings, ed. Kieran Kavanaugh (New York: Paulist Press, 1987) p. 78. The complete phrase from this poem reads: "To arrive at being all / desire to be nothing."* Trans.

28. *B:*

[. . .] Interrogation encounters the very object that the logical operation causes to pass to vertigo: like nudity excitement.

Life, in the end, is ablaze and at risk.

Something sovereignly attractive [. . .]

29. *Martin Heidegger, "What Is Metaphysics?," trans. David Farrell Krell, in* Pathmarks, *ed. William McNeill (Cambridge: Cambridge University Press, 1998) p. 82. Translation modified.* Trans.

30. *Sannyasa is the final and highest life-stage in the ashram system, reserved for male (sannyasin) and female (sannyasini) elders older than fifty and younger monks who wish to renounce all worldly thoughts and desires in favor of spiritual contemplation.* Trans.

31. *B, scattered notes:*

If I push the interrogation (supplicating) to the end, I know nothing, and man in me is only insatiable, unappeasable thirst for knowledge.

The will to know is within me so much thirst to become everything that

No difference between knowledge and being everything. Knowledge assumes at any moment whatsoever an arbitrary intervention saying with authority: this question does not exist, you know everything that you must know.

And thereby one closes the world, one enclosed it in a past: revelation, the word of God.

32. *Immanuel Kant (1724–1804) argued for the existence of a "categorical imperative" according to which one should "act only according to that maxim whereby you can, at the same time, will that it should become a universal law." See* Grounding for the Metaphysics of Morals *(1785), trans. James Ellington (New York: Hackett, 1993) p. 30.* Trans.

33. *B, scattered notes:*

The community of which I speak is that which existed virtually from the fact of Nietzsche's existence (he is its requirement) and which each of Nietzsche's readers undoes by evading—which is to say by failing to resolve the enigma he posed (not even reading it).

34. *A robe, shirt, or tunic tainted in Greek mythology with the blood of the centaur Nessus, the wearing of which led to the death of Heracles. A shirt of Nessus is thus an emblem of inescapable fate. In Shakespeare's* Antony and Cleopatra, *when*

Mark Anthony realizes he has lost the battle of Actium and betrayed himself through his ill-fated love for Cleopatra, he laments: "The shirt of Nessus is upon me" (Act 4, scene 12). Bataille borrowed Antony and Cleopatra, *in Longworth Chambrun's translation, from the Bibliothèque Nationale on December 26, 1939, returning it on June 10, 1940. Trans.*

35. *B:* Undoubtedly, more than Nietzsche, I have insisted on the sense of the night of nonknowledge (the "death of God"). He does not linger [. . .]

36. *Misdated by Bataille, corrected here. Friedrich Nietzsche,* La Volonté de puissance, *t. 2, ed. Würzbach, § 615. Trans.*

37. *Friedrich Nietzsche,* The Gay Science *(1887) § 54. Translation modified. Trans.*

38. *B:*

[. . .] a bacchant philosopher.

The pseudonym Dianus* seems to me to reunite the savor of a bearded woman and a god that dies, throat streaming with blood.

Of the ideal of a "sheltered man," key to the most vulgar prejudices commonly affirmed, I would like to remark the shame that I feel for having touched upon it, even from a distance, remark it and so anxiously that only the thickest do not share it.

It is difficult [. . .]

39. *B:*

[. . .] puts at risk. Silence and laughter as well . . . but a mode of human relation breaking with the cowardly neutrality of a rule, insignificance understood from the beginning as a principle. Thus, dying, I would imagine communicating more than writing this book (there is in the dreadful moments of death a liberty unknown to us—right up to the lowest collapse, I tremble to speak of it). A book? Without the smallest possibility of crying out when a reader touches me with a greasy paw, causes me to enter into his dirty enterprise. How I sadden myself today with my lack of rigor—at least according to appearances—which risks leading profoundly astray. What alone liberates me is the idea that a book is really let go, no longer belongs to its author.

Next we provide these scattered notes from B:

End of *Intellectual Expression of Experience*

in the end: it is only a draft and, I now know, I will never write anything else. But I also know that this is the only intellectual expression of experience that

---

*See Guilty, *p. 3.*

remains possible, for, if it is true that despite all of the obstacles we can express experience, there is one which makes the play of expression exhausting. There is nothing we can say without a new point of view adding itself after the fact: it's inexhaustible. It is only if we touch upon completely simple objects (as in mathematics) that we can hope to exhaust the possible: and no doubt this is an error. Such an obstacle, it's true, is not particular to experience but augments it by the fact that instead of wanting to evade it, it throws itself into it.

> To write my book
> I force myself
> nothing else, sickness forbids me and besides I am only interested in . . .
> and once the book is finished, after which I
> life continuing, but one more sadness, the book finished, let go, me beyond

in the void. Obliged to return to what will relay the most interest for me, will I seek in my misery a sympathy, an outstretched hand. Or on the contrary would I [*take?*] that hand to bite it cruelly, in order to die alone in the end (to rediscover a purer air and to pursue contestation, for myself and for the one whom I will have bitten just then).

Left this open—and I want to, I'm not speaking out of resignation—this infinite rejuvenation of knowledge through a change in points of view. Thus I prefer to say: I will come back to it in another book, so as to better see myself, and to let it be seen that a slipping movement is beginning that neither I nor anyone can [*complete?*]. In the end, letting it be seen that the play of light between two nights already proclaims the supremacy of the night to which experience is linked. For just as the renewal necessary for life announces that we belong to death, so that of knowledge that it is the liege of the unknown. And experience taking my life to dedicate it to the unknown, it is quite necessary that its expression, which to all appearances is removed from it, being discourse, nevertheless remains profoundly faithful to it, being only a draft, admitting with it, even with a bit of pleasure, that element of death which is the flow of a river to the sea.

Part Two

1. Ciel *means both the sky and the heavens in French.* Trans.

2. *See Marquis de Sade,* The 120 Days of Sodom and Other Writings *(1785), ed. and trans. Austryn Wainhouse and Richard Seaver (New York: Grove Press, 1966).* Trans.

3. *See Fyodor Dostoevsky,* Notes From Underground *(1864). One measure of the significance of this book to Bataille is the fact that he co-wrote, with his cousin Marie-Louise Bataille, a radio adaptation of a portion of it that was broadcast on June 19, 1946. See Bataille, "L'Esprit Souterrain" in* L'Infini, *volume 75, no. 75 (2001) pp. 46–79.* Trans.

4. *See Plutarch,* The Lives of Noble Greeks and Romans *(76 CE), from the chapter on Caesar, in John Dryden's translation: "In his journey, as he [Caesar] was crossing the Alps, and passing by a small village of the barbarians with but few inhabitants, and those wretchedly poor, his companions asked the question among themselves by way of mockery, if there were any canvassing for offices there; any contention which should be uppermost, or feuds of great men one against another. To which Caesar made answer seriously, 'For my part, I had rather be the first man among these fellows than the second man in Rome.' "* Trans.

5. *See Thomas Hobbes,* The Treatise on Human Nature *(1650) chapter 9, § 13.* Trans.

6. *An allusion to St. John of the Cross,* The Dark Night *(1578–85).* Trans.

7. *Larvatus Prodeo is a Latin phrase from René Descartes's juvenilia that means "come forward masked." Descartes writes: "So far I have been a spectator in this theatre which is the world, but I am now about to mount the stage, and I come forward masked." See René Descartes,* The Philosophical Writings of René Descartes, *volume 1, trans. John Cottingham et alia. (Cambridge: Cambridge University Press, 1985) p. 2.* Trans.

8. Ipse. *Latin: himself, herself, itself. In his review of* Inner Experience, *Jean-Paul Sartre conjectures convincingly that Bataille borrows this term from Henry Corbin's translations of Heidegger, where the term renders Heidegger's German "Selbstheit," reflecting a return toward the self as the basis of a project. See Sartre, "A New Mystic" in* Sartre, Critical Essays *(Situations, 1947), trans. Chris Turner (London: Seagull Books, 2010) p. 243. Bataille borrowed Corbin's translation of Heidegger's "What Is Metaphysics?" from the Bibliothèque Nationale on August 18, 1941, returning it March 22, 1943. Only slightly further afield, Nietzsche coins a word from this same root in* Beyond Good and Evil *§ 207.* Trans.

9. Le Dernier Homme (The Last Man) *is the title of a book by Maurice Blanchot published by Éditions Gallimard in 1957; see* The Last Man, *trans. Lydia Davis (New York: Columbia University Press, 1987).*

Part Three

1. *William Blake from "[When Klopstock England defied]" in* The Complete Poetry and Prose of William Blake. *David V. Erdman, ed. (Berkeley: University of California Press, 1982) p. 500. I have silently restored Blake's language where it differs from the translation offered in Bataille's text.* Trans.

2. *On Bataille's encounter with Henri Bergson (1859–1941), see also* The Unfinished System of Nonknowledge, *pp. 153–4.* Trans.

I Want to Carry My Person to the Pinnacle

3. Littérature. *A magazine edited by André Breton, Philippe Soupault, and Louis Aragon between 1919 and 1921. In its first year, the editors posed the open question to*

their readers: "Why Write?" On this topic, see also Bataille's fragment from the 1930s,
"Les raisons d'écrire un livre . . ." ("The reasons to write a book . . .") in Oeuvres
Complètes, *volume 2, pp. 142–3.* Trans.

Death in a Sense Is a Deception

4. *Under the title* Sacrifices, *one will find a first version of this text in Bataille,*
Oeuvres Complètes, *volume 1, pp. 87–96, 645–6. Dated "Summer 1933,"* Sacrifices *was first published by Editions G.L.M. in October 1936 with etchings by André
Masson. For an English translation of* Sacrifices, *see Bataille,* Visions of Excess, *pp.
130–6.* Trans.
5. *"Eli Eli lama sabachthani?" Words spoken by Christ on the cross, meaning
"My God, my God, why have you forsaken me?" See Matthew 27: 46 and Mark 15:
34. This quotation is the only phrase to appear in more than one Gospel. It is also
appears in Psalms 22: 1.* Trans.
6. *For Kierkegaard's thoughts on Mozart's Don Giovanni, see Søren Kierkegaard,
"The Immediate Stages of the Erotic or The Musical Erotic" in* Either/Or, *volume 1
(1843), trans. David Swenson et alia (Garden City, NY: Anchor Books, 1959) pp.
45–134.* Trans.
7. *Wolfgang Amadeus Mozart,* Don Giovanni *(1787) Act 2, scene 5: "L'ultima
prova dell'amor mio." Inaccuracies in Bataille's quotation silently corrected here.* Trans.
8. *Wolfgang Amadeus Mozart,* Don Giovanni *(1787) Act 2, scene 5: "Don
Giovanni a cenar teco."* Trans.

The Blue of Noon

9. *Reprinted from* Minotaure *n° 8 (juin 1936) pp. 50–52; see note in Bataille,*
Oeuvres Complètes, *volume 1, p. 673. Bataille's novel* Blue of Noon *[1935] also
reprints roughly the second half of this text, from "I will die in hideous conditions" to
"against all reason"; for English translation see* Blue of Noon, *trans. Harry Mathews*
(London: Marion Boyars, 1986) *pp. 23–24.*
In Minotaure, *this text accompanied a poem by André Masson, "Du Haut de
Montserrat," and reproductions of two paintings from 1935, "Aube à Montserrat" and
"Paysage aux Prodiges"; it was preceded by this note:*

What André Masson experienced at Montserrat, in particular during the
night of the *Paysage aux Prodiges*, what he has expressed in the paintings that these
pages reproduce, is closely associated with what I myself experienced and expressed
in the following text.
It is necessary to grant the greatest possible importance to the fact that the
reality in question can only be reached in religious ecstasy.

*This note leads us to reprint here the narrative that André Masson tells of his
night on Montserrat (published by Jean-Paul Clébert in* Georges Bataille et André
Masson, *"Les Lettres nouvelles" [mai 1971]):*

"*Prodigious spot. At an altitude of fourteen hundred meters, we spent, my wife and I, a winter night, lost at the summit. This is one of the most astonishing memories of my life. We were staying at the monastery. We were dressed for summer. We had lingered before the sunset that I was drawing. The sun was setting in the direction of Aragon, since this mountain is, like Mount Sinai, in a kind of sierra. I saw the sea of clouds approach, breaking like a tide. Then night fell. We had lost the path to descend. We slid ceaselessly; I could not stay in one place, I was nervous because there were shooting stars all the time. We found ourselves on a platform no larger than that and . . . the abyss.*

"*Then I had an attack of nerves (a sequel to the nervous illness which followed my war wound) and my wife said to me: we can't stay here, we have to climb back up. There was a double vertigo, the abyss and the sky with the shooting stars; the sky itself appeared to me like an abyss, which I had never felt before, vertigo from above at the same time as the vertigo from below. And I found myself in a kind of maelstrom, almost a tempest, and as though hysterical. I though that I was going crazy.*

"*Then we happened to climb up, holding onto the boxwood and cane-apple trees, and, at the summit, we waited for morning. Well, there, the spectacle was the opposite. The mountain entirely covered with clouds. Only the spot where we were emerged. And the sun rose. It was sublime. We were on our mountain like Moses awaiting the arrival of the Lord.*

"*When we arrived down below, one of the brothers was surprised to see us arrive from that direction and when my wife explained to him that we had passed the night at the summit, he cried out: Caramba! It was the first time that I heard that word that Hugo had made popular. The hostelry was not yet open, but we heard music, the children's choirs, absolutely as in Parsifal, the priests who celebrated mass. Although we were chilled to the bone, it was extraordinary. It was one of my most gripping moments. The cosmic and the religious suddenly linked by an adventure: travelers lose their way in the mountains, are present at the death of a star, at its rebirth, descend to a religious place where one appears to celebrate that event and not at all the death of Christ . . .*"

10. *All of this beginning refers to the* Dossier de l'Oeil pinéal, *in Bataille,* Oeuvres Complètes, *volume 2, pp. 13–47, 414–21. For a partial English translation, see Bataille,* Visions of Excess, *pp. 73–90.*

11. Minotaure *has for this paragraph:*

No limit, no measure can be given to the violence of those who are liberated by a vertigo experience before the vault of the sky. The least hope is regarded simply as a respect that cowardice or fatigue still accorded to the necessity of the world and there is no longer a human interest which does not sink into derision: the representation of sufferings, of miseries, or of words of which they would be guilty would make them laugh.

The ground [. . .]

12. *This city is Trento (see notes to* On Nietzsche *in Bataille,* Oeuvres Complètes, *volume 6, p. 409; for English translation of referenced material, see* On Nietzsche *(1945), trans. Bruce Boone (New York: Paragon House, 1992) pp. 106–7.*

13. Minotaure *continues:*

Prometheus moaned when a chaos of rocks fell on him.

Don Juan was drunk with carefree insolence when he was swallowed by the earth.

Beneath the dazzling light of the sky [. . .]

14. *Friedrich Nietzsche, "The Old and New Tablets," Thus Spoke Zarathustra, part three, § 23, in* The Portable Nietzsche, *trans. Walter Kaufmann (New York: Penguin, 1954).* Trans.

The Labyrinth (Or the Composition of Beings)

15. *A first version of this text appeared in* Recherches philosophiques, *volume v (1935–1936): 364–72 and is reprinted in Bataille,* Oeuvres Complètes, *volume 1, pp. 433–41; for an English translation, see Bataille,* Visions of Excess, *pp. 171–7.*

16. *Angela of Foligno (1248–1309), a tertiary of St. Francis and mystic, known for her autobiography. The Gallimard edition of* Inner Experience *notes that Bataille's text is Angèle de Foligno,* Le Livre de l'expérience des vrais fidèles *(Paris: Droz, 1927), in Latin with French translation by Ferré. Bataille also copied and translated passages from the book into his notebooks; see* Guilty, *p. 9. See Angela of Foligno,* Complete works, *translated, with an introduction by Paul Lachance; preface by Romana Guarnieri (New York: Paulist Press, 1993). The exact quotation cited here does not appear in the English text.* Trans.

17. *The German army invaded Belgium on May 10, 1940, reaching Paris by June 14.* Trans.

"Communication"

18. *In C, this paragraph precedes:*

There are not only differences in nature that are reducible (I can extract gold from sulfur): the difference between you and me is historical as well as a natural; but is not reducible, since my death could not make me you nor your death make you me.

19. *In C:*

[. . .] attack from the outside.

1. From Laughter to Anguish

It is true that [. . .]

20. *C:*

[. . .] *shattered*; but you only become this extreme point and this moment of foaming crest that is *reflection*, by being an obstacle to the shattering rush, an obstacle destined to soon be shattered.

*

To the extent [. . .]

21. La part du feu *is the title of a collection of essays published by Maurice Blanchot in 1949; for an English translation, see Maurice Blanchot,* The Work of Fire, *trans. Charlotte Mandell (Stanford: Stanford University Press, 1995).* Trans.

22. *C:*

[. . .] Thus we *sacrifice* the one we laugh at, abandoning him to a more or less pronounced, more or less lasting degradation. It also happens that our fellow being *sacrifices* himself in some way, of his own free will, that of his own movement he makes himself *sacred* (like the *madman*). However, we only ever perceive in others the way in which the spring-like movement of life has us, our pretentions, our naive illusions, at its disposal. Hardly have we grasped the vanity [. . .]

23. *In C, pages 7–12, the text continues:*

What strikes only in shared laughter and which sometimes seems to merit contempt, is the facile and superficial illusion of anguish. You laugh at seeing a woman fall on the sidewalk; you would not laugh if she had thrown herself from a window, if she had been crushed at your feet. You would not laugh because you would feel anguish, which it's true you would keep to yourself; but this anguish that you feel before a sudden and terrifying destruction, you would have felt it, perhaps less strongly but anguish, if the woman who fell on the sidewalk had not been indifferent to you. In fact, you feel anguish, you don't laugh, as soon as you feel the bonds of solidarity that unite you to the victim: this can derive from the violence of the destruction, this can derive from the bonds of a particular affection.

You would therefore have to take this for a weakness. When you laugh, you perceive yourself to be the accomplice of a destruction of what you are, you then confuse yourself with this wind of destructive life that leads everything without pity to its end (and whose disheveled joy carries away the partitions that separate you from others). But it suffices that you see yourself threatened by this same wind— you and yours—for your complicity and your joy to change immediately into fear.

2. *From Anguish to Glory*

Anguish often ties bonds around us without anything else resulting from it: it can resolve itself in the same moment. But then even while its object proves to be heavy, it can, if we have felt it for others, abandon us in the isolation of its sadness; and if it resulted from a danger that threatens us it can happen that only death brings it to its conclusion.

But anguish is far from being limited to the impasse that it sometimes is; and most often, it finds itself on the path of decisive movements. Like laughter, it breaks the barriers of isolation. When the object that provokes it is the same for everyone, it brings men close. And it is, as you will see, in this bringing together wherein breath is suspended, that human existence comes to a decisive moment of its abandonment and its laceration in the darkness of the universe.

*

At this point, I require a more profound test of your attention. What follows is not of a more demanding intelligence than the rest, but its intelligence asks that you now go right to the end of reflection. To access the deserted extremity of things assumes that a condition is realized: the silence of discourse, which discourse (the ordinary and halting steps of thought) has served only as an introduction. You now reach with me the point at which life stops, where it exhausts itself, loses itself. Where life loses itself in a remoteness so charged that everything is overwhelming. No mystery is more profound, more impenetrable, whereas we, you and I, however, have meaning only to the extent that its depths, suddenly, remain accessible to us, open.

*

It is the strange and painful fate of those who live today to be unable to approach the threshold that you now reach with me, if not guided by the markers and the traces that only an *archeological* reflection permits one, with difficulty, to discover. Such that we must arrive covered with the dusty clothes of the archeologist; how could we, in fact, arrive there, where each thing that is revealed is made *sacred*, if we had not sought the paths followed by the *sacrifices* of all times? Above all how would it have been possible to make clear the meaning of this ultimate step that we haven't had at our disposal, on those paths, from disparate facts that an indifferent lucidity has patiently established? But how vain is this science that has the *sacred* as an object and that limits itself to knowing it as crudely as a physiologist who would know life only on the dissecting table. If, before the threshold, we couldn't cast off the archeologist's clothes and lay ourselves bare, it would have been better not to have begun to take any step.

This is why, I must ask you now, since you are running over sentences wherein the silence of thought is inscribed with even more necessity than its logical sequence, to give up, if from very far away you do not feel the anguish in which I am seeking to *communicate* with you. If this reading did not have the gravity, the deadly sadness of sacrifice, for you, I would rather not have written anything.

*

SACRIFICE IS THE COMMUNICATION OF ANGUISH. Also the only true sacrifice is human sacrifice. Since the victim that the knife puts in death's power is there *for me*. In him, I was able to perceive myself beaten by the rage for destruction, in which, at least, when I was afraid to look too closely, I felt myself in solidarity with the existence that fell before me into nothingness. If I myself were dead, if I had myself been destroyed, my anguish would have been no further away than the knife. I would not have been able to recognize myself, open to the mortal winds of the outside, since all knowledge would be dissolved in me as soon as my heart had stopped beating. In order that in me this existence given to men cease to be impotently closed and *communicate*, it was necessary that another die before me. And not only before me but before others, in all ways similar to me, and, like me, adherents through anguish with the annihilation which takes place, and yet, like me, sheltered from the blow savagely turned toward the victim. For this fear, this anguish that seizes man here and there in his abandonment must not go as it has come. It must not be resolved too quickly through the deliverance of death, still less dissipate by chance, still less become interminable and sickly; it must be communicated from one man to another, it must be accumulated and charged like a storm, inscribing its point of night in the luminous order of things.

*

Anguish binds beings each time that they feel the threat of death weigh upon them. It is because they will one day be dying that they are separated from the surging excess of the world. And yet they do not have the strength to fully desire a fusion that it is not possible to know, since it annihilates. So they stop at a moving nostalgia for death, approaching it closely enough to know its terror but from far enough away to escape it. From the closed isolation that is the saddest of deaths to the fusion of physical death—where one who is at risk, as if he had never existed, is cruelly suppressed—there is neither rest nor appeasement: and anguish is only the absence of all rest and the impossibility of appeasement; there is a struggle and laceration (there is no way out), between the desire to give oneself entirely to the bacchanalia that is unleashed and destroys, and the concern to last, to participate in the bacchanalia without being dead.

*

There is no way out and the *communication of anguish*—which takes place in sacrifice—is not the solution but the introduction and the maintenance of laceration in the very center, in the heart of the human city. It is only in anguish that this being that you are maintains enough consistency and yet leaves a gaping the wound through which, rushing from all points of the universe, fatal destruction enters. Without your anguish, you would not be this faithful mirror of excess movements, of the vertiginous flight from night and day, which you have become. This is why you would be wrong to refuse this wild amplification of the pain from which you suffer, of the splendor that follows it, and of your final reality—which is sacrifice. What you feel of yourself, your isolated anguish makes you aware of everything that enters into play. But the anguish that you do not *communicate* to your fellow beings is in some way held in contempt and mistreated. Only to the weakest degree does it have the power to reflect the glory that comes from the depths of the heavens. This power derives from the place that you accord it. You must still discover your most precious possession in anguish, what you must consequently communicate to your fellow beings and, thereby, magnify without measure. Without sacrifice, anguish would only be what it is—I mean what it seems to be to the one suffering from it—it would not be the *heart* in which the movement of worlds is bound and tears itself apart.

*

You must therefore abandon yourself to your destiny or more precisely accept that it lead you to glory. This anguish that wounds you, it is necessary that it lacerate you even more so that you communicate it to your fellow beings. You must go to the public square and descry it as it is, you must descry it to your fellow beings. They must learn from you this thirst for blood that belongs to no one in isolation: the anguish that is communicated, in the darkness, from one to another, demands that blood flow; the shared desire to emerge from the neutering circle of solitude, to negate egotism without light, demands that a victim be chosen to die. Desire chooses, if it can, the one designated by divine seduction: it will designate you if you are *king*. But it does not matter that fate calls you, or anyone else. It is even necessary that you survive, so that that absolutely freezing light that death unleashes be reflected in you, in the rays of your anguish. And in the same way, when you die, you will transmit to others the hard message of light.

*

For it is true—and this truth asks that you suffer and drink deep from it—that communicated anguish changes into glory. Death or isolation stopped everything. But, in an anguished group, there is no longer either isolation or death. The isolation is resolved in the communication of anguish. And death can only strike the isolated individual; it cannot annihilate the group. From then on, just as the accumulated storm becomes lightning and thunder, anguish coming closer and closer is lost in a flash of glory. It suffices that a single individual encounter the violent destiny with which it is heavy.

[*This manuscript note follows:*]

This text is not finished: what should have emerged from what follows is that the necessity for sacrifice should not be understood in a literal sense [*crossed out*: it is a question of mystical complicity with the death of one's fellow being and not of really renewing the savage practice. Cruelty and anguish are married in this way] but as the expression of the nature of things that the most ancient men found in their rituals. It is a question of complicity with death and only of *that which* reveals itself in anguish to the mind, not of acts that must be accomplished.

    24. *Dionys Mascolo gave the editors of Bataille's* Oeuvres Complètes *access to the proofs for the first edition of* Inner Experience. *At this point in the text, Bataille anticipated a long development, in part unpublished, in part borrowed from "L'Amitié" [Friendship] (extracts of the first pages of* Guilty *published under the pseudonym Dianus in 1940 (see Bataille,* Oeuvres Complètes, *volume 6, pp. 292–306; for an English translation, see* Parallax *7: 1 [January 2001] pp. 3–15). Bataille's text here begins in italics:*

    [. . .] *the ecstatic experience from which I set out.*
    I introduced the preceding above all as a description—indirect—of the "ecstatic states" which I had attained.

*Dianus, in "Friendship" (*Mesures, *15 avril 1940), makes tangible the links between the preceding and inner experience. This emerges from a certain number of pages:*]

The path of ecstasy crosses through a necessarily deserted region: this region is nevertheless one of apparitions—seductive and agonizing. Beyond, there is no longer *anything,* if not, a lost, unintelligible movement: as if a blind man fixedly regarding the sun, eyes open and becoming in this way himself blinding light. That one imagines a change so quick, a combustion so sudden that every representation of substance becomes nonsense: place, exteriority, image, so many words lacerated by what happens, the only words that do not entirely betray themselves—*fusion, light*—are by nature ungraspable. It is more difficult to speak of *love,* such a word being burnt and without vigor, for the same reason as *subjects* and *objects* that communally sink into their impotence to love.*

Ecstasy is *communication* between terms (these terms can remain as undefined as is possible) and communication takes on a value that the terms do not yet have: it annihilates them in the same way that the luminous burst of a star annihilates (slowly) the star itself, as well as the objects near enough to be profoundly modified by the constant metamorphosis of the star in the warmth and light.

Incompletion, the wound, misery, and not completion are the condition of "communication." Communication is not completion.**

To the extent that the inaccessible opens itself up in me, I abandon the initial doubt: the fear of a delightful and dull beatitude. To the extent that I effortlessly contemplate what has become for me the object of ecstasy, I can say of this object that it lacerates me: it cuts like a razor's edge; it is, more narrowly, a point crying out, blinding, dazzling to the point of screeching, but it is not only a point since it engulfs. Provocative nudity, acidic nudity is a strident arrow drawn toward this point.

What is "communicated" from this point to a being, from a being to this point, is the fulgurating need to lose oneself. Through "communication," beings cease to be enclosed in themselves.

The "fulgurating need to lose oneself" is the most interior and most distant part of reality, the living moving part, but this has nothing to do with a supposed substance.***

---

*For the preceding paragraph, see "L'Amitié" Oeuvres Complètes, *volume 6, p. 297; compare* Guilty, *p. 25.*

**For the preceding two paragraphs, see "L'Amitié" Oeuvres Complètes, *volume 6, p. 297; compare* Guilty, *p. 26.*

***For the preceding paragraphs, see "L'Amitié" Oeuvres Complètes, *volume 6, pp. 300–1; compare* Guilty, *pp. 29–30.*

The method of ecstasy is similar to that of sacrifice: the point of ecstasy is laid bare if I shatter in myself the particularity that encloses me in myself (in the same way that a particular animal takes the place of the sacred at the moment that it is destroyed).

Thus: I turn away from an image of torture and, by turning away, I close myself; turning away is one of the access points at which my particularity is closed. If I replace the image before me, it opens the door, or rather tears it open.

But it does not follow that I can necessarily reach the exterior. Lacerating images (in the precise sense of the word) continually form on the surface of the sphere wherein I am enclosed. I only just reach the lacerations. I only glimpse a possibility of getting out: the wounds reclose. *Concentration* is necessary: a profound laceration, a lasting lightning strike should shatter the sphere; the point of ecstasy is not reached *in its nudity* without a painful insistence.

Given the decision to escape the limits of the individual and of the objects that are useful to him, it is natural to seek an outlet by multiplying the "overwhelming" images, freeing their play. These images make a glimmer appear in an elusive and pitiful reality, they create nostalgia: they do not permit access to the point where the lightning strikes.

In the first place, a state of calm equivalent to sleep must be opposed to normal movements. It is necessary to refuse every image, to become an absorption in oneself so complete that every fortuitous image slips to the surface in vain. Moreover, this absorption still needs an image to be produced: one single imprecise image of peace, of silence, of night.

There is something deceptive and irritating about this first movement. The natural movement of life towards the outside opposes it. The voluptuous or even heavy and painful torpor the mind enters is that much more debatable in that it depends upon humiliating artifices. It is inevitable to observe a position of the relaxed body, stable and nevertheless without laxity. The necessities are personal, but why not replace them from the start with some effective means: thus deep breathing, letting it be held by the bewitchment of the thorax that lifts a very slow breath. Moreover, so as to create a void in the self, the unfolding of ideas through endless associations must be avoided: this is why it is better to offer the flow of images the equivalent of a riverbed by means of obsessive words or phrases. These procedures must appear inadmissible to impatient minds. Yet the same minds ordinarily tolerate much more: they live under the command of mechanisms that these procedures want to bring to an end.

If it is true that intervention is *detestable* (but is it necessary to love that which is detestable), the submission to constraint is less serious than the risk of extreme seduction or lassitude. The first sleep weakens and enchants. After that weakening sickens. It is dull; it is not tolerable to live life enchanted for long.

For several days, it is necessary to enshroud life in an empty darkness. A marvelous relaxation results: the mind feels an unlimited power, the entire universe seems to be available to human will, but trouble comes quick.*

---

*For the preceding paragraphs, see "L'Amitié" Oeuvres Complètes, volume 6, pp. 301–2; compare Guilty, pp. 30–32, 184–5.

This can be expressed forcefully and clearly retained: that the truth is not there where men consider themselves in isolation: it begins with conversations, shared laughter, friendship, eroticism and has no place other than *passing from one to the other*. I hate the image of a being linked to separation and I laugh at the solitary who claims he reflects the world. He cannot truly reflect it because, by becoming himself the center of reflection, he ceases to be the image of *worlds* that lose themselves in every sense. On the contrary, if I see that the worlds do not resemble any separate and closed being, but *what passes from one to another* when we burst into laughter or when we make *love*: at this moment, the immensity of these worlds is opened to me and I lose myself in their flight.

Then I hardly matter to myself and the presence foreign to me hardly matters—even if it is God. I don't believe in God, due to lack of faith in myself and I am sure that one must believe absurdly in the miserable self that we are in order to believe in what seems similar to that self, in God (which is only the guarantee of the self). The one to whom life is devoted, I will say more voluntarily to itself, to life, to lose itself, to mysticism, at least that one could open one's eyes to a world wherein that which is can only have meaning if wounding, lacerating, *sacrificing*, where divinity, in the same way, could only be laceration (execution), only sacrifice.*

Most importantly: each person is a stranger to the universe, belonging to the objects, tools, meals, newspapers that enclose him in his particularity, leaving him ignorant of everything else. The only element that introduces existence into the universe is death: when a man represents death to himself, he ceases to belong to rooms, to friends and family: he returns to the free play of worlds.

To better grasp this, think of the wave–particle opposition in physics. The first accounts for this phenomenon by waves, as light, vibrations of air or sea, the second composes the world from particles—neutrons, photons, electrons—the most basic combinations of which are atoms or molecules. From love to light waves or from individual beings to particles, the relationship is perhaps arbitrary or forced. Yet the final problem of physics helps us see how two images of life, one erotic or religious, the other profane and matter-of-fact (one open and the other closed) oppose one another. Love is such a complete negation of the isolated being that we find it natural and even, in a certain sense, ideal that an insect dies from the embrace it desired (the female is no less struck down than the male, bringing a new being or beings into the world is perhaps less contrary to the law of individual isolation, which presides over life, than death). The counterpart of this excess is found in the need for possession of one by another, which does not alter singular erotic effusions: which even ordains the relations of reciprocal belonging between a believer and the presence that he discovers darkly. (God becomes a thing for the believer the way the believer becomes a thing for God). Why deny that therein lies a necessary effect? But to recognize it is not to grant grand names to the figures

---

*For the preceding paragraphs, see "L'Amitié" Oeuvres Complètes, volume 6, p. 303; compare Guilty, p. 39.

of the game. The lacerating and howling "point" I spoke of radiates life to such a degree (even if it is—or almost is—the same thing as death) that once striped bare, the object of a dream or of a desire commingled with it is animated, enflamed, and intensely present. From the moment of its supposed "apparition," the divine individual is no less available than a lover, than a woman offering her nakedness to an embrace. The god pierced with wounds or the spouse ready for pleasure is a transcription of the "cry" that ecstasy attains. The transcription is easy (it is even inevitable) given that we are obligated to fix an object before us. But someone who accedes to this object in this way does not know that he has destroyed everything that merits the name of a real object. And, just as nothing separates him from his death any longer (which he loves in acceding to this kind of fulgurating pleasure which demands its arrival), he must still link the sign of the laceration and anni- hilation to the faces that respond to his need for love.*

[*What follows is unpublished:*]

[*This spring ended in disaster—mad depression, collapse. It is not that I didn't, like any creature, conserve my power to be absent from the present time (to remain "anachronistic" like a bird whose songs the hecatomb does not interrupt). But quickly, one had to "daydream" to better face things: one saw so little that I took my shadow for another . . . Who could resist my "final address"? . . .*]**

TO WHOMEVER WISHES TO UNDERSTAND ME WELL

1

If one opens one's eyes in the street: that which is spread out before you, common and free, which believes itself to be everything and is only horror, must come up in some places against true strength: in such places, a violent feeling seizes the most coarse.

A will that obliges one to silence can only cling to anguish. Anguish is not fear of a definable ill.

If some eager will exists in you, which tramples over vulgarity and refuses to let go of glory for rest, it is vain and friable—desire for the picturesque—as long as it is not inclined toward anguish.

Compared to the most able men, the crowd is impoverished and, sadder still, in its eyes intimate values are inconsequential. There is no way to remedy this. It is as vain to speak of what no longer has any appeal for the crowd as it is to dream of the return of festivals. One draws a consequence from this: that a new value

---

*For the preceding paragraphs, see "L'Amitié" Oeuvres Complètes, volume 6, pp. 304–5; compare Guilty, pp. 40–41.

**Brackets and italics here are Bataille's.

only has meaning on the condition that it responds to a down-to-earth concern of the majority. Let me be well understood if I cry that these ideas are not only shortsighted: they betray the poverty of the "most able." It is true that in the long run, fatigue carries them away. One forgets the foundation: that the happiest people give their luck to the majority *by losing themselves.*

A *saint* is someone who loses his life—to no matter what end. But not as a soldier whose value is that much greater if he is inaccessible to fear. The *saint* inhabits anguish: he would be that much more of a *saint* if he sweated anguish.

The anguish of the neurotic is the same as that of the *saint.* The neurotic, the saint are engaged in the same struggle. Their blood flows from similar wounds. But the first wastes and the other gives.

What chance demands of men: *friendship.*

But anguish? A shameful fairy at whom one refuses to spit!

2

If you demand of thought that it betray life and dissimulate conflicts, I owe you only boredom if at least . . .

What am I waiting for? First your passivity, that the sound that you are stop. I ask you to follow me step by step into the night, better yet, into despair. I won't warn you of holes—you will fall—or of walls—you will run into them. In advance, "my heart breaks into laughter" at your awkwardness.

The Scriptures say of fools that their number is infinite. I add that in itself, the foolishness of the most wise is infinite. Night falls over a crowd in which each truth is only a gross insult for the others. Happy is he who wanted to be the child of this crowd and this night! In him human folly has entered into the kingdom of anguish.

Cunning cruelty, impudent coarseness, deception, good sense (above all dull), dissimulated interest, an old maid's gullibility, *laughter* on every occasion: these are the first words of my new "wisdom."

In a night of vomiting, to pass from this prostitution to the sadness of death: to reduce a vain uproar to an anxious silence is a "wisdom" at once *more* and *less* great.

Sovereignty alone attains a complete "wisdom." It demands silence and yet is only laughter (and if it stops laughing, it is *laughable*).

The "wisdom" is to be everyone.

The grossest weakness: to curse a constraint imposed on "everyone" and to be in control of oneself.

You are made in the image of *everyone.* You harshly constrain obscure desires within yourself. Harshness (gross ignorance) imposes itself on you in the incompatible throng of needs.

It is vain to flee pain and to want to liberate men for it. One increases it in fleeing it. The only means of suffering less is to be deaf. Pain is a cry of misfortune, a cry of hatred against chance . . .

3

What I have said comes from the heart. I find nothing in it that stops me. It makes me nauseous: the black foolishness in which I would flee it?

Empty expression, eyes white as marble, a throbbing desire that one gouge out my eyes! To be blind, deaf to the auction cries of empty words—maledictions, calumnies, errors, praise—blind! Imbeciles with scrubbed faces, my fellow beings, *whom I see* . . .

If one has not suffered enough—to the point of nausea—and if one sees me: I am only lies. One perceives me as clean and shaved: internally—covered with vomit. I am weary and cunning. I have *seen*. I have not only seen the mud into which I sink, these heavy eyes that I interrogate, but what dead eyes perceive.

What I have seen, what I know. There is no longer any power in the world: a sleep—interminable—weighs me down. It matters little that I force myself. It's vain. I will not tear out my tongue, laughing! I must continue, pass from one minute to the next—the minute measured on the dial—this tongue filling my mouth.

My fellow beings! My friends! Like stuffy houses, with dusty windows: eyes *closed*, lids open! I would like to burst them open, make the windows fall in a single crash, open to the violent wind.

What a crash of windows teaches: that everything is dead if this is not it: that it is light . . .

The one for whom I write (with whom I am familiar), he will have to weep out of compassion for what he has just read, then he will laugh, for he has *recognized* himself. No one is sun or lightning: but in him sun and lightning are prolonged . . . I offer him an enigma: his greatest danger? Would it be to weep—or to laugh? Or to survive his tears? Or to survive his laughter?

If I could know—perceive and discover—"the one for whom I write," I imagine that I would die. He would have contempt worthy of me. But I would not die of his contempt: survival needs weight.

4

He who writes with his blood does not want to be *read*? . . . One mustn't read me: I do not want to be covered with evasions. I propose a challenge, not a book. I offer nothing for insomnia.

In anguish, a brutal accident, a pool of blood, a body remains on the road, deprived of life . . . Assuming that the conclusion *made sense*, death leaves one speechless. In time, in death, there is a promise of silence, a definitive silence . . . I elude the inexorable promise, if I "dramatize" my death; the drama differs from time in that it is speech while time is mute.

But what does the vertigo that takes hold of me mean if I feel the collapse of time within myself, dark, filthy, such that one day, it will silence me? Nothing, it is obvious and it cries out: my cry is addressed to my fellow beings! Nonsense?

Nonsense rots he who remains deaf to this great cry. If silence is the truth of the universe, at least of comedy, my living mouth could not ape the silence of a dead man.

What few ears can bear, the revolting truth. With this bare truth, intelligence fades; it is no longer, in the heart of things, anything but an escape route, on the side of falsification: *man does not live by bread alone, but on poison.*

This truth is itself poison. It terrifies, withdrawing hope (of saving man, of distancing misery). It is necessary to hide it from those who avoid it; it is a proud, bewitching truth, and, like a raised stem, it is pleasing.

A joke along the way: ten behinds, of men or women, at random . . . You would take hold of the most rotten truths? They ask for love . . . Your fellow being, about whom you do not care, is the same as you: what you see, what you hear, what you are . . .

Part Four

1. *Between its initial publication in 1941 and the publication of the second edition in 1950, Maurice Blanchot substantially revised* Thomas l'obscur, *his first novel, cutting roughly one-quarter of the text. Both versions are however now currently available. For the first version, quoted by Bataille here, see Maurice Blanchot,* Thomas l'obscur: Première version 1941 *(Paris: Gallimard, 2005) p. 33. For a translation of this quotation in the context of the second revised edition of* Thomas l'obscur, *see Maurice Blanchot,* Thomas the Obscure, *trans. Robert Lamberton (Barrytown, NY: Station Hills Press, 1988) pp. 14–15.* Trans.

2. *Maurice Blanchot,* Thomas l'obscur: Première version 1941 *(Paris: Gallimard, 2005) p. 162. This quotation does not appear in the second revised edition of* Thomas l'obscur. *Trans.*

God

3. *The reference here is to the transfiguration of Jesus on Mr. Thabor; see Matthew 17: 1–6, Mark 9: 1–8, Luke 9: 28–36; see also 2 Peter 1: 16–18, John 1: 14.* Trans.

4. *Angela of Foligno,* Complete works, *trans. Paul Lachance (New York: Paulist Press, 1993) p. 202.* Trans.

5. *Angela of Foligno,* Complete works, *p. 204.* Trans.

6. *Angela of Foligno,* Complete works, *p. 315.* Trans.

7. *Angela of Foligno,* Complete works, *p. 316.* Trans.

8. *Here Bataille is paraphrasing: "When that love leaves me I nonetheless remain so totally contented, so angelic, that I can love reptiles, toads, serpents, and even devils." Angela of Foligno,* Complete works, *p. 184.* Trans.

9. *Angela of Foligno,* Complete works, *p. 126, translation modified.* Trans.

10. *Angela of Foligno,* Complete works, *p. 126.* Trans.

11. *See Angela of Foligno,* Complete works, *p. 131. Bataille copied these passages, in his own translation, in the notebook that would become the first part of* Guilty, *recording the period from September to December 1939.* Trans.

Descartes

12. *René Descartes, letter (presumed to be) to Jean Silhon, May 1637 [dated March 1637 in the Adam and Tannery edition of Descartes's complete works], in* The Philosophical Writings of Descartes, *volume 3, p. 55.* Trans.

13. *See René Descartes,* Discourse on Method *(1637) in* The Philosophical Writings of Descartes, *volume 1, p. 129.* Trans.

14. *See René Descartes,* Discourse on Method *(1637) in* The Philosophical Writings of Descartes, *volume 1, p. 113.* Trans.

15. *Paraphrasing the words of Socrates in Plato's* Republic *ln. 354c: "All I know is that I know nothing." This is the second of the two Socratic maxims that Bataille referenced in his "Socratic College" lecture, see* The Unfinished System of Nonknowledge, *p. 11.*

16. *See René Descartes, letter (presumed to be) to Jean Silhon, in* The Philosophical Writings of Descartes, *volume 3, p. 55.* Trans.

17. *See René Descartes, letter to Mersenne, March 1636, in* The Philosophical Writings of Descartes, *volume 3, p. 51.* Trans.

18. *Claude Bernard (1813–78), a celebrated nineteenth-century physician and author of an influential textbook on experimental medicine in 1865.* Trans.

Hegel

[No notes in this section.]

Ecstasy

19. Time Regained *was published in 1927. The experience in question here is therefore situated prior to 1927.*

20. *See Saint Ignatius of Loyola,* The Spiritual Exercises and Selected Works *(1522-48) ed. George Ganss (New York: Paulist Press, 1991).* Trans.

21. *"Dying from not dying." This phrase—"muero porque no muero," in Spanish—derives from a poem by St. Teresa de Avila, "Vivo Sin Vivir En Mí" (Aspirations Toward Eternal Life) (see St. Teresa of Avila,* The Collected Works of St. Teresa of Avila, *volume 3, ed. and trans. Kieran Kavanaugh et alia (Washington, DC: ICS Publications, 1985) p. 375). It is quoted most famously by St. John of the Cross in his poem, "Coplas del alma que pena por ver a Dios" (Stanzas of the Soul That Suffers with Longing to See God," by Federico García Lorca in "El Poeta pide a su amor que le escriba" (The Poet Asks His Love to Write Him), and by Paul Éluard as "Mourir de ne pas mourir," the title of a section of his* Capitale de la douleur *(Capital of Pain, 1926). Bataille references the line in 1938, during the last lecture at the Collège de*

Sociologie (see Denis Hollier, ed. The College of Sociology (Minneapolis: University of Minnesota Press, 1989) p. 340), as well as elsewhere herein. Trans.

22. *Bataille is quoting his article "The Practice of Joy Before Death" published in* Acéphale *5 (Juin 1939) 1–8; republished in Bataille,* Oeuvres Complètes, *volume 1, pp. 552–8; see p. 556 for the quoted passage. A translation of this article appears in Georges Bataille,* Visions of Excess, *pp. 235–9; see p. 238 for the quoted passage.* Trans.

23. *Here again, Bataille is quoting his article "The Practice of Joy Before Death" published in* Acéphale *5 (Juin 1939) 1–8; republished in Bataille,* Oeuvres Complètes, *volume 1, pp. 552–8; see p. 557 for the quoted passage. A translation of this article appears in Georges Bataille,* Visions of Excess, *pp. 235–9; see pp. 238–9 for the quoted passage.* Trans.

24. *Bataille is quoting "L'Amitié" (Friendship) published in* Mesures *(15 avril 1940); reprinted in Bataille,* Oeuvres Complètes *volume 6, pp. 292–306; see p. 299 for the quoted passage; compare* Guilty, *p. 28.* Trans.

25. *In the first edition:* [. . .] ecstasy before the void.

26. *As above, Bataille is quoting his article "The Practice of Joy Before Death" published in* Acéphale *5 (Juin 1939) 1–8; republished in Bataille,* Oeuvres Complètes *volume 1, pp. 552–8; see p. 556 for the quoted passage. A translation of this article appears in Georges Bataille,* Visions of Excess, *pp. 235–9; see p. 237 for the quoted passage.* Trans.

27. *Augustine of Hippo (354–430). Bataille is referencing a line from Augustine's* Confessions *[trans. R. S. Pine-Coffin (London: Penguin, 1961) p. 21; translation modified] See Bk. I: sec. 1.* Fecisti nos ad te et inquietum est cor nostrum donec requiescat in te. Trans.

28. *Jean Racine,* Phèdra *[1677] ln. 305.* Trans.

29. *Jean Racine,* Phèdra *[1677] ln. 1639–40.* Trans.

30. *Jean Racine,* Phèdra *[1677] ln. 1642.* Trans.

31. *Quoting from above, the final paragraph of "Narrative of a Partially Failed Experience."* Trans.

32. *The nocturnal excursions of the Acéphale group in the Marly forest led to a tree that had been struck by lightning. See "La Tombe de Louis XXX" in* Oeuvres Complètes *volume 4, p. 165; for an English translation, see* Louis XXX, *ed. and trans. Stuart Kendall (Prague: Equus, 2013). For a similar image, see* Guilty, *p. 188.* Trans.

Fortune

33.   *Friedrich Nietzsche,* Thus Spoke Zarathustra, *in Nietzsche,* The Portable Nietzsche, *p. 218.* Trans.

Nietzsche

34. *In his* Poésies *(1870), Isidore Ducasse, aka the Comte de Lautréamont, plagiarizes quotations from an extraordinary range of literary and philosophical sources, making small and large alterations to them. See* Maldoror and the Complete Works of the Comte de Lautréamont, *trans. Alexis Lykiard (Cambridge: Exact Change, 1994)*

pp. 221–52. The Pater is the Latin prayer Pater Noster, known in English as the Lord's Prayer. See Matthew 6: 9–13. Trans.

35. *Friedrich Nietzsche,* Beyond Good and Evil *(1886), trans. Walter Kaufman (New York: Random House, 1966) § 65a.* Trans.

36. *Friedrich Nietzsche,* Beyond Good and Evil, *§ 55.* Trans.

37. *See René Descartes,* Discourse on Method *(1637) in* The Philosophical Writings of Descartes, *volume 1, p. 113.* Trans.

38. *Marcel Proust,* In Search of Lost Time, volume 5: The Captive *(1923), trans. C. K. Scott Moncrieff and Terence Kilmartin, revised by D.J. Enright (New York: The Modern Library, 1993) p. 519.* Trans

39. *Marcel Proust,* In Search of Lost Time, volume 5: The Captive, *p. 520.* Trans.

40. *Marcel Proust,* In Search of Lost Time, volume 5: The Captive, *pp. 91–92.* Trans.

41. *Marcel Proust,* In Search of Lost Time, volume 5: The Captive, *p. 520.* Trans.

42. *Marcel Proust,* In Search of Lost Time, volume 6: Time Regained *(1927) trans. Andreas Mayor and Terence Kilmartin, revised by D. J. Enright (New York: The Modern Library, 1993) pp. 263–4.* Trans.

43. *Marcel Proust,* In Search of Lost Time, volume 6: Time Regained, *p. 264.* Trans.

44. *Marcel Proust,* In Search of Lost Time, volume 6: Time Regained, *pp. 264–5.* Trans.

45. *Marcel Proust,* In Search of Lost Time, volume 5: The Captive, *p. 347.* Trans.

46. *Marcel Proust,* In Search of Lost Time, volume 5: The Captive, *p. 346.* Trans.

47. *Marcel Proust,* In Search of Lost Time, volume 4: Sodom and Gomorrah *(1921) Trans. C. K. Scott Moncrieff and Terence Kilmartin, revised by D. J. Enright (New York: The Modern Library, 1992) p. 208.* Trans.

48. *Marcel Proust,* In Search of Lost Time, volume 4: Sodom and Gomorrah, *p. 208.* Trans.

49. *Marcel Proust,* In Search of Lost Time, volume 6: Time Regained, *p. 267.* Trans.

50. *Marcel Proust,* In Search of Lost Time, volume 6: Time Regained, *p. 267.* Trans.

51. *Marcel Proust,* In Search of Lost Time, volume 6: Time Regained, *p. 268.* Trans.

52. *Marcel Proust,* In Search of Lost Time, volume 2: Within a Budding Grove *(1919) trans. C. K. Scott Moncrieff and Terence Kilmartin, revised by D. J. Enright (New York: The Modern Library, 1993) pp. 404–8.* Trans.

53. *Marcel Proust,* In Search of Lost Time, volume 6: Time Regained, *p. 316.* Trans.

54. *Marcel Proust*, In Search of Lost Time, volume 6: Time Regained, *p. 318.* Trans.

55. *This is a reference to Orestes's last lines in scene five of Jean Racine's* Andromaque *(1667): "L'ingrate mieux que vous saura me déchirer / Et je lui porte enfin mon cœur à dévorer" (Better than you the ingrate will tear me apart / and in the end I will bring her my heart to devour).* Trans.

56. *Orestes is the hero of Jean Racine's* Andromaque *(1667), while Phaedra is the heroine of Racine's* Phèdre *(1677), quoted by Bataille above.* Trans.

57. *Marcel Proust*, In Search of Lost Time, volume 6: Time Regained, *p. 256.* Trans.

58. *André Breton, "The First Dalí Exhibit" in Breton,* Break of Day *(1934), trans. Mark Polizzotti and Mary Ann Caws. (Lincoln: University of Nebraska Press, 1999) p. 52. This article is a key document in the polemic between André Breton and Georges Bataille over Dalí's painting "The Lugubrious Game" (1929).* Trans.

59. *André Breton,* The Second Manifesto of Surrealism *(1929) in* Manifestoes of Surrealism, *trans. Richard Seaver and Helen Lane (Ann Arbor: University of Michigan Press, 1969) p. 124.* Trans.

60. *B:* A man having a parcel of genius has come to believe that it is "his" like a thing. He exploits it, he makes it give in return, like a farmer a parcel of earth, profits of vanity and money. But just as our ancestors [. . .]

61. *William Blake, "All Religions Are One" in* The Complete Poetry and Prose of William Blake. *Ed. David V. Erdman (Berkeley: University of California Press, 1982) p. 1.* Trans.

62. *Lautréamont*, Maldoror and the Complete Works of the Comte de Lautréamont, *trans. Alexis Lykiard (Cambridge: Exact Change, 1994) p. 244.* Trans.

63. *B:* [. . .] at least poetry, the poet, if a feeling of necessary ruin so profoundly lacerates him.

(What one does not grasp [. . .])

64. *B: To be known! [crossed out*: this is the bridge, the commonness that fate proposes. Before the temptation] how could he not [. . .]

65. *Marcel Proust*, In Search of Lost Time, volume 6: Time Regained, *pp. 314–15.* Trans.

66. *Marcel Proust*, In Search of Lost Time, volume 6: Time Regained, *p. 372.* Trans.

67. *Marcel Proust*, In Search of Lost Time, volume 6: Time Regained, *p. 372.* Trans.

68. *Friedrich Nietzsche,* The Gay Science *(1882), op. cited, § 125, translation modified to proximate Bataille's version.* Trans.

69. *B:* This sacrifice which man has made, that he makes of God, distinguishes itself from all others [. . .]

70. *B (on the same page as the previous note):*
[. . .] the one who sacrifices is himself reached by the blow that he strikes, he succumbs with the victim. [*see above*]

*

And what else could he be but a madman?

For a long time he held himself on the slope. It was the slope of sacrifice where he became everything and when he began to yield he could only say: Ecce homo.

The "plausibility" of the world dissipates. How beautiful the world was! *Now I have nothing.*

*

No solitude greater, more soundproof, weaker! What a moving unknown is discovered here! And what an absence of breath!

[*See page 156. The two pages that follow are described in the note below:*]
71. *Here B has:*
I imagine myself arriving on the shores of Lake Silvaplana, near the rock that Nietzsche designated, and I weep.

Having had of the eternal return the vision about which we are aware, Nietzsche wrote: "The intensity of my feelings makes me at once tremble and laugh . . . I've wept too much . . . these were not tears of self-pity, these were tears of jubilation . . ." Walking through the forest, along the length of Lake Silvaplana, he had stopped that day near an enormous block of stone that stood in the form of a pyramid, not far from Surlei. But the object of his vision, which made him tremble, was not the return (which left him from that time on indifferent) and not even time, but what the return stripped bare (just as for others another laceration), the unknown, from which I weep and which no one discovers without trembling.

One remains indifferent, seeking with great difficulty to grasp the intellectual contents of the vision instead of perceiving that through a representation of time that questions life, right to what little sense it has, Nietzsche completed losing his footing. Through it? By grace of it, perhaps.

(The return, which cannot impose itself upon the mind, is no less plausible, is equal to other imaginable conceptions. Like all perspectives on time, it questions the meaning of life, proposes its nonsense, but in a new way and, when Nietzsche had his first apprehension of it, *without any answer having been given to him*, he was happy to have found something.)

Laughter in tears. The putting to death of God [. . . *See page 154*]
72. *Friedrich Nietzsche,* Ecce Homo, Zarathustra *§ 1.* Trans.
73. *B:* [. . .] turning away from sacrifice.

[*In the margin:*]

then why go into madness
this movement must be shown starting from there

[*The following page:*]

If the poet enjoying poetry, king of the "land of treasures," has no nostalgia [. . . *see page 155; and for "land of treasures," page 148.*]

74. *B:*

[. . .] But he will feel, at this moment, *more alone*, so alone that his solitude will be like another death, the increased weight of sacrifice.

The sacrifice of God creates the desert around him. The crowd avoids him and *fails to recognize* him. The crowd is unaware that the sacrifice takes place just as it is unaware of the unknown itself.

75. *B, continues:*

To efface, to be alone, to avoid being *recognized*, is the condition of this sacrifice: the king kills himself, desiring that the communication—impossible with him—take place without him. Even more, he, the king, abolishes royalty. Abolition, necessary effacement, *without which human unity would not be discovered.* To bury thought alive, the impossible agitation that it is, to sink into nonsense to this point

To make the necessity of this solitude felt even more

Its wildflower aspect

Like that which is hidden if one laughs and must be

76 *B:* [. . .] Prolonged beyond action, seeking beyond it a distant possible, autonomous thought neither opposes nor can oppose any limit to the exercise of action. Action takes place first. A distant possible is sought when the necessities of action permit. Reciprocally, practical thought cannot oppose the rules that are valid for it to this prolonging of life in the depths of silence. And further on: the noise that action makes would be, after all, intolerable for itself if the silence did not prolong it in that way. But if it were not silence this prolongation would be a lie [*crossed out:* that which action is not, cannot be].

77. *Friedrich Nietzsche,* Beyond Good and Evil, *§ 40. Trans.*

78. *Friedrich Nietzsche,* Beyond Good and Evil, *§ 44, translation modified. Trans.*

79. *To conclude, here we offer these few scattered notes from B:*

lack of power in a path to which one is committed is repugnant against the [*forcing?*]

to suppress a part of the forcing [*of the forces?*] to dram. through instructions

but to force is not a sin, once committed one must

to force exists everywhere: in love [*in?*] poetry

it is a poison

laughter is the only outlet

profound, divine meaning of laughter in this sense

to force is the return of the project in its [*contrary?*]

*

Sometimes one would like to cry out: Have courage! With the idea that from time to time one could encounter a hand, that one would grasp it in such a way and would have one's own hand so grasped that one would in no way regret living in such difficult times, that one would become oneself gaily hardened and that beneath the cloud of sweat one would feel something pleasant in human nature.

On the last day   When the first
he won't say but he could say: it is not I who is knocking, it is the entire earth.

Isn't it curious? The English call the Germans liars and false prophets. A German begins to paint the world upside down. Ludwig, undoubtedly the greatest, has given a representation of human life that is a complete exaggeration. Nothing but the impossible, the unreal. But barely had he finished this mad painting when the English determined to prove its veracity. And to construct a world that resembles that which L. had painted, in all points faithful to his nightmare images. As if the metamorphosis in prison was an order destined for them, they decomposed the air, in the surroundings of their big shoes human nature is completely reduced to that state of unintelligible oppression. Thus without the English, one would not have had this German prophet of modern times, and how much more heartbreaking in a sense than those of ancient times.

The upheavals of these times are of another amplitude than those of epochs in which horror only entered into one valley at a time and did not spread its sheets of sweat over continents and seas.

*

Yes, I live, I pursue a light dream.

but my inner clairvoyance?
eyes apparently charged with sleep, discreet and smiling, imperceptible, it will never cease to keep watch.

*

And the day when they would all bathe in their blood, the sun, indifferent as always (sun, flies, water represent indifference), no one would think of them any more

*

How could I die in harmony without being sure that those who live will enjoy as much, more than I; death is not like I thought, the icy skeleton, but the nude bacchante—young, drunk, and beautiful. Death is quite this sun of darkness.

*

Each one draws from things the entire share of the unknown that he is able to bear without collapsing, for things reveal themselves to be great, desirable, gripping to the extent that we see the unknown that they are, not the known that they appear to be. But we only bear the unknown each time on the condition that there is much more of the known in them, and the more we can grasp it, we are reassured. At least

[digression on Marcel Proust]

The paradoxical aspect like saying of the known that in fact it is the unknown.

It is only a question of the share of the unknown that there is in communication.

And in Proust there is also communication from a dead figure to a living one, which assures perenniality, since if one can communicate from someone from the past to someone in the present one can also do so from this one to that one.

Another thing, the share of the unknown in poetry.

The charm of Proust's style derives from a kind of prolonged exhaustion in which develops that which the dissolving unfolding of time (death) leaves open. While a concise style is like a misrecognition of time (that of the pebble). But Proust's sentences are a stream, they flow, they announce, they gently murmur the flow of time toward death.

*

1) Necessary terror. Poetry renewing destruction without respite
2) The author put to death by his work

[final paragraph]

Questioning everything. It can take diverse forms. Linked to poetic genius: the form that is most separate from the crowd. Opposition between the return to the Golden Age and poetic genius: Hegel and military service. Poetic genius on the side of extremity. But what becomes of the poetic genius in solitude? (In a general way—for the introduction—from the moment when one no longer sets out from dogmatic presupposition, one sets out from poetry). The solitude of the genius necessary for the sacrifice in which everything is victim. *Unknown* (misunderstood) character of sacrifice. This is the adventure of a mind that has gone to the depth of things, has descended to hell.

Necessity of becoming everything—the possibility that genius has in solitude, but proximity to madness. Nietzsche Crucifies Dionysus Ecce Homo: megalomania.

One can in no way hope for a result analogous to that of the sacrifice of kings. The effectiveness is in fact at play in the misunderstood region. Finally poetic genius effaces itself without the crowd noticing anything. A few only.

But everything dissolves. Nothing left to oppose to the military world. Nothing left. Nothing left. All the mind's fever destroying itself in the silence of torture, of ecstasy. Total virility and transparency.

[*On the other side*:]

destruction of beings in advance, when they arrive at the salon of Princess Guermantes, the destruction of the puppets is completed—and at the summit, the execution of Berma by her own children—as if he wanted to give himself the pretext of pulling the sheet, already a pall, in advance over his face.

[*In the margin*: in regard to Terror, if one envisions that the end of expression is to suppress thought (discourse) within ourselves
and then through death it escapes from the insignificance of poetry, from the reserve of possession that belongs to it]

and according to poetic law no one escapes unless they are among those who bring Time "their heart to be devoured." Phaedra's passion which is such that she never utters a phrase that is not poetic and how many among them are so to the point of tearing one apart. But only the author has reserved for himself in his work the role of Pheadra: he was unable to find a response to his passion other than lies (and this perhaps due to the fact that he did not like the women with whom alone "communication" in the reciprocal gift of self is possible).

*

alone. Already like those of a man who has reached the extremity of the saturnalias that he has unleashed in his heart
And this is hope for him, it's the worst pain that he
(And for Nietzsche the fact that his reason foundered in megalomania was equivalent to a confirmation of the sepulchral solitude, the sacrifice of reason took the form most charged with meaning in that madness is that which separates us from the others and makes us rediscover the universe of what was separated within ourselves. Resignation failed him: it's madness despite itself, the voluntary self-effacement.)

*

The profound importance of poetry is that from the sacrifice of words, of images, and by virtue of the misery of this sacrifice (in this respect the same is true of poetry as of any other sacrifice), it causes a slipping from the impotent sacrifice of objects to that of the subject. What Rimbaud sacrificed is not only poetry as object but the poet as subject

detestable survival but much more upsetting than death
the author put to death by his work.
note that poetry is also holocaust composed with the help of words

*

communication with the unknown
the unknown that we ourselves are, infinitely fragile *ipse*, trembling, aware
of its fragility, not the *I* sure of itself imagining itself necessary and undertaking
understanding.

Rimbaud's sacrifice of poetry was not poetic in the sense that it really took
place, that it did not take form [*crossed out*: unique?] in the order of words, that
it changed life

I can have no doubt about what touches upon the principle of sacrifice

the object of sacrifice is what man in general abuses, what is exploited. Sacrifice compensates for abuse, for exploitation. In the same way the links between
sacrifice and communication are clear.

Abuse, exploitation, are what break "communication," sacrifice is what rees-
tablishes it, from whence it follows that the choice of sacrificed objects turns upon
those whose destruction is of a nature to guarantee the return to the communication
that the abuse stopped. This double source of the choice is of a nature that makes
some adjustments necessary. This is clear. I can imagine that it is incomplete but I
don't think that one can shake it for all that. Much more obscure is the particular
interpretation, bearing on this or that historical form . . .

*

Paradox of the [*illegible*]
In the solitude and renunciation of poetry, the poetic genius abandons femininity, becomes male, and it is to the extent that it effaces everything, that it is
resolved to profound silence, that it is male.

Takes upon itself the absence of satisfaction, absence of rest, absence of salvation.

With respect to the military world, the poetic genius makes it possible in
the sense that without it the passion for knowledge would divert that world into
sterile oppositions.

*

beauty, the power to seduce, necessary for poetry before destruction (par. 2).
Hence the necessity of power (par. 3).

male character of effacement?

But the only sacrifice that makes one laugh for in it bad conscience dissipates
(itself victim).

If the poet accepts immediacy . . . He can imagine a return (illusory) toward others. But he can go further, to the extremity in the path upon which he found himself, he [*illegible*] to isolate himself.

I say if the poet because . . . philosopher

To also say that the sacred is necessary to the world of action, but it must all the more withdraw from this world, reserve itself, since it is total.

*

In this unintelligible, unrecognizable sacrifice, what is attained, this time again, is the sacred, but in a form so total that one can only profoundly enshroud it.

Part Five

1. *Latin: "Gives lilies with full hands," Virgil,* Aeneid *6: 883. Mourning the death of Marcellus, nephew of Augustus. This line is quoted by Dante upon parting from Virgil in* Purgatory *XXX: 21. Trans.*

2. *Latin: "Glory to myself the highest." This is a play on* Gloria in excelsis Deo, Glory to God the highest. *Trans.*

Method of Meditation

Published by Éditions Fontaines in 1947 and reprinted (our text) in the re-edition of Inner Experience *(Gallimard, 1954).*

Extracts from this text appeared in n° 48–49 of the review Fontaine *in January–February 1946 under the title* Before an Empty Sky.

In Bataille's papers one finds:

A [Notebook 8, 1945, 37 pages, numbered in part] = first notes, equally concerning The Accursed Share *and Bataille's preface to Jules Michelet's* La Sorcière *(Paris: Éditions de Quatre Vents, 1946) [reprinted as "Michelet" in Bataille,* Literature and Evil *(London: Marion Boyars, 1985) pp. 61–74].*

B [Notebook 9, 1945–1946, 75 numbered pages] =

      Foreword (pages 1–5)

      Notes, first draft and notes for our pages 201 to 202 (pages 6–44);

      Manuscript of our pages 189 to 202 (pages 45–75).

D [Box 9, F, 76 pages] = corrected proofs for the first edition.

Additionally:

C = Before an Empty Sky

E = first edition.

Here first, notes from A:
[Pages 27–37]:
          Method [*crossed out:* Manual] of Meditation

"We were young. And the young seem to be impervious to anything except trifles. We can invest trifles with a tragic profundity, which is the world. Because, after all, there's nothing particularly profound about reality. Because when you reach reality, along about forty or fifty or sixty, you find it to be only six feet deep and eighteen feet square."

—William Faulkner, "Mistral" (1931) [in Faulkner, *The Collected Stories of William Faulkner* (New York: Vintage, 1995) p. 859.]

Foreword

If one seeks a Hindu method . . . but this is not a work of philosophy either.

4-13-45
     It is in the moment of suffering* that we return to our Gods. Or rather it is our pain—the horror that we have of it—that creates them. I will go further: we lack honesty in pain and our Gods—which matter to us—are the image or the shadow borne by our cheating.
     I suffer and I would like to tell myself: "this, at least, is worth being loved." I am able to respond: "I would only love 'what I love,' *'what is worth'* being loved if the lure opposed to the void of sufferings, a means of no longer suffering, of ordering a world wherein suffering is not the last word."
     The cruel truth is that we must avoid suffering at all cost, and our reserves of value (our churches and our [*low?*] moralities) are pharmacies.
     I affirm: what defined suffering—in that it causes suffering—is that in itself it does not have the slightest meaning. What gives a meaning to suffering is the beginning of organized lies.
     To suffer is to suffer and nothing else. If we benefit from having suffered we are lying through our teeth, people who set up, who "fake" the world.
     The worst is a deified suffering.
     How can one not laugh at the contrary of misfortune?
     The misfortune of some is the condition of happiness for others, the price that the happiness costs and if it is a "useful" proof, it is to the extent that we discover in it the void beneath our feet, the void precisely without recourse, if it enriches us, this is us reduced to the most awkward silence.

---

*Note by Bataille: An hour of vain waiting in a metro, I return alone: the forks and spoons in the room were set for diner.

4-14-45

At the final moment there are a thousand ways to have a "fly on the nose" (homage to the victim, a problem, an ambition), but there is only one way of going further.

One is wrong to say: "There is no possible return." The return is rather inevitable. If I remain distant, completely, I would have nothing to say.

A part of me that remains close recounts my departure, my stopping at the point of death.

[*At least two pages missing here.*]

comical (first movement)
4. Philosophy itself
(But how would Picasso situate himself?)

At first the child does not have the "term and beginning," then he has it in a rudimentary way, but he has no autonomy, is only a [*supplement?*] to adults.

However, the adult submits to the charm of childishness, an accomplice filled with wonder by childish stupidities.

A significant part of human life is found in the love of children (not this or that child but generally of childish *naiveté*).

The final problem for philosophers is that of the *autonomy* or *sovereignty* of a domain, admissible but subordinated to knowledge.

The comical is subordinated to the serious. The tragic is puerile, going to the end of consequences, admitting its terrible impotence.

The puerile, the tragic, pointing to the *impossible*, separated from us indefinitely by the fabric of knowledge, limiting us to the fiction of a *possible* world.

Turning our backs to those who, reasoning, admit, even *in fact*, the domination of the possible (the fabrication, the streets under the skies, the sovereignty of the political, the fictions necessary for commerce, for administrations, prisons, armies, a world wherein dressed up men have this unquestioned place to which they relate every notion, and even that of anthropomorphism).

(However never introducing outside demands into the possible: the possible [*has?*] laws, action only occurs in the possible on the condition of admitting its laws, even if intending to modify them.)

Even Heidegger's philosophy (at the height of the reason that can be derived from it) without expressly wanting to leaves unshaken the *sovereignty* of the possible. The critique of Heidegger is given in the idea of *urgency*. If Heidegger's philosophy had projected itself beyond the "fabric of knowledge," he would not have had time to write it.

*

"Who among us is not enchanted in advance, with delights and kindness, with the tears that will flow after his death on the cheeks of beings who are the flesh of his flesh." (p. 159)*

Making the tour of what I have encountered in my fellows, human experience as a whole appears to me to be diving, deeply, like a thousand feet under the water, in an irremediable ridicule.

I speak of the best, of those who have the power of attraction. Among the greatest [*crossed out*: minds] arises with the most clarity the ridiculousness of not being children—of not crying like babies do. Even the crying child is ridiculous, his inanity deriving from the serenity of the adults.

(The child but without God, without father, *alone* in the world.

Laughing?)

(A subway car, that and not Hegel decides *madness*. Hegel is only an accentuated form of it.)

*

> Only transcendence is driven to want to be everything . . .
> The will to immanence . . .

*

> Entry into matter
> First three meditations
> Philosophy as a sovereign operation
> The sovereign operation is the putting to death of the king
> The sovereign operation is a curse

*

Principles of Rhetoric

1. Recall fundamental demands. Some principles in light of deciding between things. Reasons for doing so. No concern for others.

2. The act of writing regarded as a means of exploration of the possible. Committed to representing the exploration of the possible as the only reason for writing.

3. Hatred of individuality. This is to say, a greater demand.

4. Iconoclasm. Primacy of experience over expression. Hatred of art. Impossibility of [*bringing it?*] to [*sovereignty?*]

Reference by Bataille, source unknown.

5. Whimsical nature, deprived of necessity. Suppose a planetary catastrophe.

6. [*illegible: Self or play?*]

7. Sovereign operation.

(No empty polemic. Outside of the described realm, however, envision this possibility, forfeiture such that no compromise is possible.

Put it outside of interest.)

*

[*Pages 16–17:*]

The Hatred of Poetry should be published followed by *Method of Meditation.**
In the preface (at the very least) explain the title in this way:
Poetry of the "messenger" type corresponds to the formula

a) immanence changed into transcendence, into a thing

b) profane (transcendent thing) endeavoring in vain to the transcendence of transcendence.

But,

Even the word poetry, the reference to poetry, carries in itself the movement from which the word "messenger" proceeds

The hatred of poetry is the hatred of a designation

I could generally title *Beyond Poetry:***

I. *Inner Experience*

II. [*crossed out: Guilty*] *On Nietzsche*

III. *The Hatred of Poetry*

(in this second edition, volume II will consist of two principal parts

    1) *Will to Chance*

    2) ....)

Inner Experience will be entirely revised, *On Nietzsche* considerably augmented.

Another series would include *Guilty* and *Nudity* (*Alleluia, Story of Rats,* and the dialogue, if I write it).

[*Pages 1–15*]

The procession

Or rather the two (or three)

The mass of the humble whose submission formed, at the basis of their assent as much to the ostentation of the great as to the sorcerer's pyres . . .

---

*The Hatred of Poetry *was originally published by Les Éditions de Minuit in 1947. A second edition appeared, also through Les Éditions de Minuit, with a brief new introduction and with the texts slightly rearranged, as* The Impossible *in 1962.*

**Beyond Poetry*: *These words were inscribed on the band around the first edition of* Inner Experience (1943).

They offer us, in fact, their services.

Each woman that we love undoubtedly comes from among those who burn and not from those whom one burns, but the distance is not so great: we can always reanimate this fire that extinguished the fire

*

Revolt. At first against nature. In this case the revolt is direction. Then against direction.

These two aspects of every revolt. But:

In the present state of things

The direction is what is put in question. It is regarded like nature (capitalism), identified with evil.

In the revolt against direction and only therein appears the most distant possibility of man.

If he had not first rebelled against nature, he obviously could not, rebel against a direction (he would be a wild animal: in no way differentiated from nature and as such not submitting to constraint). It is only following the revolt against nature that nature, to the extent that it opposes a particular being, appears as direction.

Finally, it is necessary to substitute for the idea of nature that of a totality of which man is part.

Here man is first the particular being, the individual but an accomplice of the others.

*

In the sacred world, I can recover the traces of the operation.

The direction (right) demolishes [*departs?*] from nature (left) but nature in rebellion against direction is no longer simple nature

> nature
> Sacred right
>   sacred left
> God   } Action of a
>   diabolical nature   single operation
> reason in nature

*

Appendices to *The Accursed Share:*
        The bullfight
        Various kinds of beauty

*

The share of revolt (what we deny to those who direct us) is *essentially*, in the experience that we make of it, something impersonal. Moreover, the value itself is the way that it burns. I call it the need for expenditure: it is always founded on a disinterestedness, on a surpassing of calculations. It is the valorization of the present, the consumption of goods, forces, resources of every kind, but not *subordinated* to some ulterior good. It is the opposite of work, wherein each expenditure is made in light of a future benefit.

It is true that, in part, a movement of revolt, once begun, has its necessities. It leads to some enterprise, wherein the defined goal is subordinate to numerous efforts. But, in the *first place*, this goal is in no way a means. *Thereafter*, it's true, the goal is given as useful to some end (and communally becomes it). One passes from revolt to revolution.

*

[*Crossed out*: In some way that we envision them, most often, our origins disarm us. So much that we don't think about them.

Childhood, if necessary . . . but uterine life? the moments that precede that? . . .

We reflect as little as possible on our parent's love life.]

Normally we are in the world as sure as if we were—confined as we are to a point in space and time*—the eternal substance of the world.

We cannot fail, however, to recall our origins, and sometimes the rigors of science, sometimes the visions of dreams return us to the processions of the past. But we normally content ourselves with the facts of scholarship that account for the state in which we live: in exchange we give the past a meaning that shows how we have come to where we are now. Sometimes, it's true, we dream without consequence: some object testifies to other periods, is useful to construct the fiction of societies less *humane* than ours.

We ask ourselves how this could be in the world with its purpose and its goals, but this is brief and insupportable: we furnish our destitution with mirages. Modern humanity has its museums.**

Nothing is more difficult than to free reflection from perspectives that are closed on themselves. Each element coming from outside is just as quickly reintroduced: a monstrous tragedy is for a critique only an object within its field. We cannot in any case claim to escape from our sleep: we live endlessly enchanted by our works and, if we had the chance to die . . .

Second draft: [. . .] were when we are in fact lost, confined to a point [. . .]

**Second draft*: [. . .] It's heavy and insupportable, and when we populate our destitution with mirages, we only blind ourselves even more.

What's more, could we know once more an obscure feeling, a fragile disquiet, by multiplying recourse to strange elements, hardly assimilable, which are only digested after a time, whose misty diversity leads us astray.

Perhaps?

One would define transcendence as well by language as language by transcendence. This word has a duty to exist. And similarly the manufactured object, responding to its rules, is transcendent.

In general, sacred language is language destroyed.

In the sacrifice of a lamb, the lamb is destroyed not only by the knife of the one who sacrifices as a living being, but as a word-identical-to-object.

But is there not from the sacred to the transcendent a fundamental slippage? The transcendence of the sacred would be its reduction to the thing. God, the effort tending to reduce to the unity of a thing the sacred realm: is it not given—fundamentally—as a cause of the world, reintroducing, in sacred speculation, profane perspectives of the world of things, which is to say of the sequence of products. God is only a *self-product* producing the world. Transcending the world like a producer his product. But transcendence assumes the two meanings of transcendence. The divine world is only a world of products, some transcending in relation to the others.

The sacred is undoubtedly the opposite of transcendence: it is contagious. We must protect ourselves from it. It is there as soon as transcendence is destroyed.

After the fact, placing ourselves in inferiority before the sacred insofar as immersed in the world of things, we define a new kind of transcendence. This is the "transcendence of the immanent."

Kojève—Jaspers

Ignorance is not atheism. It consists in denouncing the passage of the immanence (of the sacred) to the transcendence of God. It is the return to a world that is a precondition for production—language. And not, like atheism, the completion of the initial movement of the divine world.

In the same way that there is the "transcendence of the immanent," there is also the "immanence of the transcendent."

These movements check themselves in the play of moral values:

a) the position of the sacred is the position of a value in itself, unconditional, withdrawn from the circuit of production;

b) as a value, value in itself is reintroduced in the circuit of production, which is to say that we effectively bring it to production (ex.: agrarian sacrifice)—

in another way, a good of the agrarian type is introduced, this time not as external justification (insertion), but as supreme end in a movement of transcendence.

*

Michelet is no exception. He speaks of this or that, but it is finally toward a satisfying view. This clear conscience, the clarity of which depends upon the sequence of words and phrases, that sees the beam in the majesty of the oak or weight living in a herd, whose nature proceeds from an order of buildings and services, the presumption, rather the human precipitation asks that it again attain, armed with rough tools, the silent depth of things. Undoubtedly, if man himself was a stranger to this depth . . . but he is its emanation, and to the extent that he is *undone* it does not cease to belong to him.

Léon Blum did not see the inanity of a useful end (Humanity, etc.)

The most difficult problem for human beings: there is no useful end. A useful end for what? This leads to big words.

One cannot oppose the absurdity of a useless end to the absurdity of a useful one. Faced with the sequential world, a useless end is only a big word, only a void, insofar as it refers to the world of utility, it is only a plagiarism lacking an essential element: utility (this is the case with God, Humanity, etc.). Thus for God: one seeks to prove the existence of God, this goes back to saying: what is at the bottom of things is the same as a table is. Being being the attribute of a table. At bottom, the laughable aspect of God is that one must prove an existence that one gives to tables, to animals from the start (in general objects are laughable insofar as they are immobile).

We all let ourselves be enclosed in a mechanism. This is miserable and the defect of the possible.

This is not a question of a philosophical technicality. Strictly speaking, it is good to arrange all of one's resources, but they do not allow a way out (cannot in any case allow it). Escape is the fact of a nonphilosophical, nonscientific way of thinking (or of being), not limited to knowledge (all knowledge confirms judgments distinguishing the mad from the others).

In what concerns one case in particular.

Nothing is serious if one does not integrate the shame of children, phobias, laughter . . .

This is precisely what one cannot do

*

In "theopathy" the position of the transcendent overturning his transcendence above him as in a game of mirrors disappears. With the character of a commandment brought to the *object*—God commands after the fashion of a thing—substituting himself for the annihilation of the object as such.

The *forced* movement inherent in all things that only ever attempts in vain to be what it pretends to be—*the movement that causes laughter*—is suddenly absorbed in the destruction of laughter itself (this destruction is no longer centered on an object: it surpasses every object imaginable and is no longer anything other than a movement that loses itself).

In "theopathy" the world of transcendence is entirely in the background.

To theopathy—immanence returned to immanence—responds the immanence created by a suppression of transcendences borrowing their force and their pretention from immanence.

*

[*Pages 17–26*]

                                      productive expenditure
                                      useful value
a) position of the transcendent object (product) identical to language
b) counterposition of immanence, non-object, in the form of the sacred.
                                      end in itself
                                      value in itself
                                      exterior to language
                                      non-productive expenditure
c) insertion of the sacred into the world of production
d) in counterpart to c, transcendence is introduced in immanence
-- from the perspective of morality:
c = subordination of the fact of unconditional value for the *good*
c^1 = reduction of the unconditional value to the *idea* of the good.

2nd phase

A) position of the transcendence of God through alteration with immanence (inversion of the transcendence of the object in immanence).

B) reduction of the transcendence of the object through assimilation of the self with the object, principle of the immanence of the world of transcendence.

C) full development of the category of the comical, of the fact of an over-extended will to transcendence.*

The position of A is a movement that is implemented by an immanent being, but one reduced to solitude set apart.

This movement describes the route from the inferior to the superior and defines diverse possibilities in this way.

Further on, this note:

Method.

The question of the untenable and of the possibility of an ever more distant like describing the movement of the intelligence (linked to C).

the will to dominate has as an element the will to be *everything* that supposes general domination
this is the transposition of the power to produce
but
the power to produce being in relation to an inferior transcendence of objects while the will to dominate introduced the superior transcendence
but always what is essential is that making the movement of transcendence the world of immanence is changed into a thing and that it dies as immanence.

The position of personal transcendence is probably preliminary to the position of God.
Practically, the passage from immanence to transcendence is even given in the fact of directing.
Immanence, the sacred character, the exuberant generality of force are necessary for direction.
Direction is initially only a possibility exterior to transcendence.
Between a man who strikes and one who works under blows, the relations have the character of immanence, the brutality of the first, the servility of the other are of the same nature (thus the convict and the slave-driver).

*

The problem thus posed: is to escape from language, through the description of some idea.
Constructed in this way
literature helps us
being the destruction of language
Michelet is in short off the track
The slippage that one can always expect
Sight of the dregs.

What's more, the problem is posed by the very subject of the book.

In the past as today, the question was posed of knowing how one could return from the desiccation of language (the furthest possible . . .) to a movement—assuming an agreement with death—of transcendence to immanence.
the principle of sacrifice
it wears out, hence the necessity of curses
the urinal in the end.
Immanence is outside time insofar as time is a function of [eternity] language
In Plato . . . (go back to K's notes) the concept is
outside time
Aristotle . . . in time
Hegel . . . is time

But immanence—whose concept is the destruction of the concept—is outside of time: in that it is time.

Immanence is the moment—insofar as it is withdrawn from the project and flowing in time

The essence of transcendence is to be withdrawn from time as language, which is to say

Immanence is the collapse of transcendent morality (of decline).

(?) Hegel's concept is a coincidence of immanence and transcendence, but Hegel set this up to save transcendence. Evidently transcendence, in any case . . . but in one case critique entirely justifies it, in another (my perspective) transcendence is reduced to what it is as the outcome of a success: cf. *Method of Meditation*

For Method, the car entering V.

Similarly, the criteria of madness*

Transcendence is given in the corpuscle [all of its possibilities are developed on the Earth].

Hence the position of the object in language with the sacred as a consequence.

In the immense effort to resolve the sacred the position of God offers itself every position but in making an object of it (the transcendent)

Hegelianism completes the work and offers developed language the power to neutralize immanence; the immanence neutralized within language, language remains *possible* from one end to the other of its domain, particularity having become generally universal, the transcendent adequate to immanence, it is only from this or that difficulty of language (from this or that route through its domain) that the *impossible* proceeds, but from its totality, it is the fact of language adequate to the world and it is insofar as it is adequate to the world that it is impossible. And the impossibility of language is like the impossibility of the world itself: naturally the world is *possible*, "it is," but the fact of being is in no way accepted by being, *it is in no way acceptable* and even, precisely, it is the fact of not being accepted that constitutes the being, how could time exist without this (way of speaking). In this conception, the adequacy between transcendence and immanence is maintained. Transcendence is by no means condemnable, but only the stop that it is in its nature to desire. Immanence without transcendence . . .

In the margin of this page:

For *The Accursed Share*:

2nd part a) the household
            b) literature and politics
            c) (beauty)
            d) philosophy in general.

[*Manuscript Changes*]

1. *René Char,* Leaves of Hypnos *(1946), trans. Cid Corman (New York: Grossman Publishers, 1973) p. 59.* Trans.

2. *B, pages 1–5:*

Foreword

[*Crossed out:* I usually write randomly. I hardly know how to edit the results. I live beyond ideas that authorize—or demand—a state of repose.]

In time this errant and inexhaustible search, this flowing ever open wound that was up till now my books offered me a clear answer (it was hardly unexpected): "Follow without limitation, these pages will lead, in the end, to what they fled."

The feeling—slightly bitter but much more gay—of being dedicated to common foolishness commits me to flight in another way.

I attempted to define at once my effort and my method. (My method? If you prefer, my absence of method and the principles that authorize it.)

[*Crossed out:* In fact, this short text no longer implicates the ambition of the texts that preceded it.] With deliberate purpose, the ambition of these few pages is the greatest that can be offered to a human mind. It was the same, undoubtedly, in my preceding writings, but this one, from the beginning, linked itself to some limited purpose (or to delineating it), following it in every sense, avoiding ever offering an

Meanwhile the previously implicit ambition is now held tightly.

However, there remains of my habits of thought or writing (the necessities that belong to them) an invincible loathing to situate things effectively. An essential movement necessarily detached from the obligation to make an account. This is why this foreword is necessary. Here I say at the end what it is.

First I must specify that my effort is not one that results from an individual inclination. Similarly, my experience is *not in the least* morbid. I have described my experience as that of the human mind seeking its extreme possibility. On this path, I have not felt either general weakness or individual concern. No one commits himself to this path resolutely; rather it is the default of vigor (or rigor) of others and not some individual default that commits me to this, and not another.

The fact that an operation of knowledge is subordinated to another possesses in itself nothing so striking. The common critique of knowledge (I mean knowledge linked to criteria of madness), leading to the empty results of science, is, it seems, continued with more authority if one takes its most praised successes one after another. Why will we concern ourselves with a servitude linked to an operation of the mind? Look closely here.

On one side, science is in general knowledge before responding to an internal demand, refusing all external servitude. Presuppositions, various goals, all whims even negative are regarded rightly as obstacles. Thus the will to autonomy, the refusal to subordinate the being (that I am) to every demand from the outside must be regarded as [*distortions?*] to indifference. And further on, I perceive this too: between pure knowledge and freedom there is a profound incompatibility. The principle of science demands on one hand my indifference to the concern for autonomy; on the other hand I cannot remain autonomous accepting to dedicate my life to knowledge. Indeed, *I* enslave myself. I develop only one of my possibilities to the detriment of the others. I must renounce other demands within myself to the necessities of knowledge. They tell me there is no philosophical oeuvre without the consecration of an entire life: the operation of knowledge, like every complex human activity, demands of he who takes it on that he *specialize*. One must choose: remain a whole man and renounce knowledge or know and voluntarily reduce oneself to a function.

Here I'll stop the enunciation of these difficulties

What I decidedly challenge by showing it: knowledge is impossible so long as it always subordinates itself to another (change this formula).

*

3. *See notes to* On Nietzsche *in Bataille,* Oeuvres Complètes, *volume 6, p. 446.*

4. *C begins with these paragraphs* (Contestation.—The idea of silence [. . .] satisfied contemplation of an absence.) *Continuing:* I WALK WITH THE HELP OF FEET [p. 179].

5. *See G. W. F. Hegel,* Phenomenology of Spirit, *pp. 9–11.* Trans.

6. *See G. W. F. Hegel,* Phenomenology of Spirit, *p. 41.* Trans.

7. *D and E:* [. . .] my position condemns me. This feeling throws me into a void, it opens me to the light illumination "without form and without mode," to resolved ecstasy born of the certainty of infinite foolishness.

8. *C:*

[. . .] WITH THE HELP OF DRUNKS, IDIOTS, PASSERSBY. EVEN WITH THE HELP OF PHILOSOPHERS.

I enjoy the desire that a sage had to attain philosophy within me.

I incarnate the ungraspable within myself [. . .]

9. *C, continues:* Something is announced [. . . *see note 27, pages 285 and 287 below*]

10. *D and E:*

[. . .] postulate of labor. When I don't laugh, don't enjoy, *don't anything,* without opening at my feet the *impossible* as a void!

The truth, the strange and simple truth: activity [. . .]

11. *B (D and E):*

2) To say that in laughing the depth of worlds opens itself in me is a gratuitous affirmation, SOVEREIGN, the depth of worlds open [. . .]

12. *B:* [. . .] the object that does not make me laugh—I'll add: and which does not excite me* in any way—but only [. . .]

---

*Note by Bataille: an *exciting* object causes laughter, moves sexually or poetically, communicates anguish or ecstasy, in a word provokes a *sovereign* state.

13. *B*: [. . .] at the sovereign moment in which I laugh.

6) The relationships of objects of thought to sovereign moments are no more difficult to grasp than their relationships to subordinated moments, but cannot either in fact, or by right, serve thought as a point of departure.

7) Relating [. . .]

14. *In B, these paragraphs 9 and 10 read:*

9) Descartes's "I think" is linked, in any event, to our consciousness of not being subordinated to anything, but cannot be a point of departure for knowledge. It is a point of arrival: the object of thought, as submission elaborates it, follows its own movement up to the point of submitting to the power of laughter—that mocks it.

15. *D and E*:

[. . .] that it *introduces*; that will be the object of a world to be published under the title *The Accursed Share*.

[*In B, this entire note is missing.*]

16. *B (second draft)*:

[. . .] it begins to relate the known to the unknown. The known related to the unknown differs in this sense from the unknown but it is not for all that some new form of the unknown related to the known.

17. *B (second draft)*:

[. . .] (without which in the end, be it under the sign of evil, every simple sovereign moment is inscribed in the order of things) implies coincidence [. . .]

18. *B (second draft)*:

[. . .] This is the case:

– despite the aversion Heidegger inspires in me

– despite the difference in paths followed (which specifies the publication of a work begun fifteen years ago, several times abandoned—the last time, as I said (*Inn. Exp.* page 5) to write *Torture*, which follows a string of writings of the same kind—but that I am now completing and that I hope to provide, in *Fontaine*, a passage providing an idea of it).*

Such a coincidence, rare in the history of knowledge, is in my eyes full of interest.

Even more however [. . .]

19. *In B, a first draft has, for paragraphs 11 to 13 and for this note:*

10) Had the sovereign operation only occurred one time, the science relating the objects of thought to sovereign movements is possible and satisfying. However, it introduced at its birth a singular difficulty: the new subordination of operations of thought, even though it does not demand, as do theology and philosophy, a particular presupposition, no longer permitted proceeding as did classical science, randomly, advancing where it will, leaving some problems unresolved due to its methods. It was necessary *from the start* to proceed in a global way—leading *from the start* to propositions chosen for another reason than the possibility of making them.

See note 23 below.

this which is so shocking is testimony of authenticity

for all that it's not exempt . . .

11) This discipline, on the other hand, must be clearly distinguished from that of the phenomenologists. It affirms sovereign moments; the operations of thought of the phenomenologists proceed, like others, in a subordinate mode; even then they are its contestation, their methods (a professorial method) are related to the sphere of activity. I leave subordinated the operations that are: if I subordinate them to an unsubdued reality I confuse them with a sovereign operation: I am not a philosopher but a *saint*, maybe a madman.

[*In the margin:*]

11. To this difficulty is added

One cannot without counterfeiting aim at sovereignty and express oneself in a professorial way [*several illegible words*] untranslated Greek citations (Heidegger) [*crossed out*: apparent shortcoming of a professor? No, the trace of the collar.]

in a note

a hybrid method, equivocal, is an intolerable limping. Before everything else one must separate the sovereign operation and other operations: at this moment these last will lose their equivocal character and will develop into a banal science, soon calling on

never letting themselves be confused with the role played by a method losing itself in painful unfoldings and confusing itself with them.

principle of separation of the two books

20. *In B, this note reads:*

One must still envision heroism (anger). I have not done so [*crossed out*: because it is]: of all effusions it is the most distant from the sovereign operation.

say only that it is incomplete

not effusion

21. *B*: 19) In his meditation, the subject wearied of his search himself [. . .]

22. *B*: [. . .] But the comical in a comedy or the tragic in a tragedy is defined; whereas a meditating subject is prey to the comical, to undefined (unconditional) tragedy.

23. *B*: [. . .] But if it turns into a game, and the possibilities of the effects, without the help of topics, are limited, the exercise thus extended is subordinated in its turn.

[*Crossed out*: 22) Necessity of emphasizing the obstacle of all the efforts of sovereignty.

The efforts of meditation of every age have stumbled from the fact that to reach these sovereign moments one had to speak as if one had not]

Deny the value of the sphere of activity

General obstacle

Reinsertion in nature (the sphere . . .)

For this it is sufficient that it not be a totality

In fact meditation is defined from the start by a pretension (contestable) to totality

In fact meditation up till now was only possible through a slippage of sovereignty on the object, which assumed the subordinated attitude without which . . .

[*Continuing, this variation of the note for paragraph 13:*]

Sein und Zeit leaves scholarly, professorial description at the first level, leaves subordinated operations *stuck* to the sovereign (if it was not like this, I imagine, there would never even have been a hope of volume 2). For all that it is no less necessary to affirm a parallelism of results: which, in the history of knowledge, have never been obtained, other than on particular points. The paths of the method followed are, however, most different: this is what will be shown by the publication of the work that in a sense introduces this opuscule, that I abandoned, as I said (*Inn. Exp.* page 5), to write *Torture* and which is only a general economy of energy (ordering a system of relations—scientific—from objects of thought to human methods not of substance but of the expenditure of energy—to the immanent, no longer to the transcendent).

22) If poetry was not followed by the half-wild affirmation of sovereignty [. . .]

24. *B returns here to a crossed-out note*:

It is the same with God and kings.

25. *The Surrealist Group published a magazine* titled Le Surréalisme au service de la révolution *(Surrealism in the service of the revolution) from 1930 to 1933.* Trans.

26. *In B, paragraphs 30 to 33 read*:

27) So great a difficulty that the sovereign operation was only conceivable at first by a slippage.

Christianity: act of slave-subject relating sovereignty to a God-object whose purpose was to be grasped, which permitted the project. The God of the mystics is effectively sovereign but the mystic is not.

Buddhism: If Christianity is a submission to the sphere as to a pain, Buddhism is the negation of that sphere but also as a pain, which is to say that, despite everything, the Buddhists seek a sovereignty limited by a transcendence. And what also defines them as slaves is that they seek it.

28) Sovereignty cannot be acquired: it cannot be to any extent the object of a search, it is or it is not. I can define the exercise and say: if I act in this or that manner, I would lose it. At every moment I engage myself in the paths of activity. At every moment I risk being inserted. I act negatively by defining the paths of an acceptance.

29) Sovereignty cannot even be defined as a good [. . .]

27. *B title (and C)*: Before an Empty Sky

D: Facing the Void of the Sky, *corrected*: The Void of the Sky

E: The Void of the Sky

In B, a first draft of pages 201 to 202 is inscribed within a group of notes concerning effusion. Pages 6–27:

I am not speaking to professional philosophers, whose position is set, they are compromised and finished, forever deteriorated, but to someone who has turned away, now without a feeling of unease, from their sordid dispensaries only reserving a contemptuous respect founded on a awareness of a swindle at the bottom of things,
to a certain number of men injured by the shameless lie of philosophers.

Taking account of the 25 centuries of philosophy, I demonstrate that the old method results
in successive refutations
in the professoriate—
on the side of the refutations, bankruptcy, the professor's role is fraudulent banker.

I pose as a fundamental condition of knowledge
the whole character, nonservitude
thereby, 1st I make the sovereign operation of knowledge the concern where specialists of whatever kind refuse all specialty
2nd I identify experience and knowledge
(see *Inn. Exp.*)
A truth is never more than a means of knowing.

No proposition either reveals or can reveal what it is. Propositions are traces on the interior of this sphere of exteriority that is in us, modifying this sphere or linking [*it?*], that's all. If they attempt to avoid it, they transplant the methods from the sphere elsewhere (thus one arrives at the hybrid notion that is God, who even in the*

*

When I write project, it is because it is a question of some unspecified project (not of Heidegger's *Entwurf* [project]), of my project of writing or going hunting. The professor's vocabulary has more consequences than it seems. (For my part, I have written *ipseity* in Lalande's dictionary definition, because of an equivocation on individuality—identical in all points, this fly is nevertheless not that one.) The words *existential, existentialism* that I have so far as I remember never written, annoyingly

---

In margin:

mark of mind
that wanting to cause laughter wrote
critique also valuable for others
Critique of Sartre: to avoid remorse
put everything in question
life [*illegible*] entirely is project—but as such demonstrating the character of project
[*as such? so much?*] that life is [*charged? changed?*] by project: the only successes are the ways out, tears, laughter
the only *result* of the project: consciousness of death
consciousness of its impotence

accentuate a tendency of language to substitute a servile operation of intelligence for whatever claimed revelation.

Their use seems to me as foolish as can be, wanting to paint a wall, to tie a painter to his ladder. The existential school—I mean the moderns—is caught up in these stupidities.

Compared to *existential*, the word *God* itself, of hardly professorial origin, is light (causes laughter—strictly speaking, helps cause fear): with it one at least has all the come and go of a changing topic.

I do not want to be placed as a continuation of Heidegger. (I am not neglecting political criticisms that are made of him. Hegel was, after the age of thirty, as decidedly reactionary as is or was Heidegger: the substantial thought of the Marxist revolution nevertheless proceeded from him.) The little that I know of *Sein und Zeit* seems to me at once judicious and hateful. My thought, if it's possible, in some points proceeds from his. Besides, one could, I imagine, determine a parallel following from the two. I have nevertheless chosen entirely different paths and what I have finally come to say is represented, in Heidegger, only by a silence (he could not, it seems, give *Sein und Zeit* the second volume without which it remains in suspense). This means that Heidegger is no more at home in my house than the painter would be with his ladder even if he had painted the walls before.

After such a beautiful effort to cleanse the mystical [*stable? rut?*] from all mysticism, it is hard to hear it said that one is only a "new mystic."* (At least it would be hard if . . .) The accusation, it's true, comes down to saying: you claim to have made a clean slate, I don't believe it. At the same time one does not have to demonstrate the intention of seeing [*better?*], the domains that I described, men, it seems to me, don't think they are worthy of interest. Toward the end of the painful road, one assumes an attitude of impeccable rigor, a little further on one pulls out with a pirouette (disguising the intention of remaining blind in scornful criticism). That which I have really experienced (and I have described it) puts nothing less than all possible thought in question. I have specified that this interrogation had no place to be carried out in a mystical way, that no God, no morality is supported by it. Simply, an experience of human limits was given to the cultivated, reasonable man that I am. I invited one to do as I have done and if I have provided the means it is because a sovereign character placed them outside the sequences of means and ends.

*

When I will no longer publish—I'm completing at the moment that I write a work of "general economy" titled *The Accursed Share*—fragments offering gropings

---

* *"A New Mystic": the title of Jean-Paul Sartre's article on* Inner Experience, *originally published in* Cahiers du Sud *(1943), reprinted in Sartre,* Critical Essays *(1947), trans. Chris Turner (Seagull Books, 2010) pp. 219–93.*

[*equal to?*] thought, but a coherent ensemble, one will see from the paths that I have followed that they depart profoundly from those of Heidegger.

These notes on sacrifice or laughter, eroticism or anguish, that are mixed together in my book with other reflections lead to a rigorous theory.

It's laughable but what can I do?

*

1) The animal obviously cannot maintain strictly necessary consumption without danger, the necessary level can only be a minimum. So it is impossible that an animal might a priori have a surplus at its disposal

2) strictly necessary consumption for the animal as a separate being is also insufficient due to the fact that the animal is defined as a physiological system already engaged in a cycle of expenditures exceeding necessity

3) all this is made possible by the sun

*

The biosphere amasses solar energy
This in no way prevents animals from expending less energy in this labor

*

What I will say now
One day I asked a student in my class who was the laziest among us: it was me. But in the whole school? It was me.

*

Call effusion a discharge of psychic energy in which the stimulant is infinite (unlimited, undefined)

Then the stimulant is the group of available signs

To the extent that to find the stimulant someone renounces this or that possibility of discharge, it must be subordinate to him, to give him a sense external to his own

To give an external sense is an operation joined to most modes of discharge, but *after the fact*

In the calculated renunciation, the subordinated character, without being necessarily the dominant character, is more important.

The sovereignty of laughter or of eroticism is complete. That of sacrifice is doubtful. Poetry only very rarely attains the sovereign moment.

*

In every expenditure the stimulant must be envisioned
The theme of activity and the external sign

Laughter	laughter	object of laughter
Sacrifice	death	victim
Poetic rupture	id.	words
Eroticism	erotic desire	object

In effusion the theme is undefined, the sign is either the summit of signs, or the group of available signs

Laughter	sovereign character	but slightly alienated
Sacrifice	id.	but subordinated
Eroticism	id.	but shameful
Poetry	id.	

What is always threatening is an insertion into transcendence (which at bottom I call nature? No! What I have called nature is immobility not at play, stability, the static).

*

poetry is close to sovereignty but fails in that it evokes sovereignty in place of living it
embrace the group of signs
all the possible signs of an unknowable, undefined theme
passivity, transparency, in regard to this undefined theme.

*

General principle
what is partial cannot be sovereign (so laughter, poetry, etc.)
at least to establish its superiority
but one subordinates precisely to establish a superiority
relation between superiority and the totality of the possible:
to establish a superiority is to make an equation with the whole
("wanting to be everything" consists in this and not in what it seems)

There is a sovereignty of laughter, of eroticism or of poetry but neither one nor the others is always *at the level of circumstances*. Only a total expenditure envisioned as stimulating the totality of the possible is at the level of circumstances

*

Fundamentally, the obstacle in matters of poetry is the question
    "Why this particular angle?"

Effusion is what begins—or can begin—beyond poetry
     at the moment when poetry seems pointless

                              *

Human expenditure—or tragic expenditure—begins at the moment
                              play begins
with the rupture of the *continuum*, of the being himself (as *continuum* rather
than as individual being (?)).
     But how is being at play a means of obtaining a greater expenditure of energy

                              *

Sacrifice or tragedy is obviously given as superiority
Effusion begins there
Not with laughter or eroticism
Poetry is the mode of expression
     Sometimes of eroticism
     Sometimes of laughter
     Sometimes of tragedy
                         (and finally of effusion)
But first as [*rhyme?*] (immediate expenditure)
     it is a particular form beginning with
     the abandonment of themes
     in this way one discovers an amazing autonomy in it
     but poetry requires forgetfulness, the abandonment of a part of the totality.
                         (in the modern sense)
     poetry is the abandonment of a part of the totality
     but not to the total
     everything is rediscovered here (all the words)
     it abandons tragedy essentially
     through that it is already a reconciliation with nature (?)
     expenditure = putting everything that is at risk, which is to say [*surpassing?*]
nature

                              *

Poetry allied to the themes of sacrifice, eroticism, laughter, drunkenness can,
it too, be envisioned as a total operation
     in this sense one must distinguish
     tragic poetries
     erotic
     comic
     purely poetic poetry (pure holocaust of words)
     total poetry
     at the same time tragedy, erotic, comic, poetic

Even a total poetry would be limited accepting to be a part of the possible
poetry as a holocaust of words operates as a full sign, it liberates energy, really
but without a middle term from the author to the reader
in this it does not in the end differ from other operations like
sacrifice
tragedy, etc.
strictly speaking, a sacrifice implies a theme
in effusion, the difference consists in   the variety and selection of the
signs, one *tasks* with drawing a maximum of psychic discharge
effusion is fundamentally any expenditure intensified by some means
the specificity of the effusion consists in the appropriation more or less great
in relation to the expenditure
effusion is in principle sacrifice
it can also be laughter or eroticism
but effusion is *also* an intellectual operation in the sense that the signs of the
sacrifice (or of laughter, or eroticism) are in it the object of a concentrated attention
This concentrated attention signifies

B, pages 28–31, first draft of Part Three: Nudity.

At stake
something is announced in effusion
(in place of explication, of commentary on sacrifice)
everything is now at stake, suspended . . .
being in me is alone and naked before what is, all that is, if the depths
of worlds does not open itself, if I remain blind before it, it is the effect of my
impotence and whatever else may happen, what I will experience in the end, what
I will *discover*, will be the extremity of the possible,
for now I will stop only when I have advanced further, I imagine, than a
man can go.
I can "toward this end" laugh and drink and give myself up to an orgy, appeal
to the sticky disorder of words, laid out at my will, according to the power of my
imagination, tragic signs, lacerating like *the impossible* laceration,
solicit every image of what is (completely) to the point of reducing it to an
impossible equal to that of the most lacerating tragedy,
if I do not destroy within myself the sphere of activity through irreconcilable
representations, I will still only be enclosed in it,
at the mercy of subordinate operations*
unable to hope to discover anything other than a series of objects related
to my action,

In the margin: This *is not* the sovereign operation but a moment of laceration beginning with
it. There are obviously confused points of origin, but without anger at the final moment . . .

in no way capable of putting myself at risk the way an orgy, laughter, the awareness of what is from the domain of tragedy puts me at risk—that I exist—

(I risk myself in that this orgy, this laughter, this tragedy that I am pull me out of the sphere in which I have only one meaning: the sum of the responses that I can provide to the demands of utility, but to risk myself is to put myself in question, is the means that I have of exploring my possible and seeing my limits, which is to say that here the beyond of my possible strains to the point at which death is laughable

and how much at this moment the least operation is subordinated, the concern for observing the rigor of operations of knowledge appears foreign to me, I must say this while affirming it to the point of my absence of contempt

that such operations, such concerns would stop as soon as this game, without which action (labor) would enclose knowledge)

[*see below p. 285*]

B, pages 32–44:

this meeting of the possible this absence of limits defines effusion

(it is the acceptance of a limit that makes poetry return to nature, and in general all that is limited causes a return to nature: in this consists, in particular, the fact that novelty is necessary: the demand for novelty is not only linked to the incessant transcendence of objects (the profits become the property of the player) but to the fact that in our experience immanence is essentially the surpassing of itself, the impossibility of accepting a limit)

What is exciting in effusion is directly the impossibility of immanence accepting a limit, the overflowing: I must consider this as a real fact, a general discharge, an incessant destruction of limits that would be the definition (!) of energy, and that what would be received as exciting the energy discharged by the subject would be *any energy whatsoever;* the fusion of the object and the subject would be produced at the moment when every sign disappears, when the object would be "without form and without mode."

The themes in laughter or in eroticism are particular themes, the discharges of human energy at stake in laughter or eroticism.

In sacrifice, it is the same in a sense; it is the discharge provoked by the rupture of the *continuum* (whose modality is associated elsewhere, secondarily, with the themes of laughter and eros).

But this modality of sacrifice defines a negative stimulant: the sacred, which, being negative, does not have a graspable material existence. The sacred is in no way the emission of energy, but interruption (felt however in a sense by virtue of a fundamental error, as contagious).

The sacred is fundamentally a shock in return. In the sacred the constant energy of the *continuum* is interrupted but only in a point. But all the emissions of energy interrupting at the same instant on this point concentrate general attention on this point. At this moment the *continuum* that subsists is modified: what it receives in return is energy stopped. This energy is not, in any of the participants, a part of the energy of the continuum, but its totality, this energy being entirely directed toward the victim through the consecration that dedicates him to death. After the destruction, this energy tensed by the stop is then perceived at its dead point (and naturally it remains to say what these words signify . . .).

Obviously the essential interrogation of effusion cannot in any way be considered as independent of the interrogation, through the stop, specific to sacrifice.

The essence of our perception is the perception of energy—of energy emitted by others and provoking contagion (which is to say the energy that, in an individual, has, in favorable circumstances, the power to provoke in another an emission of energy of the same kind).

Disgust: inhibition to contact (corpses, excrement, etc.)

In the inhibition to contact, a stimulant is regarded as contagious

This means:

a) that in regard to the aforesaid stimulant the operation of transcendence is impossible: immanence is irreducible, inadmissible nonetheless

b) immanence however does not derive from an emission of energy

there is no possibility of this [*kind?*]: a corpse (excrement) is the sign of energy emitted, and were I to emit energy in the same mode, I would die (I would myself become refuse)

I conduct myself however as if I was going to die (etc.), as if the stimulant must at all cost be suppressed.

c) negative immanence is the result, in each case, of a previous immanence, of a *continuum* destroyed, external or inner.

The external *continuum* resulted from the power that the living being had to emit energy, by which it maintains itself in the *continuum*; the inner *continuum* resulted from the appropriation of nourishing emissions of energy and from the rejection of a residual part of this nourishment, not susceptible itself, of emitting assimilable energy, on the contrary emitting a toxic energy (destroying the tissues of the internal *continuum*): the immanence of nourishment found itself reversed from the segregation of the non-consumable residue, but the inadmissible character is only revealed to consciousness at the moment of excretion

—note that filth, disorder misappropriate energy by introducing (external) signs of immanence, of light stimulants and without the escape of energy. (At least I can account for the facts in this way.) If it is like this, one could accept this law as general: every sign of immanence provokes an unspecified emission of energy. However, if this is clear in the case of the corpse, provoking an emission of the same nature as the living, one would have to believe that an excrement, for its part, provokes an emission of the same nature as nourishment, provokes it from the moment of its release, maintains it at least for the moment in which it is visible (or felt): here there would have to be a sudden stop, a reversal. Same reaction in regard to vomit and—to a certain extent—in regard to each excretion (snot, ear wax).

But

the reactions are different

—according to the origin (each feels good . . .)

—according to the nature of the product (blood, some horror that one had in regard to it, can provoke a nourishing reaction: the value of blood is intelligible in consideration of the bearing of signs; to the extent that the principle of reversal is not dissociated from the interior of a coherent group, blood is an object of horror; menstrual blood is never dissociated; but the blood of a wound is dissociable: the nourishing reaction in its regard is possible, at least if it is a question of one's personal blood; on the other hand horror is reinforced in that blood is the sign of violent death: there are, in the reactions in regard to blood, great mixtures with, at bottom, a correct reaction, that of nourishing immanence, inhibited by the play of signs (fundamental association, entered into a new association)).

d) the emission of energy is stopped.

The transcendence of animals is not realized in them as an object
However, the rupture of the continuum in animals is at stake in sexuality
Separated self, then copulation
The play of expenditure is therefore from the departure of transcendence and immanence. But the rupture of the continuum is accentuated by the death of the other
It is sexual play inserted in society, lived by society, which animal societies are unable to do (?), if not in a rudimentary way (the murder of males in bees)

There is in nature a general dialectic of immanence and transcendence

Nature is to be seen in two ways
a) as subordinating all that is in itself or subordinating itself to its own laws
b) as sovereign totality

Within nature, a tiger, a star appear as sovereign totality

All that is I am signifies consciousness of the continuum

Sovereignty is transcendence destroying itself

It is to want to be everything and to remain transcendent that . . .

[B, pages 65–70, recopied in the first draft, reprinted without notable variation in C and D:]

BEFORE AN EMPTY SKY

Something announces:
[. . .]
action (labor) would enclose knowledge.)

[A note:]

This is not the sovereign operation. But [*engaged?*] in the operation. Undoubt-edly, the [*illegible*] origins confuse (they hardly matter). It is not only possible, it is good to err (if not, why be free?). And besides without anger . . .

> [*And in the margin:*]
> The Earth before history
> in principle everything, clearly impossible
> but to define the impossible
> it is not rare to behave in a sovereign way
> but no one thinks in a sovereign way

[*This note is then rewritten in its near final version, reprinted in C and D:*]

What I call *sovereign operation* obviously can only be defined in the night [. . .] under this blow, instantly, the night would change into lightning, into the light of day, frozen terror into a smile).

Post-Scriptum 1953

Written in January and February 1953 in Orléans, where Bataille was librarian at the municipal library, to serve as a post-face to the re-edition of Inner Experience.
This Post-Scriptum *is in some ways the final avatar of a* preface for Inner Experience, *undoubtedly initially conceived as a response to Gabriel Marcel's criti-cal review of that book, "The Refusal of Salvation and the Exaltation of the Man of Absurdity" (see* Revue de la Table Ronde, *n° 3 (March 1945)—reprinted in Marcel,* Homo Viator *(Aubier, 1945); trans. Emma Craufurd and Paul Seton (South Bend, IN: St. Augustine's Press, 2010) pp. 178–204). That preface became "The Sovereign," a text published in the spring of 1952 in* Botteghe Oscure, *n° IX (English translation in Bataille,* The Unfinished System of Nonknowledge, *pp. 185–95).*
On January 8, 1952, Bataille wrote to Jean Bruno:
I have finally written, just the past few days, the preface for *Inner Experi-ence*, the purpose of which is to oppose the possibility of the *spirit of rebellion* to the *spirit of submission*.
On January 23, 1952, he noted [notebook 11, p. 1]:
Finished the preface the day before yesterday and sent it to Madame de Bassiano.* Aside from this text, the edition will include some *addenda,*** *Method of Meditation* (and *Theory of Religion****?).

---

*Madame de Bassiano, Princess Caetani, publisher of the review Botteghe Oscure.

** *We have not been able to identify the addenda referenced here.*

****See Georges Bataille,* Theory of Religion (1948), *trans. Robert Hurley (New York: Zone Books, 1992).*

The *addenda* will be partly linked to the existing text, some are already written in the collated copy. Moreover extracts of the following articles can be arranged in their place: "Dernier Instant," "Mères profanées," "Existentialisme," "Ivresse," reviews on Proust and Racine, on Blanchot.* I will have to write on yoga, Mallarmé, laughter for *Critique*.

I will also have to reconsider "Hiroshima," "Baudelaire," "Gide," "Leonardo," "Huizinga," some notes from *Critique*, and the articles from *Troisième Convoi, Deucalion,* etc.**

Reconsider in particular the absence of community and insist on the idea of negative community: the community of those who have no community.

How do they say "temple of several or of numerous divinities"? This is the name that must be given to the *addenda*. It should have structure, ordered as much as possible but not more than that.

Elsewhere [Envelope 57] one finds these few scattered notes in drafts for "The Sovereign":

---

* *"Dernier Instant"* Critique *n° 5 (octobre 1946) pp. 448–57, reprinted in* Oeuvres Complètes, *volume 11, pp. 116–25; English translation by Thomas Walton, "The Ultimate Instant" Transition 48, n° 1 (January 1948) pp. 60–69 [This article is a review of a play by Gabriel Marcel]; "Marcel Proust et la mère profanée" Critique n° 7 (décembre 1946) pp. 601–11, reprinted in* Oeuvres Complètes, *volume 11, pp. 151–61; "Existentialisme" Critique n° 41 (octobre 1950) pp. 83–86, reprinted in* Oeuvres Complètes, *volume 12, pp. 11–13; "L'Ivresse des taverns et la religion" Critique n° 25 (juin 1948) pp. 531–9, reprinted in* Oeuvres Complètes, *volume 11, pp. 322–31; "Marcel Proust" Critique n° 31 (novembre 1948) pp. 1133–6, reprinted in* Oeuvres Complètes, *volume 11, pp. 391–4; "Racine" Critique n° 37 (juin 1949) pp. 552–6, reprinted in OC 11, pp. 497–501; "Le Bonheur, l'érotisme, et la Littérature" Critique n° 35 (avril 1949) pp. 401–11 and n° 36 (mai 1949) pp. 447–54, reprinted in* Oeuvres Complètes, *volume 11, pp. 434–52; English translation by Michael Richardson in* The Absence of Myth: Writings on Surrealism *(London: Verso, 1994) pp. 186–208.*

** *See "À propos de récits d'habitants d'Hiroshima" Critique n° 8–9 (janvier–février 1947) pp. 126–40, reprinted in* Oeuvres Complètes, *volume 11, pp. 172–87; "Baudelaire 'mis à nue' " Critique n° 8–9 (janvier–février 1947) pp. 3–27, reprinted* La Littérature et le mal *(1957), English translation by Alastair Hamilton (London: Marion Boyars, 1985) pp. 31–61; on Gide, see, for example, "Le Journal, jusqu'à la mort," Critique n° 46 (mars 1951) pp. 212–18, reprinted in* Oeuvres Complètes, *volume 12, pp. 58–64; on Leonardo, see "Léonard de Vinci (1451–1519)" Critique n° 46 (mars 1951) pp. 261–7; on Johan Huizinga, see "Sommes-nous là pour jouer ou pour être sériux?" Critique n° 49 (juin 1951) pp. 512–22 and n° 51–52 (août–septembre 1951) pp. 734–48, reprinted in* Oeuvres Complètes, *volume 12, pp. 100–25. The articles Bataille published in* Troisième Convoi *are collected in* The Unfinished System of Nonknowledge.

Preface to *Inner Experience*

The interest of Gabriel Marcel's critique: he understood what Sartre did not see.*

I am on the side of Gabriel Marcel in a sense, because his thought extends that of a spiritual line.

drawbacks of the absence of the search for salvation

absence of discipline, of solidarity, but this is a strength, finally,

no humility, but this resembles that of Christians, like the Christians, I want to exist in a sovereign way

humility is always false

radicalism

but I will never condemn the world and do not accuse what others call God with having made the world a trap, as Christians practically do.

[*One or several pages missing.*]

for us. I see that the world is founded on a division, a separation: from this division our thoughts again go astray, which I wanted to avoid through the discipline demanding the night of nonknowledge. I recognize that this is a challenge. But it has the merit of excluding nothing, condemning nothing, the way those who want to reduce the world to a determinate form do.

I voluntarily ask forgiveness for having introduced my readers to an unfortunate agitation.

[*In the margin:* a story is required to provide the image of suppression]

it seems to me that the fundamental thought of G. Marcel would have benefited from not being founded on a disdain that, for example, betrays a truly facile irony to such a degree

have it appear at the same time as L'Érotisme (Mercure [*crossed out:* Synthèses?])

notes

the only passages that seem to me to still have a meaning (?) even though my mind has foundered since then

mention my regret that I had to live in a world in which I so rarely had someone with whom to speak. A conversation with a Jesuit priest. Certainly I pre-

---

*In "Un nouveau mystique" (A New Mystic, 1943); *reprinted in* Situations I *(Paris: Galli-mard, 1947)*; *English translation by* Christ Turner, "A New Mystic," *in Jean-Paul Sartre,* Critical Essays *(Calcutta: Seagull Books, 2010) pp. 219–93. For Bataille's partial response to Sartre, see* On Nietzsche, *pp. 179–87; see also the translator's introduction to this volume for additional information.*

fer talking to others more often but I am nostalgic for encountering people who [*brought together?*] the principle of equivalence. My sadness at finding the absence of rigor everywhere. Description of Weil and Kojève.

*

End like this: far from turning one's back . . . (?)
Opposition between Sartre and Hegel, the first giving a conceptual form to existence, the second reducing concepts and existence in their unity (?)
    what I have done
        describe a state of impossibility turning into repose
Shamanism
Sartre and the Church
Church in this sense = absence of Church
    absence of community
        see text published on surrealism

*

For the preface to *Inner Experience*: science in itself is nothing, learns nothing, but it has destroyed the teachings of religion.
    Science does not respond to religious teachings, yet it makes faith impossible.
    in regard to surrealism
    Inviability of immanence. The fact of not condemning the world entails a nonexistence

*

There is no philosophical question when there is no question of knowledge. It is not the unintelligible that is the object but the sensible. It is a question of experiencing the world in itself or oneself in the world. It is a question

*

The infinite inferiority of God in relation to man resides in the faculty of man to limit himself to the stupid, the sly, the guilty [*crossed out:* who feel the egg], to the sub-mistress, to the colonel . . . endlessly, from the wings of the theater to the prison office, from childhood class to the writer's room.

*

My pretension: to respond without knowing philosophy. It is that it seems to me in general to exhaust its possibility there where it clarifies an absence of a way out as in God, in freedom, etc. It is for this reason that I stopped myself at

Hegel's thought, which situated itself in these absences so as to surpass them. But in this way it only attains an extremity. And what I have personally done is not to prolong an extreme situation but generally to have substituted for a search conceived as a given possibility, a search conceived from the outset as impossible: this is the meaning of attaining the extremity, for impossible is not to say that the facts caused an error from the outset but that they would be missing at an otherwise indeterminate point since we cannot reach this point without losing the power to determine it. In fact it is in every way and *only in every way* that—I will not say: according to *me*, for on this point I can force agreement—that we can reach the extremity. It is of course possible to refuse the search for extremity, but no one can tell me anything if I respond that this is in advance to want to put what is essential between parentheses, essential to knowledge, in fact the *situation* of the one, I will say more readily of *those* who seek. At this moment, it's true that the search is in a dilemma: or else I put my situation between parentheses and I cold-bloodedly pose the question, or I attach myself to the fact that, in the question, my situation is at stake, and that—reciprocally—my situation is truly given only if I have posed the question. Now this is also to say that being unable to remain indifferent I add a given *sensible* to a process that

putentirely differently, philosophy is at stake

    what I find annoying is not the abuse that I have done to the word torture but the little abuse that I have made of torture itself and the little grace from torture from M. Marcel, who permits himself to see the abuse of a word

      connect through glorifying

    For finally I have seen this same torture in all the extreme points attained by human beings—in sacrifice—and that it was always like this

    I added that this was no less torture

    sense from nonsense therefore nonsense from sense—but there is the question of the nonsense of [*art?*]

*

    It is a pretension to silence and to death, to such a degree that it swells the voice, as slight as it is, like the words silence, and death certainly, to engage in this paradoxically would be to desire an error [*sic*]* in a ritual. Sovereignty in fact only exists at the moment when the one who speaks is going to disappear, silence himself, or die such that the words that announce his death only ever open the path of a dead man and that this is only recognized by surprise, the feeling of discomfort, of mad gaiety and of incongruity with those who, having only figured it out can only experience it suddenly as an absence.

*

Bataille's correction. Trans.

my "pretension"

assuming that M. Marcel is right, this would not strongly testify against the principles that I have defended. Similarly I cannot concern myself for a long time with knowledge. We will remain ignorant of what we are in history and no one could do anything he did not have the strength to pretend, if only to himself.

I even admit that Mr. Marcel's rather dry judgments and limited sensibility could not know how to entail the weakness of the propositions that he put forward. It seems to me that he would have to give these propositions more authority if he were not limited to judging presumptuous the fact of having wanted (or required?) to go "beyond the limits" ([*Homo Viator*] p. 193).

*

This debate cannot be clear-cut

There only remains for us a judgment of value to pronounce between rebellion and submission

The fact is that the spiritual Christians or others indicate a wealth of open spiritual possibilities; on the contrary, from the side of rebellion. Nietzsche is an exception, recognized by M. Marcel.

The entire question of the preface is here (and precisely of my book from the beginning)

M. Marcel was right to attempt to [*try to?*] with authority. He represents me as the clown of my situation, from the fact that [*illegible*] counts for me. He should have been able to show, it's true, honestly, that I had opened a breach, but he mocked me. What is there to say?

*

The final question

How could God, if he existed, condemn me? I seek him no less than . . . I seek him more: beyond a shelter, a security that I no longer seek, in the absence of shelter which is itself the death of god

I know it, I put myself in the worst position. *On Nietzsche, L'Abbé C.*

*

develop in part in *eroticism* and in part only in the preface to *Inner Experience*: where I will have to insist on *L'Abbé C.* and Sade.

*

but the author knows that he cannot be sovereign: to be sovereign he would have to silence himself, no longer be an author.

Returning to Post-Scriptum 1953. *Below one will find a first draft [Envelope 74, 11 manuscript pages of which only the first six are numbered], then variants from the manuscript [Box 9, E, 17 numbered pages].*

a) *First draft:*

There is in *Inner Experience*—and in *Method of Meditation* (which remedies rather poorly the insufficiency of my first book)—an irreparable weakness. In the usual sense, these writings have nothing to do with a desperate attitude (their author is even, in fact, most often happy). But this *enterprise* could not lead to anything satisfying. These are, in short, inert books.

The desire to escape from the servility of thought is at the origin of these strange structures, in which the only solidity would be collapse. The assumed task condemned me, it seems to me, to deception, to trickery. A trickster! But how can I be believed? Perhaps I'm lying right now . . .

I must nevertheless say that a closed situation is not necessarily unlivable. It leaves no equilibrium possible, but no slipping either. It only demands rigor. It requires a kind of awareness without collapse of which a difficult indifference is key: the smallest error here is not permitted. This is not the business of imprecise and weak minds: if they accept it, if they persist, such minds devote themselves, in order to save face, to a kind of affected suffering that is not very honorable. Moreover, such is the hard and comical destiny of man: almost always, the limp admiration and the blunders of the minority who occupy themselves with this respond to the strongest tension.

This proof is neither discouraging nor anything else: I can easily endure it. But I feel myself bound to remark on the degree to which I am distanced from a way of seeing that often seems close to mine. What counts most in my eyes is the intensity of the feeling, but nothing is more contrary to this than the agreement offered without control to vague feelings. I bring rigor to each thing: if I am weak, I go to the end of my weakness; I can sink into hesitation, but I hate the waste toward which good intentions turn. It is difficult for me to defend myself from the contempt that verbal feelings inspire in me. It is also difficult for me to be hard, but I refuse an emotion asked of me with big words.

Perhaps it is sometimes having had recourse to moving language that forces me to open myself to these practices of pity and sentimentality that ordinarily mask greed, egotism, and a base ferocity. The great movements that command this and that part of human activity—illusory impulses that shatter a lasting weightiness—will not cease to take place within these limits. But I want to withdraw thought—or, if one prefers, experience—which I have distinguished from confusion.

I can only say that most of those who have read my books have not fallen into the mystic state of mind that I take to be the opposite of my own. But I then show by an example how and to what extent I differ from them.

Toward this end, I must first specify a point about which, so it seems to me, defenders of various schools agree against me. No one places all beings on the same level: for man must be granted a dignity that raises him above the other animals. Listen, it is not important to know if one says: "in this way man is divine, supernatural, or free"; this is not necessary, but rather: "it is abominable to kill a man, to eat a man, to exploit a man . . ." Such is the fundamental mysticism common to almost the entire human race. It is acceptable to kill, eat, or exploit an animal, not a man. Of course, nothing is more common than men exploiting their fellows, and we kill each other often without moderation, this is no less theoretically condemnable; similarly anthropophagy in fact coexists in principle with the taboo of which it is the ritual violation.*

[*Non-numbered pages*]

Beginning with the exceptional character of man among beings, humanity constructs itself
    there is something extraordinary that belongs to each man in common
    everything that separates men is the object of judgment, etc., and reciprocally dissimulated

I maintain, on the contrary, even though this initially appears rather far from my older books, notably from *In. Exp.* that the exceptional character of humanity consists in this will to separation. Neither reason nor freedom nor spirituality nor anything of this type, but this disgust with animality that pursues itself through the human species [*enters*] in the disgust for the enemy or for the class, etc.

I think that man is an animal that abuses itself, that knows nothing of what he thinks he knows, which is linked to the difference of man, that on the contrary man must first detach himself from what he thinks he knows

    work of destruction
    that we have perched ourselves on a shoddy pedestal
    rigor and certainly not romantic facility
    In place of mysticism, it is possible to envision

Note by Bataille: This form of mysticism has remained the common basis of thought even though it apparently differs from the original mysticism, wherein animals are often placed on the same footing as man. I imagine that from the outset it has been a question of the same attitude: from the outset men have held themselves to be sacred, but they were not logical; they sometimes saw their fellows in other animals, in other beings. This kind of assimilation of the animal and the human being has not ceased to be possible. Secondly, locally, it is at work in contemporary humanity but it leaves a fundament intact: what is evil, atrocious, horrible to bear undermines the being that we are. This responds to the eternal nausea that orders human life. We pass our time on earth making a kind of escape from this nausea.

in order to escape from nausea men must avoid contact with those of their
fellows who live in conditions that they themselves could not bear without nausea.
What one thinks, for example, of men who live in [*filth?*]. There is a process of
classification beginning with a first step

Nausea founds the feeling of being human: in the eyes of their fellows, men
are beings who experience the same horrors and manifest these horrors by observing given taboos. At bottom, this nauseous distancing before the apparition of a
determined object, or for the manifest change of an object, that characterizes a man.
The newborn never knows this distancing, but a newborn is human only to the
extent that it is susceptible, one day, to share this humanity. The determination of
objects and of changes that cause nausea is the result of experience: it is therefore
very random; it varies among peoples, places, even among individuals

Nausea is evidently the limit of play; it is not play that is proper to man, but
nausea—suffering having the aura of death. The life of animals is play but animal
play is profoundly altered by nausea.

Human equivocality derives from the fact that it is play despite the nausea
that is the final value, but that the nausea itself constitutes human nature.

In religion, the positive forms of nausea are the ones that count: there is
inversion. Thereafter the picture is complex.

In simple anthropogenesis

[*Manuscript Changes*]

1. [. . .] nor satisfying.

Outside of my present intention to express my thought more simply, with
greater coherence (to which responds a general work on the "effects of nonknowledge," slowly elaborated, following a plan), one single thing matters to me on the
subject of my first books.* Often, those who enjoy them in fact associate them
with a vague mind and sentimentality: by this I mean to say that I would flatly
disappoint, I'm sure, most of those who have read me. I would disappoint them if
they knew and I want them to know the extent to which my taste for dry precision
and my horror of facility distances them from me.

For a long time I have felt myself incapable of preparing myself, even in
appearance, for the weakest mystical slippage. Once I had a less clear attitude.

Note by Bataille: In this way I point to not only *Inner Experience* but *Guilty* and *On Nietzsche*.
The general work upon which I am now working will again take up the themes that I have
developed over several years in a coherent series of lectures at the Collège Philosophique
[*crossed out*: under the title: *To die laughing, and laugh to death*]. [*For the texts of these lectures,
see Bataille*, The Unfinished System of Nonknowledge, *pp. 111–50*. Trans.]

In particular, *Inner Experience, Method of Meditation* which prolongs it (without mentioning *Guilty* or *On Nietzsche*) in my eyes today are open to criticism . . .

I am more and more linked to the dryness of intellect and it seems to me a good idea to add these pages to my first book to situate it in relation to my present feeling and to better oppose myself to the mysticism that, in error, it is possible to find here, to denounce that which still alienates almost all human thought.

I will stop myself on a point [. . .]

2. [. . .] But these reactions are arbitrary. They are convenient: without them, humanity would not be what it is. It is servile, however, to see anything in this other than the religious attitude. The thought that does not limit this arbitrariness to what it is is not only mystical, it is servile since it submits humanity to a condition. By exploiting, etc., I could not in fact maintain the communication that links me to other human beings, but it is to the extent that, at the outset, I separate myself from the mass of humanity that exploits and that puts to death that which, following its mood, it regards negatively.

What makes mystical humanism an irritating platitude [. . .]

3. [. . .] stop themselves en route.

In this grand movement, the initial rejection of animality and the violence of humanism appear in their narrowness with another meaning than that of naive mysticism, unconscious of its arbitrary origins and of its slippery motion. I experience human destiny, in a sense, as if it alienated me profoundly. But from then on *what am I?*

This I will never know.

This is my final word, my absence of presuppositions, my refusal of all mysticism.

But for all that I do not cease to exist on this side of this final word, in the way from which it is the way out—the only way out.

In these strange conditions, in this maze of reactions, there is no movement that does not have a meaning ignored by the one who is committed to it. Our human form in its corporeal or moral implications is so dependent on a tangled history that I must first demand of myself a wakefulness that never fails me. The slightest naiveté is perhaps at bottom only drowsiness, it is perhaps weak. I know that this effort is in principle also an enslavement, but not doing it, returning to nonchalance, is to accept servitude. In the end, the secular machinery that I am can only make a sovereign *use* of the servile reactions that have always ordered themselves within it. Often, the nonchalance of poetry dissimulates the life of a victim, only escaping through suffering agonies, sometimes by death, the insidious servility that engenders foolishness.

To give oneself up to nonchalance, one will say, is no less a humiliation. It's true, but would the most hardened nonchalance know how to withdraw itself without trickery?

Here the role of *play*, which makes activity uncertain, is apparently decisive, but must I discern in my loathing the malediction that asks a desperate man to denigrate—to take his vanity for sovereignty, the false superiority of "transcendence" for divine "immanence"—I say this with a firmness that does not tremble, I want nothing without consciousness of it. I know that unconsciousness is always the gauge of servitude, and that the choice of unconsciousness, since consciousness is the effect of servitude, demands first, *more consciousness*. In other words, this choice wouldn't know how to be made halfway, *unconsciously!*

This is perhaps the negation of the books, including this almost unchanged new edition. It is not, at least, it's denial. Already in these books, experience was constituted through reflection upon it. It is true that I have given the beautiful part to *experience* . . . that reflection here, *without which experience would not exist*, is stammering, uncertain. I cannot contest the weakness implied in the open expression of a thought whose object, experience itself, would not permit it to mature. Must I "put off till later" speaking of it? But the experience that does not maintain itself in duration, community, or tradition required that a literary expression at least still linked me to other men. Without hope, the fundamental contradiction of a sovereign effusion and of the existence of man put us in a false situation. My present effort, substituting the firm voice for the stammer, will ultimately leave me with this chance of a way out. There will never be anything more than a refusal to accept fate. What's more, I still cannot complete it; if I come to the point that I have fixed, I still will not have completed it. I am placed in such a way that the immutable incompletion of my effort resembles the incompletion of humanity as a whole.

In myself as in its immensity, humanity takes up again, without respite, the contestation of its limits.

Orléans, January–February 1953.

Index of Names

Adamov, Arthur, xvi, xviii
Angela of Foligno, ix, 91, 105–107, 124, 232, 243
Angélique, Pierre, viii
Anselme, St., 107
Aquinas, St. Thomas, vii
Aragon, Louis, 229
Ariadne, 39
Aristotle, 264
Augustine of Hippo, St., 124, 245

Bassiano, Madame de, 280
Baudelaire, Charles, xviii, xx, 281
Beauvoir, Simone de, xviii
Beethoven, Ludwig, 72, 151
Bergson, Henri, 70, 103, 229
Bernard, Claude, 108, 177, 244
Blake, William, ix, xi, 69, 149, 229, 247
Blanchot, Maurice, x, xi, xiii, xvi, xviii, xx, xxiii, 14, 19, 58, 65, 103, 198, 220, 222, 229, 232, 243, 281
Blum, Léon, 262
Boldt, Leslie Anne, xxii
Breton, André, xxiv, 54, 148, 229, 247
Bruno, Jean, xvi, xxiii
Buddha, 29

Caesar, Julius, 49
Caillois, Roger, x
Camus, Albert, xi, xvi, xviii, xx, xxiv
Chabrun, Jean-François, 53

Char, René, 168, 266
Christ, xiii, 27, 52, 56, 120, 134, 156, 230, 243
Corbin, Henry, ix, xvii

Dalí, Salvador, 247
Damiens, xiii
Daniélou, Jean, xviii
Dante Alighieri, 254
Deguy, Madeleine, xvi
Demeny, Paul, xv
Descartes, René, xvii, 51, 107, 108, 109, 110, 124, 134, 190, 229, 244, 268
Dianus, 227, 237
Dionysius, xiii, xv, 33, 34, 153, 156, 251
Dostoevsky, Fyodor, 49, 55, 228
Dubarle, Henri, xviii
Dumas, Georges, 120
Durkheim, Émile, xvii

Eckhart, Meister, ix, xi, 10, 104, 218
Éluard, Paul, 244

Fardoulis-Lagrange, Michel, xi, 220
Faulkner, William, 255
Foucault, Michel, xiii
Fou-Tchou-Li, xiii, 120, 122
Freud, Sigmund, xv

Galletti, Marina, xxiv
Gandillac, Maurice de, xv, xviii
Genet, Jean, xviii
Gide, André, 281
Goya, Francisco, 180

Hardy, Thomas, x
Hegel, G.W.F., ix, xvii, 33, 48, 49, 83,
    84, 90, 110, 111, 113, 124, 150,
    177, 180, 183, 211, 216, 251,
    257, 264, 265, 267, 272, 283,
    284
Heidegger, Martin, ix, xvii, 14, 31,
    111, 193, 220, 225, 229, 256, 268,
    269, 270, 271, 272, 273
Heloise, 121
Heraclitus, x
Hobbes, Thomas, 49, 229
Hollier, Denis, xxiii, 219
Huizinga, Johan, 281
Hyde, Lewis, xxiii
Hyppolite, Jean, xviii

Ignatius of Loyola, ix, xiii, 20, 120,
    122, 220, 244
Isaac, 57
Isolde, 121

Janet, Pierre, ix, 217, 220
Jaspers, Karl, ix, xvii, 261
Job, 214
John of the Cross, St., ix, xvi, 10, 19,
    28, 52, 57, 218, 226, 229, 243

Kant, Immanuel, 4, 32, 33, 226
Keynes, John Maynard, 191
Kierkegaard, Søren, ix, xi, 19, 49, 80,
    111, 230
Klossowski, Pierre, x, xviii
Kojève, Alexandre, 111, 261, 283
Kotcoubey de Beauharnois, Diana, xix

Lautréamont, Comte de, ix, 131, 149,
    245, 247

Langevin, Paul, 86
Le Bouler, Jean-Pierre, xxiii
Leiris, Michel, xi, 220
Leonardo da Vinci, 281
Lescure, Jean, xi, 220
Lorca, Federico García, 244
Louis XIV, 225

Mallarmé, Stéphane, 281
Marcel, Gabriel, xvi, xviii, xx, xxiii,
    280, 282, 284, 285
Martini, Joëlle Bellac, xxiii
Masson, André, x, 209, 230
Maydieu, Auguste, xviii
Michelet, Jules, xx, 254, 262, 264
Moré, Marcel, viii, xvii, 210
Mozart, Wolfgang, 80, 230

Nietzsche, Friedrich, vii, x, xii, xiii, xiv,
    xv, xvi, xvii, xviii, xix, xx, xxiv, 2,
    3, 25, 27, 32, 33, 34, 35, 83, 111,
    129, 131, 132, 152, 153, 154, 156,
    189, 211, 213, 225, 226, 227, 229,
    232, 245, 246, 247, 248, 249, 251,
    252, 285

Oedipus, xv
Ollivier, Louis, xi, 220
Orestes, 147, 247

Pascal, Blaise, xvii
Paulhan, Jean, xviii
Peignot, Colette Laure, xii
Pelorson, Georges, xi, 220
Peter, St., 105, 243
Petitot, Romain, xi, 220
Phaedra, 147, 252
Picasso, Pablo, 256
Plato, 34, 244, 264
Plutarch, 229
Prévost, Pierre, x, xi, xviii, 220
Proust, Marcel, viii, ix, xi, 114, 135,
    137–146, 149, 151–152, 246, 247,
    251, 281

Pseudo-Dionysius the Areopagite, ix, 10, 218

Queneau, Raymond, xi, xix, xx, 220

Racine, Jean, 245, 281
Rembrandt, 151
Rimbaud, Arthur, ix, xv, 46, 55, 148, 252, 253
Rollin, Denise, 210

Sade, D.W.F. de, xx, 48, 49, 228, 285
Sahagun, Bernardino de, ix
Sartre, Jean-Paul, x, xvii, xviii, xxiii, xxiv, 229, 271, 272, 282, 283

Schelling, F.W.J., 177
Shakespeare, William, 226
Soupault, Philippe, 229
Surya, Michel, xxii, xxiv

Teresa of Avila, St. ix, 10, 26, 121, 218, 244
Twain, Mark, 170

Ubac, Raoul, xi, 220

Wahl, Jean, ix, xx
Weil, Simone, xx, 283
Würzbach, Friedrich, 35